teach®
yourself

russian grammar

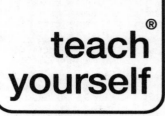

russian grammar
daphne west

For UK order queries: please contact Bookpoint Ltd, 130 Milton Park, Abingdon, Oxon OX14 4SB. Telephone: +44 (0) 1235 827720, Fax: +44 (0) 1235 400454. Lines are open 9.00–18.00, Monday to Saturday, with a 24-hour message answering service. You can also order through our website www.madaboutbooks.com

For USA order queries: please contact McGraw-Hill Customer Services, PO Box 545, Blacklick, OH 43004-0545, USA. Telephone: 1-800-722-4726. Fax: 1-614-755-5645.

For Canada order queries: please contact McGraw-Hill Ryerson Ltd, 300 Water St, Whitby, Ontario L1N 9B6, Canada. Telephone: 905 430 5000. Fax: 905 430 5020.

Long renowned as the authoritative source for self-guided learning – with more than 30 million copies sold worldwide – the *Teach Yourself* series includes over 300 titles in the fields of languages, crafts, hobbies, business, computing and education.

The publisher has used its best endeavours to ensure that the URLs for external websites referred to in this book are correct and active at the time of going to press. However, the publisher has no responsibility for the websites and can make no guarantee that a site will remain live or that the content is or will remain appropriate.

British Library Cataloguing in Publication Data: A catalogue entry for this title is available from The British Library.

Library of Congress Catalog Card Number: on file

First published in UK 2000 by Hodder Headline Ltd., 338 Euston Road, London, NW1 3BH.

First published in US 2000 by Contemporary Books, a Division of The McGraw Hill Companies, 1 Prudential Plaza, 130 East Randolph Street, Chicago, IL 60601 USA.

This edition published 2003.

The 'Teach Yourself' name and logo are registered trade marks of Hodder & Stoughton Ltd.

Copyright © 2000, 2003 Daphne West

Typeset by Transet Limited, Coventry, England.
Printed in Great Britain for Hodder & Stoughton Educational, a division of Hodder Headline Ltd., 338 Euston Road, London NW1 3BH by Cox & Wyman Ltd, Reading, Berkshire.

Impression number   10 9 8 7 6 5 4 3 2 1
Year   2007 2006 2005 2004 2003

The author would like to thank Elena Kelly for her help in the preparation of the manuscript and Tatyana Izmailova for her constant support.

v

acknowledgements

contents

introduction

Teach Yourself Russian Grammar is a reference and a practice book in one. It is intended for learners with very little Russian, but will also be useful for anyone who feels they need more explanation and practice of basic Russian grammar. The explanations are clear and simple, and answers to the exercises are provided in the key at the end, making it an ideal book for self-study. The left-hand page of each unit introduces and explains one particular point of grammar, which can then be practised by doing the exercises on the right-hand page. At the end of most units you will find cross-references to other units on the same or related points.

How to use this book

You can either work through the book progressively, or dip into specific grammar points which you need to clarify and practise. You can select the grammar items you have found difficult while using the language, or units which supplement the material in the coursebook you are working with. You will find all the grammar points listed in the contents and/or index. There is also a glossary of grammatical terms at the end of the book. Most students of Russian find that they need lots of practice to help them master the case endings of nouns, adjectives and pronouns, so this book gives lots of opportunity for that (and that's why each case is treated separately, singular and plural – so you can just practise the points you feel you need to reassure yourself about). You will find it helps you to learn points of grammar if you say the examples on the left-hand pages out loud (and you can do the same with your answers to the exercises, of course). English translations are given for most of the examples on the left-hand pages and for most of the material used in the exercises.

Abbreviations

sing.	singular	acc.	accusative
pl.	plural	gen.	genitive
masc.	masculine	dat.	dative
fem.	feminine	instr.	instrumental
adj.	adjective	prep.	prepositional
nom.	nominative	infin.	infinitive

The Cyrillic alphabet is made up of 33 letters. Here they are in their printed and handwritten forms.

ру́сский алфави́т – printed		ру́сский алфави́т – cursive	
А а	*a* in f*a*ther	*А*	*а*
Б б	*b* in *b*ank	*Б*	*б*
В в	*v* in *v*isit	*В*	*в*
Г г	*g* in *g*oat	*Г*	*г*
Д д	*d* in *d*aughter	*Д*	*g ∂*
Е е	*ye* in *ye*t	*Е*	*е*
Ё ё	*yo* in *yo*nder	*Ё*	*ё*
Ж ж	*s* in plea*s*ure	*Ж*	*ж*
З з	*z* in *z*oo	*З*	*з*
И и	*ee* in f*ee*t	*И*	*и*
Й й	*y* in bo*y*	*Й*	*й*
К к	*k* in *k*ite	*К*	*к*
Л л	*l* in bott*l*e	*Л*	*л*
М м	*m* in *m*otor	*М*	*м*
Н н	*n* in *n*ovel	*Н*	*н*
О о	*o* in b*o*re (when stressed; otherwise like *a* in sof*a*)		
П п	*p* in *p*each	*П*	*п*
Р р	*r* in *r*at	*Р*	*р*
С с	*s* in *s*ip	*С*	*с*
Т т	*t* in *t*ired	*Т*	*m, т*
У у	*oo* in sh*oo*t	*У*	*у*
Ф ф	*f* in *f*unny	*Ф*	*ф*
Х х	*ch* in lo*ch*	*Х*	*х*
Ц ц	*ts* in ra*ts*	*Ц*	*ц*
Ч ч	*ch* in *ch*eese	*Ч*	*ч*
Ш ш	*sh* in *sh*eep	*Ш*	*ш*
Щ щ	*shsh* in English *sh*ampoo	*Щ*	*щ*
ъ*	hard sign – makes a tiny pause between syllables		*ъ*
ы*	approximately like *i* in *i*ll	.	*ы*
ь*	soft sign – adds a soft, gentle 'y' sound after a consonant		*ь*
Э э	*e* in l*e*t	*Э*	*э*
Ю ю	*u* in *u*niversity	*Ю*	*ю*
Я я	*ya* in *ya*rd	*Я*	*я*

* Do not occur at the beginning of words.

1 Match the Russian words on the left with their English meaning on the right.

1 компью́тер	**a** *floppy disk*
2 фло́ппи-диск	**b** *laser printer*
3 ла́зерный при́нтер	**c** *Internet*
4 программи́ст	**d** *computer programmer*
5 Интерне́т	**e** *computer*

2 The words in the following list all sound like their English equivalents. Fill in the missing letter from each word. (Cover up the list on the right unless you are stuck!)

1	т_ри́ст	*tourist*
2	с_уде́нт	*student*
3	_урнали́ст	*journalist*
4	ба_ки́р	*banker*
5	бале_и́на	*ballerina*
6	пи_ни́ст	*pianist*
7	про_е́ссор	*professor*
8	а_три́са	*actress*
9	ме́недж_р	*manager*
10	д_ктор	*doctor*

3 Look at the following details of what's on television and answer the questions:

1 At what time is the dog show?
2 On which channel is there a film about Hollywood?

1	ОРТ	2	НТВ
10.15	Макси-шоу	10.00	Сегодня
10.40	Каламбур. Юмористический журнал	10.25	Сериал «Комиссар Рекс»
11.25	Сериал «Дженни едет в Голливуд»	11.30	Дог-шоу «Я и моя собака»
12.00	Новости	12.00	Сегодня

A The importance of the stress syllable; some spelling rules which will apply to all forms of words (e.g. nouns, adjectives, verbs).

If a Russian word has more than one syllable, it is important in terms of both pronunciation and grammar to know which syllable is 'stressed'. For example, in the Russian word for *engineer* there are three syllables: инженéр and the accent over the relevant letter (é) shows you that the third syllable is the one to emphasize. The good news is that you never need to write the 'stress mark' in – it's just there to help you, while you're learning. In this book stress marks are always indicated, unless an exercise is based on a real advertisement or ticket, as you would not normally see them in printed materials.

Of course, Russian isn't the only language where emphasis is important. In English, emphasizing the wrong part of the word can sometimes change the meaning (think of *record* and *record)*, and there are many words where it would sound odd if we emphasized each syllable equally (think how we emphasize the first syllable of *ever, everything* and *father* and how we 'throw away' the second or the second and third). This is what happens in Russian: pronounce the stressed syllable clearly and deliberately, but skim over the others – don't give them any emphasis (much as we deal with the last syllable, the *-er* of *ever*). The stress mark is perhaps most important of all in words which feature the letter o. If the o occurs in a word of only one syllable, or if it is the stressed syllable in a word composed of several syllables, then it will be pronounced, like *o* in 'b*o*re':

нос   *nose*   нóвый   *new*

If the letter o is not stressed it is pronounced like the 'a' in 'sof*a*', for example, хорошó *good*.

B Spelling rules

Remember! There are two important spelling rules in Russian:
1   Never write ы, ю, я after г, к, х, ж, ч, ш, щ; instead write и, у, а
2   Never write an unstressed o after ж, ч, ш, щ, ц
In order to apply Rule 2 accurately, it is important to know which syllable of a word is stressed. Unfortunately, there is no foolproof way of knowing where a word is stressed... other than to make a point of learning where the stress is when you first come across the word!

➤ For change of stress, see Units 5 and 39.

1 Here is a list of 15 of the words you have seen in stressed form so far in Units 1 and 2. Mark in their stresses and, when you have checked your answers in the Key, practise saying each word.

актриса	*actress*
балерина	*ballerina*
банкир	*banker*
доктор	*doctor*
журналист	*journalist*
компьютер	*computer*
менеджер	*manager*
новый	*new*
пианист	*pianist*
программист	*computer programmer*
профессор	*professor*
собака	*dog*
студент	*student*
турист	*tourist*
хорошо	*good*

2 Vladimir has been writing a story for homework, but has made five serious spelling mistakes. Underline and explain them. (A translation of Vladimir's masterpiece can be found in the Key.)

Ваня наконец спрашивает Машю
«Где собакы? Почему они молчят?»
Маша не отвечает, Ваня берёт
свои книгы и уходит к другу, Сашю.

Nouns are words which name someone or something (people, places, animals, objects, concepts). All Russian nouns have a gender.

A Russian words are divided randomly into three groups, known as 'genders'. These groups are *masculine, feminine* and *neuter*. Russian has no direct article (*the*) or indirect article (*a*), so we have to look at the ending of each word to determine its gender.

Gender	Endings	Example	
Masculine	consonant	журна́л	*magazine*
(dictionary symbol м)	й	музе́й	*museum*
	ь	автомоби́ль	*car*
Feminine	а	газе́та	*newspaper*
(dictionary symbol ж)	я	неде́ля	*week*
	ия	Росси́я	*Russia*
	ь	дочь	*daughter*
Neuter	о	ме́сто	*place*
(dictionary symbol ср)	е	по́ле	*field*
	ие	зда́ние	*building*

Б So, the only ending 'shared' by more than one gender is the soft sign (ь). These are the only nouns where you have to *learn* the gender, but they are a small group (and three-quarters of them are feminine); often they are 'naturally' masculine or feminine – e.g. царь (*tsar*) is masculine and дочь (*daughter*) is feminine.

В It will be helpful when you are learning case endings to distinguish between feminine nouns which end in я and those which end in ия as they often behave differently (and similarly for neuter nouns ending in е and ие).

Г There are a few exceptions to these patterns.
- The following nouns are masculine (because of their meaning):

де́душка	*grandfather*	мужчи́на	*man*
дя́дя	*uncle*	па́па	*daddy*

- The diminutive form of men's first names have feminine endings (e.g. Алекса́ндр → Са́ша).
- Nouns ending in -мя are neuter (вре́мя, *time*); ко́фе is masculine.

1 Look at the endings of the words that follow and decide on their gender; write м, ж or ср (or if you prefer to do it in English: *m*, *f*, or *n*) in the brackets which follow each word.

1	ра́дио	*radio*	( )	6	письмо́	*letter*	( )
2	телеви́зор	*television*	( )	7	де́рево	*tree*	( )
3	ма́рка	*stamp*	( )	8	дочь	*daughter*	( )
4	ку́хня	*kitchen*	( )	9	царь	*tsar*	( )
5	А́нглия	*England*	( )	10	геро́й	*hero*	( )

2 Match the words from the box to the pictures and indicate the gender (м, ж, ср).

ла́мпа	ра́дио	соба́ка	автомоби́ль	компью́тер	де́рево

1

2

3

4

5

6

3 There is one 'rogue' word in each of the following gender lists. Which words are in the wrong lists and which list should they be in?

М		**Ж**		**СР**	
па́спорт	*passport*	медсестра́	*nurse*	окно́	*window*
докуме́нт	*document*	инжене́р	*engineer*	ме́сто	*place*
ме́сяц	*month*	биоло́гия	*biology*	понима́ние	*understanding*
ви́за	*visa*	шко́ла	*school*	эне́ргия	*energy*
гид	*guide*	газе́та	*newspaper*	метро́	*metro*
ю́ноша	*young man*	деклара́ция	*declaration*	письмо́	*letter*

Cases show the roles that nouns play in a sentence. There are six cases in Russian and the endings of nouns change according to their case. The nominative case shows us who or what is performing the action of a verb (the subject); singular means there's only one actor/subject.

A The nominative case of a noun is the form you find in a dictionary, vocabulary or glossary.

год (м) *year*   шко́ла (ж) *school*
свида́ние (ср) *appointment, date*

The endings for each gender are: masculine: consonant, й, ь
feminine: а, я, ия, ь
neuter: о, е, ие

Б The nominative case 'names' the person or the thing doing the action of the verb (the subject).

Subject	Verb	Meaning
Студе́нт	чита́ет	*The student is reading*
О́льга	рабо́тает	*Olga is working*
Письмо́	лежи́т (на столе́)	*The letter is lying (on the table)*

В Since there are no words for *the* or *a* in Russian, a noun in the nominative case can mean either:

ме́сяц (м) *a month* or *the month*   медсестра́ (ж) *a nurse* or *the nurse*
окно́ (ср) *a window* or *the window*

Г Since there is no present tense of the verb 'to be' in Russian, the nominative case will appear with no apparent verb.

Subject	No verb 'to be'	Meaning
Бори́с	студе́нт	*Boris (is a) student*
Медсестра́	о́чень до́брая	*(The) nurse (is) very kind*
Письмо́	интере́сное	*(The) letter (is) interesting*

Д Russian word order is very flexible, so the subject is not always at the beginning of a sentence or phrase. The word order may be the same as English:

The lecture begins at seven o'clock.
Ле́кция начина́ется в семь часо́в.

or the subject may appear later in the phrase (without affecting the meaning):

В семь часо́в начина́ется ле́кция.

1 Look at the English sentences that follow and underline the subject of each sentence.

e.g. <u>Moscow</u> is the capital of Russia.
1 My husband works in the centre of town.
2 Viktor always stays at home on a Friday evening.
3 Is Olga a journalist?
4 Where is the dog?
5 Does the student know the new teacher?

2 Look at the Russian sentences that follow and underline the subject of each sentence (translations of these sentences are given in the Key):

e.g. Обы́чно <u>Влади́мир</u> отдыха́ет в Я́лте.
1 Соба́ка игра́ет в саду́.
2 Теа́тр о́чень краси́вый.
3 Когда́ начина́ется конце́рт?
4 Где моя́ кни́га?
5 Мой сын о́чень хоро́ший футболи́ст.

3 Complete the following sentences with the appropriate nominative singular noun, using the English sentences as a guide.

e.g. _____ начина́ется в семь часо́в. *The concert begins at seven o'clock.* (Конце́рт начина́ется в семь часо́в)

1 _____ не о́чень интере́сная. *The lecture is not very interesting.*
2 К сожале́нию э́то_____не свобо́дно. *Unfortunately this place is not free.*
3 _____ чита́ет кни́гу по фи́зике. *The student is reading a book on physics.*
4 _____ смо́трит телеви́зор. *Grandfather is watching TV.*
5 _____ до́рого сто́ит. *The car is (costs) expensive.*
6 Где нахо́дится_____? *Where is (situated) the stadium?*

If you want to talk about more than one subject, you use the plural. In Russian there are different forms of the plural, depending on the gender of the noun.

А Regular masculine nouns end in either a consonant, -й or -ь. The plural ending depends on which of these three kinds of noun you are using:

To a consonant, add ы:	студе́нт	→ студе́нты	*students*
Remove й, then add и:	музе́й	→ музе́и	*museums*
Remove ь, then add и:	автомоби́ль	→ автомоби́ли	*cars*

Б Regular feminine nouns end in either -а, -я, -ия or ь. The plural ending depends on which of these four kinds of noun you are dealing with:

Remove а, add ы:	актри́са	→ актри́сы	*actresses*
Remove я, add и:	неде́ля	→ неде́ли	*weeks*
	ста́нция	→ ста́нции	*stations*
Remove ь, add и:	дверь	→ две́ри	*doors*

NB For plurals of feminine nouns which end in -а, remember: never write ы after г, к, х, ж, ч, ш, щ. So, for example, кни́га → кни́ги *books*.

В Regular neuter nouns end in either -о, -е or -ие. The plural ending depends on which of these three kinds of noun you are dealing with:

Remove о, add а:	ме́сто	→ места́	*places*
Remove е, add я:	зда́ние	→ зда́ния	*buildings*

Г The stress in some regular nouns changes in the nominative plural, as you can see in the word ме́сто. This can happen in all genders. For example:

Masculine: стол (*table*) → столы́	стари́к (*old man*) → старики́
Feminine: игра́ (*game*) → и́гры	рука́ (*hand, arm*) → ру́ки
	сестра́ (*sister*) → сёстры
Neuter: окно́ (*window*) → о́кна	мо́ре (*sea*) → моря́

Dictionaries usually indicate any movement of stress in the Russian–English section and the best thing is to look out for this when you first come across a word (and try to learn it by saying both singular and plural out loud).

Д Some regular nouns 'lose' a vowel from their last syllable in all forms except nominative singular. (Vowels which disappear in this way are called 'fleeting vowels'.) Some common ones are: оте́ц → отцы́ (*fathers*); ковёр → ковры́ (*carpets*); це́рковь → це́ркви (*churches*).

➤ **For spelling rules, see Unit 2.**

1 In the following sentences which nouns are in the plural form? Underline them. (Translations of these sentences are given in the Key.)

1 Бо́льше всего́ Ви́ктор лю́бит чита́ть газе́ты.
2 Ма́рки до́рого сто́ят.
3 Я не зна́ю, где компью́теры.
4 Да, я ча́сто смотрю́ кинофи́льмы.
5 Я не понима́ю, почему́ он смо́трит телесериа́лы.

2 Match up each noun with a suitable plural ending.

e.g. конце́рт + ы → конце́рты

-ы	-и	-а	-я

1 балери́на   *ballerina*   6 свида́ние   *appointment*
2 журнали́ст   *journalist*   7 инжене́р   *engineer*
3 соба́ка   *dog*   8 ме́сяц   *month*
4 самолёт   *'plane*   9 буты́лка   *bottle*
5 исто́рия   *story*   10 письмо́   *letter*

3 Write the plural form of the following nouns.

1 же́нщина   *woman*   6 ло́шадь (ж)   *horse*
2 ма́льчик   *boy*   7 мо́ре   *sea*
3 де́вушка   *girl*   8 деклара́ция   *(currency) declaration*
4 мужчи́на   *man*   9 зда́ние   *building*
5 ко́шка   *cat*   10 геро́й   *hero*

4 Match the sentences on the left with the appropriate nominative plural noun phrase on the right.

1 О́льга и Ви́ктор игра́ют в те́ннис.   **a** Они́ журнали́сты
2 Они́ беру́т интервью́.   **b** Они́ программи́сты
3 Они́ лю́бят компью́теры.   **c** Они́ теннисисты

Some nouns do not work in the way described in Unit 5. Fortunately, irregular plural nouns in Russian fit into convenient groups.

A One group of irregular masculine nouns all behave in the same way. Instead of ending in ы or и they must end in a stressed á (or, in the case of учи́тель, a stressed я́). Here are the most common nouns which behave in this way:

а́дрес	→ адреса́	*addresses*	но́мер	→ номера́	*hotel rooms*
бе́рег	→ берега́	*banks/shores*	о́стров	→ острова́	*islands*
ве́чер	→ вечера́	*evenings/parties*	па́спорт	→ папорта́	*passports*
глаз	→ глаза́	*eyes*	по́езд	→ поезда́	*trains*
го́род	→ города́	*towns*	профе́ссор	→ профессора́	*professors*
дом	→ дома́	*houses*	тра́ктор	→ трактора́	*tractors*
до́ктор	→ доктора́	*doctors*	учи́тель	→ учителя́	*teachers*
лес	→ леса́	*forests*	цвет	→ цвета́	*colours*

Try not to confuse the last word on this list with the plural noun цветы́ (*flowers*, singular: цвето́к).

Б A second group of masculine nouns takes the nominative plural ending -ья:

брат	→ бра́тья	*brothers*	лист	→ ли́стья	*leaves*
друг	→ друзья́	*friends*	стул	→ сту́лья	*chairs*
сын	→ сыновья́	*sons*			

В A third group of masculine nouns ends in the singular in -анин or -янин. To make the nominative plural of these nouns, simply remove -ин and add -е:

англича́нин → англича́не *Englishmen* граждани́н → гра́ждане *citizen*

Г Feminine and neuter nouns have very few irregulars. The most common are:

дочь (ж)	→ до́чери	*daughters*	коле́но (ср)	→ коле́ни	*knees*
мать (ж)	→ ма́тери	*mothers*	плечо́ (ср)	→ пле́чи	*shoulders*
вре́мя (ср)	→ времена́	*times*	у́хо (ср)	→ у́ши	*ears*
де́рево (ср)	→ дере́вья	*trees*	я́блоко (ср)	→ я́блоки	*apples*
и́мя (ср)	→ имена́	*names*			

The good news is that some neuter nouns do not change at all in the plural, so the following are both the singular and the plural forms:

бюро́	*office*	метро́	*metro*	такси́	*taxi*
ви́ски	*whisky*	пиани́но	*piano*		
кафе́	*cafe*	ра́дио	*radio*		

Note that all these 'indeclinable' words (i.e. words that do not change) have been borrowed by Russian from western European languages.

Д The nouns for 'children' and 'people' are the most strikingly irregular of all:

ребёнок → де́ти *children*   челове́к → лю́ди *people*

➤ **For change of stress, see Units 5 and 39.**

1 Translate the following irregular nominative plural words into Russian.

1 brothers
2 names
3 children
4 mothers
5 addresses

6 eyes
7 trees
8 friends
9 people
10 towns

2 Кроссво́рд

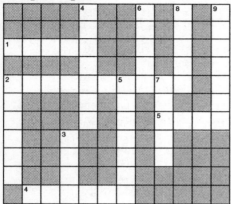

По вертика́ли

2 More than one train
3 Lots of forests
4 Plural of teacher
5 More than one son
6 Underground railway(s)
7 Radio(s)
8 More than one colour
9 Times

По горизонта́ли

1 Scottish drink in singular or plural
2 More than one top university teacher
4 Not sisters, but...
5 More than one house

The accusative case is used for the direct object of a sentence. The direct object is the person or thing that has an action done to it.

A Most sentences include the formula

Subject (person or thing performing an action) + Verb (action performed) + Object (person or thing that has action done to it)

Subject	Verb	Object	Meaning
Áнна	смóтрит	телевúзор	*Anna is watching television*
Борúс	читáет	газéту	*Boris is reading the newspaper*
Мы	слýшаем	рáдио	*We are listening to the radio*

Б In the singular, masculine nouns only change in the accusative case if they are animate (i.e. a person or an animal). All inanimate nouns (i.e. things) remain the same as in the nominative:

Хорошó, я возьмý журнáл. *OK, I'll take the magazine.*

If masculine singular nouns are animate (i.e. a person or an animal), their endings in the accusative are formed as follows:

To a consonant, add a: студéнт → студéнта
Remove й, then add я: герóй → герóя
Remove ь, then add я: учúтель → учúтеля

Вы знáете Борúса? Мы вúдим учúтеля кáждый день.
Do you know Boris? We see the teacher every day.

В The overwhelming majority of neuter nouns are inanimate, and they do not change in the accusative case: Письмó интерéсное? Дáйте мне письмó, пожáлуйста. *Is the letter interesting? Give me the letter, please.* A common animate neuter noun is лицó (when it means *person*, not *face*); its animate accusative is лицá.

Г Feminine singular nouns always change in the accusative case, whether animate or inanimate, except for soft-sign nouns (e.g. дверь *door*). Accusative endings of feminine nouns are formed as follows:

Remove a, add y: актрúса → актрúсу
Remove я, add ю: недéля → недéлю
Soft sign stays the same: дверь → дверь

Вы знáете Татья́ну? *Do you know Tatyana?*

➤ For change of stress, see Units 5 and 39.

1 Underline the object noun in each of the following sentences.

e.g. Always buy comfortable <u>shoes</u>.

1 I often watch the television.
2 Pass the water, please.
3 Have you seen the cat anywhere?
4 I've never visited the Kremlin.
5 He bought the least expensive watch available.

2 Match the two halves of each sentence, then find the English translation below.

1 Я предпочита́ю фи́зику   **a** но его́ бра́та я не зна́ю.
2 Я зна́ю его́ сестру́,   **b** А́ню и Вади́ма
3 Вы ви́дите апте́ку напра́во   **c** и врача́.
4 Я хочу́ пригласи́ть   **d** и не люблю́ хи́мию.
5 Мы уже́ зна́ем медсестру́   **e** и по́чту нале́во?

1 *I know his sister, but I don't know his brother.*
2 *I want to invite Anya and Vadim.*
3 *We already know the nurse and the doctor.*
4 *I prefer physics and I don't like chemistry.*
5 *Do you (can you) see the chemist's on the right and the post office on the left?*

3 Put the following words into the accusative case.

e.g. инжене́р → инжене́ра

1	дочь (ж)	*daughter*
2	ба́бушка	*grandmother*
3	мать (ж)	*mother*
4	дя́дя	*uncle*
5	тётя	*aunt*
6	стол	*table*
7	по́ле	*field*
8	октры́тка	*postcard*
9	ло́шадь (ж)	*horse*
10	брат	*brother*

08 accusative plural

If a plural noun is the object in a phrase or sentence its endings must change. The endings depend on whether the noun is animate (a person or an animal) or inanimate (a thing).

A The good news is that if a noun is inanimate, the ending for the accusative plural is exactly the same as the ending for the nominative plural. This applies to all three genders.

Subject	Verb	Object	Meaning
Áнна	смóтрит	фи́льмы	*Anna watches films*
Бори́с	чита́ет	газе́ты	*Boris reads newspapers*
Мы	мóем	óкна	*We are cleaning the windows*

Б If a noun is animate, then its ending must change. The animate accusative plural and the genitive plural are the only cases where the endings are different for the three genders. So, the bad news is that there are quite a few endings to learn for the animate accusative, but the good news is that by the time you get to Unit 11 you will already know the endings of the genitive plural!

В Masculine animate accusative plural:

To a consonant, add ов   студе́нт   →   студе́нтов
Remove й, then add ев   герóй (*hero*)   →   герóев
Remove ь, then add ей   писа́тель (*writer*) →   писа́телей
Care is needed if the masculine singular nominative ends in ж, ч, ш, щ. If it does, add ей, not ов: e.g. врач (*doctor*) → врачéй.

Г Feminine animate accusative plural:

Remove а, add nothing   актри́са   →   актри́с
Remove я, add ь: сóня (*dormouse*)   →   сонь
For nouns ending in ия, remove я, add й: Мари́я → Мари́й
Remove ь, add ей: лóшадь (*horse*)   →   лошадéй
Care is needed with feminine nouns ending in а. If you are left with a cluster of consonants when you have removed the -а you usually need to insert the vowel о, е or (very occasionally) ё. Three common examples you might find in the animate accusative are: де́вушка → де́вушек, ма́рка → ма́рок, сестра́ → сестёр

Вы зна́ете этих де́вушек?   *Do you know these girls?*
Нет, но я зна́ю их сестёр.   *No, but I know their sisters.*

Д There are *very* few neuter animate nouns. A common one is лицó (when it means *person*). The animate accusative plural is formed simply by removing the last letter.

> **For formation of irregular animate accusative plural see Unit 9; for genitive plural nouns see Unit 11.**

1 Underline the plural nouns in the following sentences which would need to be in the inanimate accusative in Russian and circle those which should be in the animate accusative.

e.g. Have you ever seen these (actors) and these plays before?
1 We always like to watch the boats and the seagulls when we are by the sea.
2 I forgot to buy tickets for the concert.
3 Please send the customers and their purchases to the cash desk.
4 Do you prefer to read books or newspapers?
5 She says she's going to get two dogs.

2 Write sentences saying what you want to buy, adding the correct accusative plural ending to each singular noun (they're all inanimate).

e.g. биле́т (*ticket*) → Я хочу́ купи́ть биле́ты
1 телефо́н
2 зда́ние
3 буты́лка
4 по́ле
5 ма́рка

3 Write sentences saying who you know, adding the correct accusative plural ending to each singular noun (they're all animate).

e.g. тури́ст → Я зна́ю тури́стов
1 инжене́р
2 медсестра́
3 футболи́ст
4 балери́на
5 врач

4 Explain who or what you're photographing by putting each singular noun in the accusative plural (animate or inanimate?).

e.g. собо́р (*cathedral*) → Я фотографи́рую собо́ры
1 коро́ва   *cow*
2 музыка́нт   *musician*
3 ло́дка   *boat*
4 магази́н   *shop*
5 пти́ца   *bird*

Some nouns do not work in the way described in Unit 8.
Fortunately, irregular accusative plural nouns fit into convenient
groups (just like irregular nominative plural nouns).

A Nouns which have irregular endings still follow the same pattern
for the accusative plural outlined in Unit 8: if a noun is inanimate,
the ending for the accusative plural is exactly the same as the
ending for the nominative plural.

Он зна́ет все адреса́.   Вы купи́ли сту́лья?
He knows all the addresses   *Did you buy the chairs?*

Б Animate nouns which have an irregular nominative plural
ending in a stressed á take -óв in the accusative plural: Я уже́
зна́ю профессоро́в. The irregular nominative plural учителя́
becomes учителе́й.

В If animate nouns have an irregular nominative plural ending in
-ья, then the accusative plural ending is either -ьев (if the
nominative plural is stressed on the stem) or éй (if the nominative
plural is stressed on the end):

Nominative singular	Nominative plural	Accusative plural
брат *brother*	бра́тья *nom. pl. stressed on stem*	бра́тьев
друг *friend*	друзья́ *nom. pl. stressed on end*	друзе́й
сын *son*	сыновья́ *nom. pl. stressed on end*	сыиове́й

Г For animate nouns whose nominative singular ends in -нин, this
is what happens:

Nominative singular	Nominative plural	Accusative plural
англича́нин	англича́не	англича́н
граждани́н	гра́ждане	гра́ждан

Д The accusative plural of the irregular feminine nouns мать and
дочь are:

Nominative singular	Nominative plural	Accusative plural
дочь	до́чери	дочере́й
мать	ма́тери	матере́й

Е And finally, the accusative plural for 'children' and 'people'
comes from their strikingly different nominative plural form:

Nominative singular	Nominative plural	Accusative plural
ребёнок	де́ти	дете́й
челове́к	лю́ди	люде́й

➤ For formation of irregular nominative plural, see Unit 6.
For animate accusative plural of regular nouns, see Unit 8.

1 Ask about people's preferences by putting the nouns given below into the accusative plural:

e.g. лес/о́стров → Что вы лю́бите бо́льше, леса́ и́ли острова́?

1 де́рево/бе́рег
2 по́езд/тра́ктор
3 стул/цвет
4 дом/го́род

2 Match the two halves of each sentence, then find the English translation in the sentences that follow.

1 Он уже́ зна́ет   a англича́н в аэропорту́.
2 Вы ви́дели   b учителе́й.
3 Гид встре́тил   c друзе́й в рестора́н.
4 Нет, я не зна́ю   d бра́тьев Влади́мира.
5 Она́ ча́сто приглаша́ет e его́ сынове́й вчера́?

1 *No, I don't know Vladimir's brothers.*
2 *She often invites friends to the restaurant.*
3 *Did you see his sons yesterday?*
4 *He already knows the teachers.*
5 *The guide met the Englishmen at the airport.*

3 Boris and Elena complete a questionnaire about their visit to England. They have made a list of what they have liked most (✔) and what they have liked least (✖). Complete the account of their visit by giving the accusative plural in Russian of their likes and dislikes (reminder бо́льше = *more*; ме́ньше = *less*).

✔	✖
towns	trains
houses	evenings
people	
hotel rooms	

Мы тури́сты в А́нглии. Что мы люби́ли бо́льше? Что мы люби́ли ме́ньше?

Мы люби́ли бо́льше_____, _____, _____, и_____.

Мы люби́ли ме́ньше_____ и_____.

The genitive case is the Russian way of saying 'of', so it indicates possession and is also used when talking about quantities.

A The principal meaning of the genitive case is *of*, but it is also used with quantities (e.g. *a lot, a bottle, not any*, and after the numerals 2, 3 and 4):

Это паспорт студе́нта.	*It is the passport of the student (the student's passport).*
Здесь нет телефо́на.	*Here there is no (not any) telephone.*

Б There are two possible endings for the genitive singular of masculine nouns: either -a or -я.

To a consonant, add a:	лимона́д →	лимона́да
Remove й, then add я:	Серге́й →	Серге́я
Remove ь, then add я:	И́горь →	И́горя
Вот буты́лка лимона́да.	*Here is a bottle of lemonade.*	
Где пиджа́к Серге́я?	*Where is Sergei's jacket?*	
Серге́й брат И́горя.	*Sergei is Igor's brother.*	

В There are two possible endings for the genitive singular of feminine nouns: either -ы or -и.

Remove a, add ы:	вода́ →	воды́
Remove я, add и:	Росси́я →	Росси́и
Remove ь, add и:	свекро́вь →	свекро́ви
Да́йте, пожа́луйста, буты́лку воды́.	*Give me a bottle of water, please.*	
Москва́ столи́ца Росси́и.	*Moscow is the capital of Russia.*	

Remember: never write ы after г, к, х, ж, ч, ш, щ (e.g. ко́шка → ко́шки *of the cat*).

NB мать and дочь have irregular genitive singular forms: ма́тери and до́чери.

Г There are two possible endings for the genitive singular of neuter nouns: either -a or -я.

Remove o, add a:	ме́сто →	ме́ста
Remove e, add я:	зда́ние →	зда́ния
	по́ле →	по́ля

Neuter words which end in -мя have the irregular ending -мени: вре́мя → вре́мени, и́мя → и́мени.

Здесь нет ме́ста.	*There's no room (not any place) here.*
У меня́ нет вре́мени!	*I have no (not any) time!*

> **For use of genitive case with prepositions, see Units 83, 84, 85, 88, 89, for use of genitive singular with numerals, see Units 41 and 45, for use of genitive with comparatives, see Unit 37.**

1 In the following sentences which nouns would be in the genitive in Russian? Underline them.

e.g. Have you seen <u>Olga's</u> book?

1 There isn't any cheese in the fridge.
2 I'd like half a kilo of ham, please.
3 Rome is the capital of Italy.
4 The tourist's passport is on the floor.
5 Igor's e-mail address is on this piece of paper.

2 Look at the drawings and then make up sentences to describe who owns what:

e.g. Ольга/багáж

→ Это багáж Ольги.

1 Борис/собáка

2 Андрéй/автомобиль

3 Анна/телефóн

4 Игорь/рáдио

3 Complete the phrases by putting the word in brackets into the genitive singular.

1 Бутылка	(винó)	*a bottle of wine*
2 Полкилó	(сыр)	*half a kilo of cheese*
3 Бáнка	(икрá)	*a jar/tin of caviar*
4 Пáчка	(чáй)	*a packet of tea*
5 Бутылка	(вóдка)	*a bottle of vodka*

4 The restaurant has run out of everything – the waiter is explaining what isn't on the menu. Complete his statements by putting the word in brackets into the genitive singular.

e.g. курица → У нас нет курицы. *We haven't got any chicken.*

1 У нас нет_____(ветчинá). *We haven't got any ham.*
2 У нас нет_____(пиво). *We haven't got any beer.*
3 У нас нет_____(хлеб). *We haven't got any bread.*
4 У нас нет_____(говядина). *We haven't got any beef.*
5 У нас нет_____(шоколáд). *We haven't got any chocolate.*

The genitive plural has different endings for each gender. You need this case if you want to say, for example, 'a big group of tourists'.

A There are three endings for the genitive plural of masculine nouns: -ов, -ев, -ей.

NB If a masculine word ends in ж, ч, ш, щ, add ей, not ов: e.g. нож (*knife*) → ножéй.

Nominative singular		Genitive plural
турúст	*tourist*	турúстов
трамвáй	*tram*	трамвáев
портфéль	*briefcase*	портфéлей

Б There are four endings for the genitive plural of feminine nouns: remove a and add nothing, or remove я or ь and add, -ь, -й or -ей.

Nominative singular		Genitive plural
шкóла	*school*	школ
недéля	*week*	недéль
стáнция	*station*	стáнций
дверь	*door*	дверéй

NB If the feminine word ends in -a and when you remove it you are left with a consonant 'cluster' (i.e. more than one), it is sometimes necessary to insert either о, ё or е (е if the 'cluster' you are left with is жк, чк, шк). E.g.:

Nominative singular		Genitive plural
мáрка	*stamp*	мáрок

В There are two endings for the genitive plural of neuter nouns: if the word ends in о remove it; otherwise add й:

Nominative singular		Genitive plural
мéсто	*place*	мест
пóле	*field*	полéй
здáние	*building*	здáний

NB If the neuter word ends in -о and when you remove it you are left with a consonant 'cluster' (i.e. more than one), it is sometimes necessary to insert either о or е. Two very common examples are окнó (*window*) → óкон and письмó (*letter*) → пúсем (notice that here the е replaces ь).

1 Underline the words in the following sentences which are in the genitive plural.

e.g. Он купи́л мно́го <u>сувени́ров</u>. *He bought a lot of souvenirs.*

1 В кла́ссе мно́го ма́льчиков. *There are many boys in the class.*

2 Вот докуме́нты студе́нтов. *Here are the students' documents.*

3 Он дал мне мно́го книг. *He gave me a lot of books.*

4 У нас нет пи́сем. *We have no letters.*

5 Полкило́ помидо́ров, пожа́луйста. *Half a kilo of tomatoes, please.*

2 Give the genitive plural of the following nominative singular nouns.

e.g. су́мка → су́мок

1 час	*hour*	6 мо́ре	*sea*
2 река́	*river*	7 гости́ница	*hotel*
3 музе́й	*museum*	8 ня́ня	*nanny*
4 танцо́р	*dancer*	9 геро́й	*hero*
5 дверь (ж)	*door*	10 строи́тель	*builder*

3 Complete the shopping list by putting the word in brackets into the genitive plural.

1 полкило́ _____ (апельси́н) *half a kilo of oranges.*
2 коро́бка _____ (конфе́та) *a box of sweets*
3 коро́бка _____ (спи́чка) *a box of matches.*
4 па́чка _____ (сигаре́та) *a packet of cigarettes.*
5 гроздь _____ (бана́н) *a bunch of bananas.*

4 Put the words in column A into the genitive plural, then match them up with the words in column B in order to produce the meaning in column C.

e.g. A ма́льчик B гру́ппа C *a group of boys* → гру́ппа ма́льчиков

A	B	C
ма́льчик	гру́ппа	*a group of boys*
докуме́нт	нет	1 *lots of stations*
ма́рка	гру́ппа	2 *a bunch of roses*
врач	мно́го	3 *there are no stamps*
ро́за	па́чка	4 *a group of doctors*
ста́нция	буке́т	5 *a bundle of documents*

There are a number of very common nouns which have irregular forms in the genitive plural.

А The important thing is to know which nouns have irregular nominative plurals, because their genitive plural forms will be based on this.

Б This is what happens to masculine nouns in the genitive plural: if the nominative plural ends in stressed á, then the genitive plural ending is óв (so not strikingly irregular, just be aware of the stressed ending).

If the nominative plural ends in:

- ья and the word is stressed on the stem, the genitive plural ending is -ьев
- stressed ья́, then the genitive plural ending is -éй
- -не, then the genitive plural ending is... nothing!

Nominative singular		Nominative plural	Genitive plural
го́род	*town*	города́	городо́в
стул	*chair*	сту́лья	сту́льев
друг	*friend*	друзья́	друзéй
англича́нин	*Englishman*	англича́не	англича́н

В There are very few irregular genitive plural endings for feminine nouns. The most common are the words for *mother* and *daughter*:

мать → матерéй   дочь → дочерéй

NB Some feminine nouns with a 'cluster of consonants' before their ending form their genitive plural by inserting the letter ё: звезда́ (*star*) → звёзд, сестра́ (*sister*) → сестёр, серьга́ (*ear-ring*) → серёг

Г Although a number of common neuter nouns have irregular nominative plural forms, only a few have irregular genitive plurals, e.g.:

врéмя   (*time*)   → времён   у́хо   (*ear*)   → ушéй

и́мя   (*name*)   → имён

Д And finally, the genitive plural for 'children' and 'people' comes from their strikingly different nominative plural form:

Nominative singular	Nominative Plural	Genitive plural
ребёнок	дéти	детéй
человéк	лю́ди	людéй

NB After a numeral the genitive plural of человéк is человéк (5 человéк, *5 people*).

➤ For irregular nominative plurals, see Unit 6.

1 You are showing your holiday photographs. Explain what they are of by putting each noun into the genitive plural.

e.g. друг → Вот фотогра́фии друзе́й. *Here are photographs of friends.*

1	брат	6	англича́нин
2	де́рево	7	сын
3	ребёнок	8	дочь
4	звезда́	9	граждани́н
5	го́род	10	лист

2 If you want to buy quantities of things, you'll need the genitive plural. Make sentences by using the following words (NB a mixture of regular and irregular).

e.g. конфе́та → Я хочу́ купи́ть мно́го конфе́т. *I want to buy a lot of sweets.*

1	стул	*chair*
2	апельси́н	*orange*
3	отркы́тка	*postcard*
4	блу́зка	*blouse*
5	конве́рт	*envelope*
6	ру́чка	*pen*
7	сувени́р	*souvenir*
8	дом	*house*
9	я́блоко	*apple*
10	письмо́	*letter*

3 The following words are in the genitive plural. Put them into the nominative singular (NB another mixture of regular and irregular).

e.g. адресо́в → а́дрес

1 ли́стьев
2 матере́й
3 гости́ниц
4 англича́н
5 фотогра́фий
6 уше́й
7 бу́лок
8 автомоби́лей
9 времён
10 люде́й

The principal meaning of the dative case is *to* or *for*. It is used for the indirect object (the person or thing that is shown, told etc. something). The dative case also follows some common verbs, e.g. помогáть (to help), звонѝть (to ring).

A The dative case is needed for the indirect object of a sentence:

Subject +	Verb +	Object +	Indirect object
Vadim	*gave*	*a bunch of roses*	*to Katya*
Вадѝм	дал	букéт роз	Кáте

Б There are two endings for the dative singular of masculine nouns: -у and -ю.

Nominative singular		Dative singular
брат	*brother*	брáту
Сергéй	*Sergei*	Сергéю
учѝтель	*teacher*	учѝтелю

В There are two endings for the dative singular of feminine nouns: -е and -и.

Nominative singular		Dative singular
сестрá	*sister*	сестрé
Кáтя	*Katya*	Кáте
Марѝя	*Maria*	Марѝи

NB The two most common irregular dative feminine forms are for *mother* and *daughter*: мать → мáтери and дочь → дóчери.

Г There are two endings for the dative singular of neuter nouns: -у and -ю.

Nominative singular		Dative singular
окнó	*window*	окнý
мóре	*sea*	мóрю
здáние	*building*	здáнию

NB The neuter words врéмя and ѝмя form their dative singular as follows: врéмя → врéмени; ѝмя → ѝмени.

➤ For use of dative case with prepositions, see Units 85 and 89; for use of dative with expressions of possibility, impossibility and necessity, see Unit 77; for use of dative with impersonal verbs, see Unit 81.

1 Which of the words in the following passage are in the dative singular? Underline them.

e.g. Она́ звони́т <u>инжене́ру</u> ка́ждый день. *She rings the engineer every day.*

Бори́с никогда́ не помога́ет дру́гу, Ви́ктору. Éсли у Ви́ктора пробле́ма, он звони́т тёте и́ли дя́де. Дя́дя лю́бит помога́ть племя́ннику.
Boris never helps (his) friend. If Viktor has a problem, he rings (his) aunt or uncle. (His) uncle likes to help (his) nephew).

2 Who gave what to whom? Make sentences using the words given (the direct objects – the presents – have already been put into the accusative case for you; the meaning of your completed sentence is on the right).

e.g. Серге́й/ру́чку/Еле́на → Серге́й дал ру́чку Еле́не.
Sergei gave a pen to Elena.
Еле́на/носки́/Серге́й → Еле́на дала́ носки́ Серге́ю.
Elena gave socks to Sergei.

1 Он/кни́гу/Светла́на	*He gave a book to Svetlana.*
2 Дочь/духи́/мать	*The daughter gave perfume to (her) mother.*
3 Он/цветы́/медсестра́	*He gave flowers to the nurse.*
4 Áня/мотоци́кл/Андре́й	*Anya gave Andrei a motorbike.*
5 Она́/письмо́/дире́ктор	*She gave the letter to the director.*

3 Put the following words into the dative singular.

1 врач	*doctor*	6 Ита́лия	*Italy*
2 журнали́ст	*journalist*	7 Зо́я	*Zoya*
3 Ѝгорь (м)	*Igor*	8 ку́хня	*kitchen*
4 по́ле	*field*	9 писа́тель	*writer*
5 у́лица	*street*	10 свекро́вь (ж)	*mother-in-law*

4 Complete the passage by putting the words in brackets into the dative singular.

Вади́м звони́т _____ (мать), _____ (Татья́на) ка́ждый день в 4 часа́. Он ча́сто звони́т _____ (брат), _____ (Константи́н) и _____ (друг), _____ (Анто́н).

If the indirect object of a sentence is plural then its ending must change to the dative plural; it must also change to the dative if the noun follows those verbs which always take the dative (e.g. помогáть, to help, звонúть, to ring and совéттовать, to advise).

A The dative plural endings for nouns are the same for all genders. There are two possible endings (-ам, or -ям) and to determine which one should be used, look at the last letter of the nominative singular.

Б The ending for dative plural nouns ending in a consonant, -а or -о in the nominative singular is -ам. Add this ending to nouns ending in a consonant; to nouns ending in -а or -о, remove the last letter of the nominative singular, then add -ам, for example:

спортсмéн → Врач совéтует спортсмéнам. *The doctor advises the sportsmen.*

сестрá → Брат совéтует сёстрам. *The brother advises (his) sisters.*

В The ending for dative plural nouns which end in anything else in the nominative singular (i.e. -й, -ь, -я, -ия, -е, -ие) is -ям. Remove the last letter of the nominative singular and add -ям, for example:

герóй → Президéнт дал герóям медáли. *The president gave medals to the heroes.*

стройтель → Банкúр совéтует стройтелям. *The banker advises the builders.*

Г Nouns which have irregular nominative plurals form their dative plural from the nominative plural:

Nominative singular	Nominative plural	Dative plural
друг	друзья́	друзья́м
ребёнок	дéти	дéтям
человéк	лю́ди	лю́дям

The words дочь, врéмя and úмя form their dative plurals as follows: дочь → дочеря́м, врéмя → временáм, úмя → именáм.

➤ For use of dative case with prepositions, see Units 85 and 89, for use of dative with expressions of possibility, impossibility and necessity see Unit 77, for use of dative with impersonal verbs, see Unit 81, for irregular nominative plurals, see Unit 6.

1 Build sentences from the three Russian words given in each line. The third word is in the nominative singular – you will need to put it into the dative plural.

e.g. Бабу́шка/конфе́ты/ребёнок → Бабу́шка даёт конфе́ты де́тям

1 Кассирша/сда́чу/клие́нт — *The cashier gives change to the customers.*

2 Ученики́/кни́ги/учи́тель — *The pupils give the books to the teachers.*

3 Медсестра́/лека́рство/пацие́нт — *The nurse gives medicine to the patients.*

4 Гид/биле́ты/англича́нин — *The guide gives the tickets to the Englishmen.*

5 Он/пода́рки/друзья́ — *He gives presents to (his) friends.*

2 Give the dative plural of the following nouns.

1 трамва́й	*tram*	6 почтальо́н	*postman*	
2 де́рево	*tree*	7 преподава́тель	*teacher (in higher education)*	
3 карти́на	*picture*	8 зда́ние	*building*	
4 худо́жник	*artist*	9 ло́шадь (ж)	*horse*	
5 сын	*son*	10 официа́нтка	*waitress*	

3 Match the phrases on the left with those on the right so that they accord with the English translations which follow.

1 Мини́стры сове́туют — **a** актёрам
2 Продю́сер звони́т — **b** ме́неджерам
3 Врач помога́ет — **c** писа́телям
4 Программи́ст помога́ет — **d** пацие́нтам
5 Секрета́рь сове́туёт — **e** поли́тикам

1 *The producer rings the actors.*
2 *The secretary advises the managers.*
3 *The ministers advise the politicians*
4 *The computer programmer helps the writers*
5 *The doctor helps the patients.*

The instrumental case is used to describe the means by which an action is performed (*I write <u>with a pen</u>*). It is also used for the complement of a verb (*I work <u>as a doctor</u>*), in some time phrases, for nouns following some reflexive verbs and with certain prepositions.

A The principal meaning of this case is 'by/with' to explain how an action is achieved. The words underlined below would be put into the instrumental case:

> *Ivan went to Moscow by <u>train</u>. He took photos with his <u>camera</u>.*

NB If a phrase including 'with' means 'accompanied by' (e.g. 'tea with lemon', 'I'm going with my sister'), then the preposition **c** must be used before the noun in the instrumental: e.g. 'Я е́ду в Ло́ндон по́ездом с сестро́й' *I'm going to London with my sister*. Note that the vowel o is sometimes added to the preposition **c** when it is followed by a word which starts with a cluster of consonants, e.g. со внима́нием *with attention*.

Б The instrumental case is used when a verb is followed by a 'complement' (which gives more information about the subject of a sentence). For example: *Ivan works as a <u>photographer</u>*.

В The instrumental ending is found in time phrases relating to seasons and parts of the day, e.g.:

| ле́том | *in summer* | у́тром | *in/during the morning* |
| зимо́й | *in winter* | ве́чером | *in/during the evening* |

Г Common reflexive verbs followed by the instrumental are занима́ться (*to be busy, occupy oneself*) and интересова́ться (*to be interested in*): он интересу́ется рисова́нием, *he is interested in drawing*.

Д To form the instrumental case:

- Masculine nouns ending in a consonant add -ом, otherwise remove the last letter and add -ем: ве́чер (*evening*) → ве́чером, трамва́й → трамва́ем, учи́тель → учи́телем. Remember that you can't have unstressed o after ж, ч, ш, щ, ц! So instrumental of муж (*husband*) → му́жем.

- Feminine nouns: remove last letter and add -ой to words which end in -a; add -ей to words ending in -я or -ия. If a word ends in -ь, don't remove it, just add -ю. Eg: зима́ (*winter*) → зимо́й, А́нглия → А́нглией, о́сень (*autumn*) → о́сенью. (**NB** мать → ма́терью, дочь → до́черью). Remember that you can't have unstressed o after ж, ч, ш, щ, ц! So instrumental of у́лица → у́лицей.

- Neuter words: just add -м! у́тро (*morning*) → у́тром, зда́ние → зда́нием (**NB** вре́мя → вре́менем).

> **➤ For use of instrumental case with prepositions, see Unit 84.**

1 Underline the nouns in the following passage which you would need to put into the instrumental case in Russian.

In the evening I am going by <u>train</u> with <u>Elena</u> to Viktor's. Viktor works in Novgorod as an <u>architect</u>. Viktor's interested in <u>sport</u>. In the <u>summer</u>, he plays tennis with Sasha twice a week.

2 Here is the same passage in Russian. Complete it by putting the words in brackets into the instrumental singular.

Ве́чером я е́ду _поездом_ (по́езд) с _Еленой_ (Еле́на) к Ви́ктору. Ви́ктор рабо́тает в Но́вгороде, _архитектором_ (архите́ктор). Ви́ктор интересу́ется _спортом_ (спорт). _Летом_ он игра́ет в те́ннис с _Сашей_ (Са́ша) два ра́за в неде́лю.

3 Each customer in the restaurant wants something slightly different. Make up their requests by giving the instrumental of the following words.

e.g. рис → Мне, пожа́луйста, ры́бу с ри́сом. *For me, please, fish with rice.*

1 хлеб	bread	Мне (салат) рыбу с хлебом
2 сала́т	salad	мне рыбу с салатом
3 карто́шка	potato	мне рыбу с картошкой

e.g. са́хар → Мне, пожа́луйста, чай с са́харом. *For me, please, tea with sugar.*

4 молоко́	milk	Мне чай с молоком
5 лимо́н	lemon	Мне чай с лимоном
6 пече́нье	biscuit	Мне чай с печеньем

4 Who is going to the cinema with whom? Complete the details by putting the names in brackets into the instrumental case:

e.g. Бори́с → Мы идём в теа́тр с Бори́сом.

1 И́горь (м) — Я еду в кинотеатр с Игорем
2 профе́ссор — Ты идёшь в кинотеатр с профессором
3 Мари́я — Он идёт в кинотеатр с Марией
4 друг — Вы идёте в кинотеатр с другом
5 Ка́тя — Он идёт в театр с катей

The instrumental plural endings are needed if a plural instrument is being described, or a plural noun is following the prepositions, or a verb which requires the instrumental.

A The instrumental plural endings for nouns are the same for all genders. There are two possible endings (-ами or -ями) and to determine which one should be used, look at the last letter of the nominative singular.

Б The ending for instrumental plural nouns ending in a consonant, -a or -o in the nominative singular is -ами. Add this ending to nouns ending in a consonant. To nouns ending in -a or -o, remove the last letter of the nominative singular, then add -ами, for example:

гриб (*mushroom*)	→ суп с грибáми	*soup with mushrooms (i.e. mushroom soup)*
мáрка (*stamp*)	→ интересовáться мáрками	*to be interested in stamps*
письмó (*letter*)	→ занимáться пúсьмами	*to be busy with letters*

В The ending for instrumental plural nouns which end in anything else in the nominative singular (i.e. -й, -ь, -я, -ия, -е, -ие) is -ями. Remove the last letter of the nominative singular and add -ями, for example:

гость (*guest*) → Он éдет в тeáтр с гостями.	*He is going to the theatre with guests*

Г Nouns which have irregular nominative plurals form their instrumental plural from the nominative plural (but the choice is still only between the endings -ами, or -ями), for example:

Nominative singular	Nominative plural	Instrumental plural
врéмя	временá	временáми
гóрод	городá	городáми
друг	друзья́	друзья́ми
стул	стýлья	стýльями
ýхо	ушú	ушáми

NB The following are exceptions and do not end in -ами, or -ми:

дочь	дóчери	дочерьмú
ребёнок	дéти	детьмú
человéк	лю́дей	людьмú

➤ **For uses of instrumental case, see Unit 15, for further uses with prepositions, see Units 84, 88, 89, for irregular nominative plurals, see Unit 6.**

1 Put the following words into the instrumental plural.

e.g. магазин (*shop*) → магазинами

1	аптека	*chemist's*	6 дерево	*tree*
2	здание	*building*	7 друг	*friend*
3	предмет	*subject*	8 экскурсия	*excursion*
4	писатель	*writer*	9 дочь	*daughter*
5	открытие	*discovery*	10 компьютер	*computer*

2 Who is interested in what? Make sentences by putting the singular noun into the instrumental plural:

e.g. Сергей/книга (*book*) → Сергей интересуется книгами.

1 Ирина/симфония (*symphony*)
2 Валентин/фильм (*film*)
3 Архитектор/окно (*window*)
4 Гитарист/гитара (*guitar*)
5 Студент/писатель (*writer*)

3 Complete the menu by putting the words in brackets into the instrumental plural.

e.g. суп с _____ (гриб) → суп с грибами *mushroom soup*

МЕНЮ

1 суп с _____ (помидор) — *tomato soup*
2 салат с _____ (огурец) — *cucumber salad*
  рыба с жареной картошкой — *fish with fried potato*
  бефстроганов — *beef stroganoff*
  курица с овощами — *chicken with vegetables*
3 торт с _____ (орех) — *walnut cake*
4 мороженое с _____ (фрукт) — *ice-cream with fruits*

The prepositional case has no 'meaning' of its own. As its name suggests it is used in phrases which indicate position and specifically with the prepositions в (*in, at*) and на (*on, at*).

A There is one regular ending for masculine nouns: -e.

Nom. sing.	Prep. sing.	Example	Meaning
óфис	óфисе	Я рабóтаю в óфисе.	*I work in an office.*
музéй	музéе	Он рабóтает в музéе.	*He works in a museum.*
стол	столé	Кни́га на столé.	*The book is on the table.*

Б There are two regular endings for feminine nouns: -e and -и.

Nom. sing.	Prep. sing.	Example	Meaning
гости́ница	гости́нице	Я рабóтаю в гости́нице.	*I work in a hotel.*
дерéвня	дерéвне	Он живёт в дерéвне.	*He lives in a village.*
Áнглия	Áнглии	Я живу́ в Áнглии.	*I live in England.*
тетрáдь	тетрáди	Упражнéние в тетрáди.	*The exercise is in the exercise book.*

NB *Mother* – мать → мáтери and *daughter* – дочь → дóчери.

В There are two regular endings for neuter nouns: -e and -и.

Nom. sing.	Prep. sing.	Example	Meaning
письмó	письмé	Нóвости в письмé.	*The news is in the letter.*
пóле	пóле	Палáтка в пóле.	*The tent is in the field.*
здáние	здáнии	Óфис в здáнии.	*The office is in the building.*

NB Irregular forms for *time* – врéмя (врéмени) and *name* – и́мя (и́мени).

Г Some masculine nouns have the irregular prepositional ending -ý. The most common of these are:

аэропóрт (*airport*) → аэропортý   пол (*floor*) → полý

бéрег (*bank, shore*) → берегý   сад (*garden*) → садý
год (*year*) → годý   снег (*snow*) → снегý
лёд (*ice*) → льдý*   ýгол (*corner*) → углý*

лес (*forest*) → лесý   шкаф (*cupboard*) → шкафý
*(Fleeting vowels.)

> **For fleeting vowels, see Unit 5. For other prepositions used with prepositional case, see Unit 89, for restrictions on use of в, see Unit 83.**

1 **Make up sentences explaining who works where.**

e.g. учи́тель/шко́ла → Учи́тель рабо́тает в шко́ле.

1	врач/в/больни́ца	*the doctor works in the hospital*
2	архите́ктор/в/зда́ние	*the architect works in the building*
3	моря́к/на/мо́ре	*the sailor works at sea*
4	официа́нт/в/рестора́н	*the waiter works in the restaurant*
5	садо́вник/в/сад	*the gardener works in the garden*

2 **Make up sentences explaining where things are.**

e.g. су́мка/на/пол → Су́мка на полу́. *The bag is on the floor*

1	самолёт/в/аэропо́рт	*The 'plane is at the airport*
2	ви́за/в/па́спорт	*The visa is in the passport*
3	шу́ба/в/шкаф	*The fur coat is in the cupboard*
4	компью́тер/на/стол	*The computer is on the table*
5	Мадри́д/в/Испа́ния	*Madrid is in Spain*

3 **Put the following words into the prepositional case.**

1	ме́сто	*place*
2	бассе́йн	*swimming pool*
3	автомоби́ль (м)	*car*
4	лаборато́рия	*laboratory*
5	лёд	*ice*
6	музе́й	*museum*
7	трамва́й	*tram*
8	по́чта	*post office*
9	ку́хня	*kitchen*
10	по́ле	*field*

4 **Match each question with an appropriate answer.**

1 Ро́зы в шкафу́?	**a**	Нет, она́ в саду́
2 Соба́ка в университе́те?	**b**	Нет, он в теа́тре
3 Официа́нт в лаборато́рии?	**c**	Нет, они́ в буке́те
4 Актёр в о́фисе?	**d**	Нет, он на стадио́не
5 Спортсме́н на ку́хне?	**e**	Нет, он в рестора́не

18 prepositional plural

The prepositional plural endings are needed if a plural noun is following the prepositions в (*in, at*) or на (*on, at*).

A The prepositional plural endings for nouns are the same for all genders. There are two possible endings (-ах or -ях) and to determine which one should be used, look at the last letter of the nominative singular.

Б The ending for prepositional plural nouns ending in a consonant, -a or -o in the nominative singular is: -ах. Add this ending to nouns ending in a consonant. To nouns ending in -a or -o, remove the last letter of the nominative singular, then add -ах, for example:

ресторáн → Они́ обéдают в ресторáнах. *They have lunch in restaurants.*

квартúра → Они́ живýт в квартúрах. *They live in flats.*

мéсто → Они́ сидя́т на местáх у окнá. *They are sitting in seats by the window.*

В The ending for prepositional plural nouns which end in anything else in the nominative singular (i.e. -й, -ь, -я, -ия, -е, -ие) is -ях. Remove the last letter of the nominative singular and add -ях, for example:

автомоби́ль → Води́тели ждут в автомоби́лях. *Drivers are waiting in (their) cars.*

стáнция → Пассажи́ры ждут на стáнциях. *Passengers wait at stations.*

Г Nouns which have irregular nominative plurals form their prepositional plural from the nominative plural (but the choice is still only between the endings -ах, or -ях), e.g.:

Nominative singular	Nominative	Prepositional plural plural
гóрод	городá	городáх
друг	друзья́	друзья́х
ребёнок	дéти	дéтях
стул	стýлья	стýльях
человéк	лю́ди	лю́дях

The words мать, дочь, врéмя and и́мя form their dative plurals as follows: мать → матеря́х, дочь → дочеря́х, врéмя → временáх, и́мя → именáх.

➤ For other prepositions used with prepositional case, see Unit 89, for restrictions on use of в, see Unit 83, for irregular nominative plurals, see Unit 6.

1 Put the following nouns into the prepositional plural:

1	дере́вня	*village*	6	парфюме́рия	*perfume shop*
2	го́род	*town*	7	портфе́ль (м)	*briefcase*
3	центр	*centre*	8	по́ле	*field*
4	страна́	*country*	9	но́мер	*hotel room*
5	ме́сто	*place*	10	стул	*chair*

2 Make sentences from the words that follow.

e.g. Тури́сты отдыха́ют/пляж → Тури́сты отдыха́ют на пля́жах. *Tourists rest on beaches.*

1 Продавцы́ рабо́тают/магази́н *Shop assistants work in shops.*

2 Студе́нты у́чатся/университе́т *Students study at universities.*

3 Фе́рмеры рабо́тают/фе́рма *Farmers work on farms.*

4 Хи́мики рабо́тают/лаборато́рия *Chemists work in laboratories.*

5 Учителя́ рабо́тают/шко́ла *Teachers work in schools.*

3 Complete the passage about tourists below by putting the words in brackets into the prepositional plural. Use the English translation which follows to help you.

Тури́сты живу́т в _____ (гости́ница) и в _____ (ке́мпинг). Они́ проводя́т не́которое вре́мя в _____ (музе́й), в _____ (галере́я), в _____ (собо́р) и к концу́ дня, в _____ (универма́г). Они́ то́же проводя́т не́которое вре́мя в _____ (клуб), в _____ (са́уна) и в _____ (рестора́н).

Tourists live in hotels and on campsites. They spend a certain amount of time in museums, galleries, cathedrals and, towards the end of the day, in department stores. They also spend a certain amount of time in clubs, saunas and restaurants.

The function of each of the six cases is summarized in this unit. The first trick is to know when which case is needed. The second is to know the endings well enough so that you can use the ranges of cases you might need in any one sentence.

The six cases are as follows.

А Nominative *shows us who or what is performing the action of a verb. Remember that nouns are listed in dictionaries in their nominative singular form.*
<u>Мария</u> даёт бутылку вина Сергею.
<u>Maria</u> gives the bottle of wine to Sergei.

Б Accusative *shows us the person or thing that has an action done to it (the direct object). Also used after certain prepositions.*
Мария даёт <u>бутылку</u> вина Сергею.
Maria gives <u>the bottle</u> of wine to Sergei.

В Genitive *is the Russian way of saying 'of', so it indicates possession and is also used when talking about quantities (also used after certain prepositions and sometimes with the comparative):*
Мария даёт бутылку <u>вина</u> Сергею.
Maria gives the bottle of <u>wine</u> to Sergei.

Г Dative *shows us the indirect object of a sentence or phrase (the person or thing that is shown, told etc. something). Its basic meaning is 'to', 'for' (also used after certain prepositions and verbs).*
Мария даёт бутылку вина <u>Сергею.</u>
Maria gives the bottle of wine <u>to Sergei.</u>

Д Instrumental *is used to describe the means by which an action is performed (eg 'by train', 'with a pen'), to describe accompanying circumstances (e.g. 'tea with lemon' with the preposition c), for the complement of a verb and after certain reflexive verbs.*
Сергей любит ездить <u>поездом</u>. *Sergei likes to travel <u>by train</u>.*
Мне салат с <u>помидорами</u>, пожалуйста. *<u>Tomato</u> salad for me, please.*

Е Prepositional: *this case has no 'meaning' of its own; it is used in phrases which indicate position and specifically with the prepositions в (in, at) and на (on, at).*
Мария купила бутылку вина <u>в супермаркете</u>. *Maria bought the bottle of wine <u>at the supermarket</u>.*

> For nominative case endings, Units 4, 5, 6, accusative Units 7, 8, 9, genitive Units 10, 11, 12, dative Units 13, 14, instrumental Units 15, 16, prepositional Units 17, 18.

1 Match the phrases on the left with those on the right, then find the matching English translation.

1 В о́фисе мно́го   **a** враче́й
2 В больни́це мно́го   **b** актёров
3 В шко́ле мно́го   **c** профе́ссоров
4 В университе́те мно́го   **d** компью́теров
5 В теа́тре мно́го   **e** учи́телей

1 *There are lots of actors in the theatre.*
2 *There are lots of professors at the university.*
3 *There are lots of computers in the office.*
4 *There are lots of teachers in the school.*
5 *There are lots of doctors in the hospital.*

2 Look at the list of words a-e in Exercise 1 again.
1 Which case are they all in?
2 Now put each of them back into the nominative singular.

3 Underline the words in the following sentences which are in the accusative case (animate and inanimate).

e.g. Я люблю́ <u>спорт</u> и <u>му́зыку</u>.   *I like sport and music.*
1 Бори́с зна́ет бра́та Ива́на.   *Boris knows Ivan's brother.*
2 Вы хоти́те смотре́ть телеви́зор? *Do you want to watch television?*
3 Она́ купи́ла сту́лья.   *She bought the chairs.*
4 Ви́ктор уви́дел друзе́й в теа́тре. *Viktor saw (his) friends at the theatre.*
5 Мы заказа́ли ку́рицу с ри́сом.   *We ordered chicken with rice.*

4 Complete the following sentences by putting the word in brackets into the appropriate case (if the word in brackets is plural, you will need to put it into a plural case form).
1 Серге́й лю́бит _____ (де́рево).
2 Мы живём в _____ (го́род).
3 О́льга дала́ _____ (Вади́м) _____ (карти́на).
4 Я зна́ю _____ (студе́нты).
5 Я люблю́ е́здить _____ (по́езд) с _____ (друзья́).
6 Он смо́трит фильм с _____ (брат).
7 А́нна рабо́тает _____ (медсестра́) в _____ (больни́ца).

20 adjectives: unstressed

An adjective describes a noun (e.g. shows the colour, the size, the mood). In Russian an adjective must agree with its noun, i.e. a masculine adjective with a masculine noun. Adjectives with unstressed endings are the most common type in Russian.

A Adjectives are made up of a 'stem' and an 'ending' (the 'ending' is the last two letters). The adjectives dealt with in this unit all have stressed stems (and, therefore, unstressed endings). There are different endings for masculine, feminine and neuter singular, but the nominative plural ending is the same for all genders. Dictionaries always give the masculine singular nominative form of the adjective and it is this form which tells us what sort of adjective it is (unstressed, stressed or soft).

Б The ending for masculine unstressed adjectives is -ый: но́вый телеви́зор, *new television.* Some masculine unstressed adjectives end in -ий, rather than -ый because the last letter of their 'stem' is г, к, х, ж, ч, ш, щ (first spelling rule). Two of the most common are the adjectives meaning *small* and *good*: ма́ленький ма́льчик, *small boy*; хоро́ший журна́л, *good magazine.*
NB Although some nouns with masculine meanings have feminine endings (e.g. мужчи́на (*man*), де́душка (*grandfather*)) adjectives used to describe them must be masculine: ста́рый де́душка, *old grandfather.*

В The ending for feminine unstressed adjectives is -ая (easy to remember, because feminine nouns usually end in -а or -я): но́вая гости́ница, *new hotel*, ста́рая ку́хня, *old kitchen.*

Г The ending for neuter unstressed adjectives is -ое (easy to remember, because neuter nouns usually end in -о or -е): но́вое окно́, *new window.* Some neuter unstressed adjectives end in -ее, not -ое, because of the second spelling rule, which does not allow an unstressed о to appear after ж, ч, ш, щ, ц: све́жее яйцо́, *fresh egg*, хоро́шее ме́сто, *good place.*

Д The ending for all nominative plural adjectives of all genders is -ые. However, if the last letter of an adjective's 'stem' is г, к, х, ж, ч, ш, щ, then the ending must be -ие (in accordance with the first spelling rule): но́вые телеви́зоры, *new televisions,* ста́рые ку́хни, *old kitchens*, хоро́шие места́, *good places.*

➤ For For spelling rules, see Unit 2, for stressed and soft adjectives, see Unit 21, for possessive adjectives, see Unit 22, for adjectival cases other than the nominative, see Units 24–30.

1 Choose the appropriate adjectives from the box to describe each person – give the adjectives appropriate endings.

высо́кий	ма́ленький	стро́йный	то́лстый
tall	*small*	*slim*	*fat*

же́нщина, *woman*

мужчи́на, *man*

1 _____ же́нщина *woman*
2 _____ мужчи́на *man*

2 Match the phrases on the left with those on the right, using the English translation as a guide.

1	хоро́шая	**a**	ле́кции	*a good opera*
2	интере́сные	**b**	фильм	*interesting lectures*
3	моско́вское	**c**	о́пера	*the Moscow metro*
4	ма́ленький	**d**	метро́	*a small theatre*
5	ску́чный	**e**	теа́тр	*a boring film*

3 The adjectives in brackets are in the masculine singular form. Make them 'agree' with their noun (e.g. make sure you put a feminine adjective ending on the adjective if it is describing a feminine noun).

e.g. (вку́сный) то́рты *delicious cakes* → вку́сные то́рты

1 _____ (краси́вый) шко́ла   *a beautiful school*
2 _____ (жёлтый) окно́   *a yellow window*
3 _____ (све́жий) молоко́   *fresh milk*
4 _____ (хоро́ший) журнали́ст   *a good journalist*
5 _____ (до́брый) у́тро   *good morning*

The most common kind of adjectives are those whose stems are unstressed (see Unit 20). In this unit we meet stressed adjectives – adjectives whose endings are stressed. Soft adjectives are a third, relatively small, group of adjectives; their endings are composed only of 'soft' vowels (ий, яя, ее, ие).

A A stressed adjective can be identified by looking at the masculine singular nominative form – it will end in -ой: молодóй футболúст, *a young football player.*

Б The feminine form of a stressed adjective is exactly the same as that of an unstressed adjective – it will end in -ая: молодáя актрúса, *a young actress.*

В The neuter form of a stressed adjective is exactly the same as that of an unstressed adjective – it will end in -ое: молодóе дéрево, *a young tree.*
NB The Russian word for *big* is большóй. Because the ending is stressed the letter ш *can* be followed by the letter ó – this applies both to the masculine singular and to the neuter singular: Большóй теáтр, *Bolshoi Theatre,* большóе окнó, *a big window.*

Г Plural stressed adjectives in the nominative end in -ые, whatever the gender of the noun they are describing: молодые люди, *young people.* If the adjective's stem ends in г, к, х, ж, ч, ш, щ, then the ending must be -ие (in accordance with the first spelling rule): другúе люди, *other people.*

Д There are only about 40 soft adjectives. You can recognize them because their masculine singular will end in -ний: послéдний автóбус, *the last bus.* The feminine ending for a soft adjective is -яя; the neuter ending is -ee and the plural is -ие: вечéрняя газéта, *evening paper,* зúмнее ýтро, *a winter morning,* послéдние нóвости, *the latest news.*
Most soft adjectives are connected with time and seasons, as in the last examples. Others indicate location (e.g. Дáльний Востóк *the Far East*) and two indicate colour:

сúний дивáн   кáрие глазá
a navy blue sofa   *hazel eyes*

NB кáрий is the only soft adjective whose stem does not end in н.

➤ For explanation of role of adjective in a sentence and of stems and endings, see Unit 20, for spelling rules, see Unit 2, for possessive adjectives, see Unit 22; for adjectival cases other than the nominative, see Units 24–30.

1 Underline the soft adjectives in the following sentences (not all the adjectives in the sentences are soft!).

1 Я читáю интерéсную ýтреннюю газéту.   *I'm reading an interesting morning paper.*

2 Нúжняя пóлка óчень удóбная.   *The bottom bunk is very comfortable.*

3 Вот сúняя лéтняя ю́бка.   *Here's a dark blue summer skirt.*

4 Сосéдний дом óчень стáрый.   *The neighbouring house is very old.*

5 Вот зáвтрашняя прогрáмма. *Here's tomorrow's programme.*

2 In the following exercise there is a mixture of stressed and soft adjectives. Make them agree with their nouns.

1 (плохóй) _____ погóда   *bad weather*

2 (послéдний)_____ останóвка   *the last (bus) stop*

3 (новогóдний) _____ подáрки   *New Year presents*

4 (молодóй) _____ дéрево   *a young tree*

5 (кáрий) _____ глазá   *hazel eyes*

6 (большóй) _____ здáние   *a big building*

3 Match the phrases on the left with those on the right, using the English translation as a guide.

1 послéдняя   **a** ýтро   *the last station*

2 весéннее   **b** жéнщина   *a spring morning*

3 плохúе   **c** проблéмы   *bad news*

4 большúе   **d** нóвости   *big problems*

5 зáмужняя   **e** стáнция   *a married woman*

4 Translate the following phrases into Russian (all the vocabulary is in this unit).

1 a young actress

2 other theatres

3 a summer programme

4 a bad morning

5 the last problem

The possessive adjectives (*my, your* etc.) indicate possession or a relationship; for example твой дом, *your house*, мой тётя, *my aunt*, Это твоё письмо? *Is this your letter?*

A Possessive adjectives indicating *my, your, our* etc. must agree in number, gender and case with the noun they qualify, rather than with the possessor:

«Это моя сестра,» говорит Борис.
'This is my sister,' says Boris.

These are the forms for the nominative singular and plural.

	Masculine	Feminine	Neuter	Plural
my (mine)	мой	моя	моё	мой
your(s), *belonging to* ты	твой	твоя	твоё	твой
our(s)	наш	наша	наше	наши
your(s), *belonging to* вы	ваш	ваша	ваше	ваши

Это ваше место?
Is this your seat?

Б Possessive adjectives indicating *his/hers, theirs* are invariable (i.e. never change):

Это её место?
Is this her seat?
Это их место?
Is this their seat?

belonging to он→ его	belonging to она→ её	belonging to оно→ его	belonging to они→ их

В Possessive adjectives are used less frequently in Russian than in English. Виктор увидел друзей в театре, *Viktor saw (his) friends at the theatre.* In particular, Russian tends not to use possessive adjectives when referring to parts of the body:

У меня болит голова.
My head aches.

➤ For reflexive possessive, see Unit 23, for possessive pronouns, see Unit 50. For use of reflexive pronoun себя, see Unit 54.

1 **Change the English adjectives or pronouns given into their corresponding Russian forms.**

e.g. (*My*) соба́ка в саду́ → Моя́ соба́ка в саду́. *My dog is in the garden.*

1 Вот (*our*) биле́ты.
2 Где (*your* (formal)) ви́зы?
3 (*His*) сестра́ прие́дет за́втра.
4 Куда́ идёт (*your* (informal)) брат?

5 (*Their*) сад о́чень большо́й.
6 (*My*) ба́бушка живёт в Ки́еве.
7 (*Your* (informal)) сын – студе́нт?
8 Э́то (*her*) журна́л и́ли (*theirs*)?
9 (*Our*) друг в Москве́

2 **Match the phrases on the right and the left, using the English translations as a guide.**

1 Она́ не зна́ет,
2 Мы не зна́ем,
3 Вы не зна́ете,
4 Они́ не зна́ют,
5 Ты не зна́ешь,

a где их гости́ница.
b где ва́ши кни́ги.
c где её ключ.
d где на́ша соба́ка.
e где твоё письмо́.

1 *She doesn't know where her key is.*
2 *We don't know where our dog is.*
3 *You don't know where your books are.*
4 *They don't know where their hotel is.*
5 *You don't know where your letter is.*

3 **Fill in the gaps by giving the appropriate form of the possessive adjective in order to complete the conversation.**

1 Здра́вствуйте. Э́то _____ (*your*) бага́ж?
2 А где (*my*) _____ ключ?
3 Вот _____ (*your*) ключ. У вас есть па́спорт и ви́за?
4 Да, вот _____ (*my*) ви́за и _____ (*my*) па́спорт.

4 **Complete these sentences using the appropriate possessive adjective.**

e.g. Он не зна́ет, где ____ сестра́. Он не зна́ет, где его́ сестра́. *He doesn't know where his sister is.*

1 Я не зна́ю, где _____ соба́ка.
2 Мы не зна́ем, где _____ друзья́.
3 Вы не зна́ете, где _____ каранда́ш?
4 Ты не зна́ешь, где _____ биле́ты?
5 Они́ не зна́ют, где _____ паспорта́.

Reflexive possessives indicate possession by the subject of the nearest verb and it can mean *my own, your own, his/her own, our own, their own*. The reflexive possessive in Russian is свой (masculine form; feminine своя, neuter своё).

A As far as я, ты, мы, вы are concerned, свой is an *alternative* to мой, твой, наш, ваш (and is in fact more common in conversational Russian, especially as an alternative to твой). So, if you want to say *I am reading my magazine*, you can say either Я читаю мой журнал or Я читаю свой журнал

Б Свой is **not** an alternative to его, её, их. If you want to say *his, her, their*, you must work out whether you mean *his own, her own, their own* or not (i.e. you must work out whether you mean that the subject of the verb is the owner). For example:

Анна и Андрей любят свой сад means that the garden in question belongs to Anna and Andrei: *They love their (own) garden.*

Анна и Андрей любят их сад means that Anna and Andrei love a garden – but it belongs to someone else.
They love their (friends', daughter's etc.) garden.

В Свой must indicate *possession* by the subject of the verb; it cannot just describe the subject of the verb. To describe the subject of the verb, you must use мой, твой, его, её, наш, ваш, их:

Его дети говорят по-русски.   *His children speak Russian.*

Г Sometimes you need both an ordinary possessive and a reflexive possessive in one sentence:

Его дочь не очень любит свой офис.
His daughter doesn't really like her office.

In this sentence свой is needed in the second part of the sentence to indicate that the daughter doesn't like her own office (*possession* by the subject of любит). In the first part of the sentence the word *'his'* is describing the subject of the verb and therefore the reflexive possessive cannot be used.

➤ **For possessive adjectives, see Unit 22.**

1 Underline the words in the following passage where it would be appropriate to use the reflexive possessive (hint: there are five).

Last year we set off on holiday in our car. Unfortunately Ivan lost his passport before we reached our destination. My brother, Nikolai, tried to help him find it. Nikolai is a very impatient person and soon lost his patience with Ivan. Whilst they were arguing, I looked in his suitcase and found that his passport was right at the bottom. How I love my brothers!

2 Complete the following phrases by choosing the appropriate word from the box. You will need to use one of the words in the box twice.

1 _____ сестра́ рабо́тает в Но́вгороде.
Her sister works in Novgorod.

2 Константи́н чита́ет _____ пи́сьма.
Konstantin is reading his (own) letters.

3 _____ бра́т лю́бит _____ велосипе́д.
My brother likes his own bicycle.

4 _____ друзья́ купи́ли _____ дом.
Our friends have bought their own house.

5 _____ ба́бушка потеря́ла _____ письмо́.
Their granny has lost her (own) letter.

её их мой наши своё свой свой

3 Translate the following phrases into Russian (possessive or reflexive possessive?).

1 Their house is in the town.
2 They like their house.
3 We like your house (formal).
4 Their mother likes our house.
5 Ivan's house? I like his house!

An adjective must always agree with the noun it is describing. So, if the noun is in the accusative case, the adjective also must be in the accusative case.

A If an adjective is describing a masculine or a neuter inanimate noun this is not a problem: the ending is just the same as it is in the nominative singular:

Я чита́ю интере́сный журна́л
I am reading an interesting newspaper

Б If an adjective is describing a masculine animate noun (e.g. врач, *doctor*), the ending of the adjective must change; there are two possible endings, -его for soft and possessive adjectives and for unstressed adjectives whose stem ends in ж, ч, ш, щ or ц; otherwise, use -ого:

хоро́ший но́вый врач → Я зна́ю хоро́шего но́вого врача́
I know a good new doctor

твой дре́вний → Я зна́ю твоего́ дре́внего врача́
I know your ancient doctor

In the unlikely event of a neuter noun being animate, the adjective which describes it takes the same endings as a masculine adjective, for example ва́жное лицо́, *VIP (very important person)*.

Вы зна́ете э́того ва́жного лица́?
Do you know this very important person?

В Adjectives describing feminine nouns always change in the accusative, whether the noun they are describing is animate (e.g. актри́са, *actress*) or inanimate (e.g. кварти́ра, *flat*). The four possible endings are -ую, -юю, -у or -ю.

Type of adjective	Nominative singular	Animate accusative singular	Example
unstressed	но́вая	но́вую	Я люблю́ но́вую кварти́ру.
stressed	молода́я	молоду́ю	Я люблю́ молоду́ю актри́су.
soft	дре́вняя	дре́внюю	Я люблю́ дре́внюю кварти́ру.
possessive	твоя́	твою́	Я люблю́ твою́ кварти́ру.
	наш	на́шу	Он лю́бит на́шу кварти́ру.

> **For nominative singular adjectives, see Units 20, 21, 22, 23; for accusative singular nouns, see Unit 7.**

1 Underline all the adjectives which are in the accusative case in the passage. A translation is given to help you.

Вчера́ мы бы́ли в го́роде. В рестора́не мы ви́дели на́шего дру́га, Ива́на. Он уже́ сде́лал свои́ поку́пки. Он показа́л нам свой но́вый сви́тер, дороги́е джи́нсы и шика́рный пиджа́к.

Yesterday we were in town. In the restaurant we saw our friend, Ivan. He had already done his shopping. He showed us his new sweater, expensive jeans and stylish jacket.

2 Explain what Anya has bought by putting the phrases in the following list into the accusative case:

e.g. А́ня купи́ла _____ (краси́вая блу́за) А́ня купи́ла краси́вую блу́зу. *Anya bought a beautiful blouse.*

1	больша́я соба́ка	*big dog*
2	но́вый дива́н	*new sofa*
3	пуши́стый кро́лик	*fluffy rabbit*
4	деревя́нный стол	*wooden table*
5	но́вое окно́	*new window*
6	вку́сный торт	*delicious cake*
7	шика́рная ю́бка	*stylish skirt*
8	интере́сная кни́га	*interesting book*
9	купа́льный костю́м	*swimming costume*
10	си́няя бро́шка	*dark blue brooch*

3 Explain who Viktor met at Konstantin's yesterday evening. Put each phrase into the accusative case.

Вчера́ ве́чером Ви́ктор был у Константи́на. Там он встре́тил...

1	моя́ сестра́	*my sister*
2	молодо́й профе́ссор	*young professor*
3	дре́вний писа́тель	*ancient writer*
4	интере́сная актри́са	*interesting actress*
5	ску́чный журнали́ст	*boring journalist*

An adjective must always agree with the noun it is describing. So, if the noun is in the accusative plural, the adjective also must be in the accusative plural. This is easy if the noun is inanimate – for all genders the ending is the same as it would be in the nominative. For animate nouns (people, animals) a special animate accusative ending is needed for all genders.

A If the plural object which the adjective is describing is inanimate, the adjective endings are the same as they would be in the nominative plural – i.e. -ые or -ие. This applies to all genders.

Type of adjective	Nominative singular	Inanimate accusative plural	Example
unstressed	нóвый *new* хорóший *good*	нóвые хорóшие (no unstressed о after ж, ч, ш, щ, ц)	Я читáю нóвые кнѝги. Я знáю хорóшие ресторáны.
stressed	плохóй *bad*	плохѝе	Он передáл плохѝе нóвости. *He passed on the bad news.*
soft	дрéвний *ancient*	дрéвние	Я люблю́ дрéвние городá.
possessive	твой *your* наш *our*	твой нáши	Я вѝжу твой дом. Он читáет нáши пѝсьма.

Б If the plural object is animate, then the two possible endings for the adjective are -ых or -их. This applies to all genders.

Type of adjective	Nominative singular	Animate accusative plural	Example
unstressed	нóвый *new* хорóший, *good*	нóвых хорóших (no unstressed о after ж, ч, ш, щ, ц)	Я знáю нóвых студéнтов. Я знáю хорóших врачéй.
stressed	плохóй *bad*	плохѝх	Он критикýет плохѝх актёров.
soft	дрéвний *ancient*	дрéвних	Я люблю́ дрéвних писáтелей.
possessive	твой *your* наш *our*	твоѝх нáших	Я знáю твоѝх сестёр. Он знáет нáших друзéй.

➤ For nominative plural adjectives, see Units 20, 21, 22, 23, for nominative plural nouns, see Units 5 and 6.

1 **What/whom does Viktor like to photograph? Complete the following sentences by choosing the correct ending for each adjective.**

-ые	-ие	-ых	-их

Ви́ктор лю́бит фотографи́ровать...

1 сво____ дете́й   *his children*
2 краси́в__ пля́жи   *beautiful beaches*
3 молод__ лошаде́й   *young horses*
4 истори́ческ___ места́   *historical places*
5 нов___ друзе́й   *new friends*

2 **Meet the artist – what/whom does Katya like to paint? Put the phrases into the accusative plural (animate or inanimate?).**

e.g. Ка́тя лю́бит рисова́ть _____ (высо́кий
человек) →
Ка́тя лю́бит рисова́ть высо́ких люде́й *Katya likes to paint
tall people.*

1 больша́я соба́ка   *big dog*
2 краси́вая ло́шадь   *beautiful horse*
3 зелёное де́рево   *green tree*
4 дре́вний дом   *ancient house*
5 стра́нная пти́ца   *strange bird*
6 свой брат   *her brother*
7 молода́я ко́шка   *young cat*
8 ма́ленькая кварти́ра   *small flat*
9 иностра́нный го́род   *foreign town*
10 изве́стный писа́тель   *famous writer*

3 **Make sentences explaining what you want to buy by putting the phrases into the accusative plural.**

e.g. Я хочу́ купи́ть_____ (но́вая руба́шка) →
Я хочу́ купи́ть но́вые руба́шки.
I want to buy new shirts.

1 ма́ленький соба́ка   *small dog*
2 хоро́ший костю́м   *good suit*
3 ва́ша кни́га   *your book*
4 но́вое окно́   *new window*
5 интере́сная кассе́та   *interesting cassette*

An adjective must always agree with the noun it is describing; if the noun is in the genitive singular, so must the adjective describing it. There are special genitive singular adjective endings for each gender.

A The endings for masculine and neuter adjectives are the same: either -ого or -его (if you know the accusative adjective endings, you'll recognize that these are the same as the masculine singular animate accusative).

- All unstressed adjectives take the ending -ого unless their stem ends in ж, ч, ш, щ, ц (spelling rule number 2), in which case the ending is -его: па́спорт англи́йского (хоро́шего) актёра, *the English (good) actor's passport*; недалеко́ от ма́ленького по́ля, *not far from the small field*.
- All stressed adjectives take the ending -ого: дире́ктор Большо́го Теа́тра, *the director of the Bolshoi theatre*.
- All soft adjectives take the ending -его: цена́ си́него дива́на, *the price of the dark blue sofa*.
- All possessive adjectives take the ending -его: недалеко́ от на́шего зда́ния, *not far from our building*.

Б If an adjective is describing a feminine noun which is in the genitive singular, then the adjective should end either in -ой or -ей.

- All unstressed adjectives take the ending -ой unless their stem ends in ж, ч, ш, щ, ц (spelling rule number 2), in which case the ending is -ей: па́спорт англи́йской (хоро́шей) актри́сы, *the English (good) actress' passport*.
- All stressed adjectives take the ending -ой: дире́ктор большо́й компа́нии, *the director of the big company*.
- All soft adjectives take the ending-ей: цена́ си́ней руба́шки, *the price of the dark blue shirt*.
- All possessive adjectives take the ending -ей: дом мое́й сестры́, *the house of my sister.*

➤ For spelling rules, see Unit 2, for different categories of adjective, see Units 20–3, for genitive singular of nouns, see Unit 10, for prepositions taking the genitive case, see Units 83, 84, 85, 88, 89.

1 Underline all the genitive singular adjectives in the following passage. A translation is given to help you.

Наша школа находится недалеко от красивого парка. Налево от нашей школы есть большая аптека, где работает мать моего друга, Ивана. Друг моей сестры тоже работает в этой большой аптеке.

Our school is situated not far from a beautiful park. To the left of our school there is a big chemist's, where the mother of my friend Ivan works. The friend of my sister also works in this big chemist's.

2 The words много *(a lot, much)* and мало *(little, few)* are both followed by the genitive case. Explain what you have a lot of and what you're short of by putting the following phrases into the genitive singular.

e.g. свежий/сыр → У меня мало свежего сыра. *I have little fresh cheese.*

1 мало/русская водка   *Russian vodka*
2 много/французское вино   *French wine*
3 мало/китайский рис   *Chinese rice*
4 много/вкусный салат   *delicious salad*
5 мало/свежая колбаса   *fresh sausage*

3 Look at the pictures and make sentences to explain who owns what:

высокая стройная женщина

маленькая старая бабушка

маленький толстый мужчина

e.g. Это кролик маленькой старой бабушки.
1 Это собака _____ _____ _____
2 Это кошка _____ _____ _____

An adjective must always agree with the noun it is describing; if the noun is in the genitive plural, so must the adjective describing it. There are only two genitive plural adjective endings (irrespective of gender).

A The two possible endings for genitive plural adjectives are -ых and -их (which are actually the same endings used for the animate accusative plural of adjectives). These endings apply to all three genders.

B Stressed and unstressed adjectives always take the ending -ых, unless their stem ends in г, к, х, ж, ч, ш, щ (spelling rule 1).

Examples of the ending -ых
паспортá молоды́х тури́стов *the passports of the young tourists*
кни́ги совреме́нных писа́телей *the books of the modern writers*
фотогрáфии иностра́нных куро́ртов *photographs of foreign resorts*

The genitive plural adjective ending is -их if:
• the adjective's stem ends in г, к, х, ж, ч, ш, щ (spelling rule 1)
• the adjective is soft (e.g. си́ний *dark blue*)
• the adjective is possessive (e.g. мой)

Examples of the ending -их
The adjective's stem ends in г, к, х, ж, ч, ш, щ: паспортá англи́йских тури́стов *passports of English tourists*
The adjective is soft: кни́ги дре́вних писа́телей *books of the ancient writers*
The adjective is possessive: фотогрáфии на́ших друзе́й *photographs of our friends*

➤ **For spelling rules, see Unit 2, for different categories of adjective see Units 20–3, for genitive plural of nouns, see Units 11 and 12, for prepositions taking the genitive case, see Units 83, 84, 85, 88, 89.**

1 Using the expressions нале́во от (*to the left of*) and напра́во от (*to the right of*) make up sentences by giving the genitive plural of each phrase.

e.g. Нале́во от/молодо́й спортсме́н → Нале́во от молоды́х спортсме́нов. *To the left of the young sportsmen.*

1 *to the left of/*у́тренняя газе́та   *morning paper*
2 *to the right of/*наш велосипе́д   *our bicycle*
3 *to the right of/*дорога́я ю́бка   *expensive skirt*
4 *to the left of/*деревя́нный стул   *wooden chair*
5 *to the left of/*огро́мное зда́ние   *huge building*

2 Explain which groups are visiting the museum today by using the genitive plural in the following phrases.

e.g. гру́ппа/молодо́й ма́льчик → гру́ппа молоды́х ма́льчиков

1 италья́нский/тури́ст   *Italian tourist*
2 изве́стный/врач   *famous doctor*
3 но́вый/студе́нт   *new student*
4 пожило́й/челове́к   *elderly person*
5 серьёзный/исто́рик   *serious historian*

3 Match the two halves of each sentence, using the English translation as a guideline:

1 У вра́ча мно́го   **a** интере́сных студе́нтов
2 У профе́ссора мно́го   **b** ста́рых книг
3 У такси́ста мно́го   **c** больны́х пацие́нтов
4 У банки́ра мно́го   **d** но́вых автомоби́лей
5 У библиоте́каря мно́го   **e** серьёзных пробле́м
6 У фе́рмера мно́го   **f** тяжёлых пи́сем
7 У президе́нта мно́го   **g** краси́вых коро́в
8 У почтальо́на мно́го   **h** америка́нских до́лларов

1 *The doctor has many sick patients.*
2 *The professor has many interesting students.*
3 *The taxi driver has many new cars.*
4 *The banker has many American dollars.*
5 *The librarian has many old books.*
6 *The farmer has many beautiful cows.*
7 *The president has many serious problems.*
8 *The postman has many heavy letters.*

28 dative singular

An adjective must always agree with the noun it is describing; if the noun is in the dative singular, so must the adjective describing it. There are special dative singular adjective endings for each gender.

А If an adjective is describing a masculine noun which is in the dative singular, then the adjective should end either in -ому or -ему.

- All unstressed adjectives take the ending -ому unless their stem ends in ж, ч, ш, щ, ц (spelling rule number 2), in which case the ending is -ему: Гид дал паспорт английскому (хорошему) актёру, *the guide gave the passport to the English (good) actor.*
- All stressed adjectives take the ending -ому: Он позвонил молодому директору, *he rang the young director.*
- All soft adjectives take the ending -ему: Он позвонил прежнему директору, *he rang the former director.*
- All possessive adjectives take the ending -ему: Он позвонил моему брату, *he rang my brother.*

Б If an adjective is describing a feminine noun which is in the dative singular, then the adjective should end either in -ой or -ей.

- All unstressed adjectives take the ending -ой unless their stem ends in ж, ч, ш, щ, ц (spelling rule number 2), in which case the ending is -ей: Гид дал паспорт английской (хорошей) актрисе, *the guide gave the passport to the English (good) actress.*
- All stressed adjectives take the ending -ой: Он позвонил молодой англичанке, *He rang the young Englishwoman.*
- All soft adjectives take the ending-ей: Он позвонил прежней учительнице, *He rang the former teacher.*
- All possessive adjectives take the ending -ей: Он позвонил моей сестре, *He rang my sister.*

В If an adjective is describing a neuter noun which is in the dative singular, then the adjective should end either in -ому or -ему (just like masculine adjectives). In the examples below the preposition к *towards/to the house* of (which must always be followed by the dative case) is used.

- All unstressed adjectives take the ending -ому unless their stem ends in ж, ч, ш, щ, ц (spelling rule number 2), in which case the ending is -ему: к новому (хорошему) зданию, *towards the new (nice) building.*
- All stressed adjectives take the ending -ому: к большому окну, *towards the big window.*
- All soft adjectives take the ending -ему: к соседнему зданию, *towards the neighbouring building*
- All possessive adjectives take the ending -ему: к моему месту, *towards my seat (place) .*

➤ For spelling rules, see Unit 2, for different categories of adjective, see Units 20–3, for dative singular of nouns, see Unit 13, for prepositions with the dative case, see Units 85 and 89.

1 Make sentences explaining who Ivan helps every day.

e.g. ста́рый почтальо́н → Ка́ждый день Ива́н помога́ет ста́рому почтальо́ну. *Every day Ivan helps the old postman.*

1 ру́сский студе́нт   *Russian student*
2 больна́я стару́шка   *sick old lady*
3 пре́жний ме́неджер   *former manager*
4 на́ша мать   *our mother*
5 молодо́й пиани́ст   *young pianist*

2 Who is walking towards what? Make up sentences from the information given.

e.g. Еле́на/шика́рный магази́н → Еле́на идёт к шика́рному магази́ну. *Elena is walking towards a stylish shop.*

1 Татья́на/краси́вая карти́на   *beautiful picture*
2 И́горь/дре́вняя ва́за   *ancient vase*
3 Вади́м/большо́й мост   *big bridge*
4 А́ня/сосе́дний дом   *neighbouring house*
5 Па́вел/но́вая лаборато́рия   *new laboratory*

3 Look at the pictures and make sentences to explain who is giving what to whom.

ма́ленькая ко́шка

больша́я соба́ка

пуши́стый кро́лик

e.g. Ба́бушка даёт морко́вку пуши́стому кро́лику.
1 Же́нщина даёт конфе́ту _____ _____.
2 Мужчи́на даёт ры́бу _____ _____.

An adjective must always agree with the noun it is describing; if the noun is in the dative plural, so must the adjective describing it. There are only two dative plural adjective endings (irrespective of gender).

A The two possible endings for dative plural adjectives are -ым and -им. These endings are used for all three genders.

B Stressed and unstressed adjectives always take the ending -ым (unless their stem ends in г, к, х, ж, ч, ш, щ (spelling rule 1)).

Examples of the ending -ым
гид даёт билеты молодым туристам *the guide gives the tickets to the young tourists*
гид часто помогает иностранным актрисам *the guide often helps foreign actresses*
фотограф подходит к зелёным полям *the photographer is walking towards the green fields*

C The dative plural adjective ending is -им if:
• the adjective's stem ends in г, к, х, ж, ч, ш, щ (spelling rule 1)
• the adjective is soft (e.g. синий, *dark blue*)
• the adjective is possessive (e.g. мой)

Examples of the ending -им
The adjective's stem ends in г, к, х, ж, ч, ш, щ: гид даёт билеты английским туристам *the guide gives the tickets to the English tourists*
The adjective is soft: мы подходим к соседним домам *we are approaching the neighbouring houses*
The adjective is possessive: мы помогаем нашим друзьям *we are helping our friends*

➤ For spelling rules, see Unit 2, for different categories of adjective, see Units 20–3, for dative plural of nouns, see Unit 14, for prepositions with the dative case, see Units 85, 86, 89.

1 **Explain who sends a letter to whom by matching the two halves of each sentence, using the English translation as a guideline.**

1 врач пишет письмо   **a** иностранным политикам
2 профессор пишет письмо   **b** больным пациентам
3 дирижёр пишет письмо   **c** потенциальным клиентам
4 журналист пишет письмо   **d** ленивым студентам
5 банкир пишет письмо   **e** известным музыкантам

1 *The doctor writes a letter to the sick patients.*
2 *The professor writes a letter to the lazy students.*
3 *The conductor writes a letter to the famous musicians.*
4 *The journalist writes a letter to the foreign politicians.*
5 *The banker writes a letter to potential customers.*

2 **Make sentences explaining who you intend to buy presents for.**

e.g. мой друг → Я хочу купить подарки моим друзьям.
1 твоя дочь   *your daughter*
2 наш учитель   *our teacher*
3 молодая собака   *young dog*
4 прежний директор   *former director*
5 русский студент   *Russian student*

3 **Complete the sentences by putting the adjective in brackets into the dative plural.**

1 Официант подходит к _____ (большой стол).
2 Архитектор подходит к _____ (маленькое окно).
3 Татьяна подходит к _____ (новый офис).
4 Катя подходит к _____ (свой ребёнок).
5 Иван подходит к _____ (старые друзья).

An adjective must always agree with the noun it is describing; if you put the noun in the instrumental singular, you must put the adjective describing it in the instrumental singular too. There are special instrumental singular adjective endings for each gender.

A The endings for masculine and neuter adjectives are the same: either -ым or -им:

- All unstressed and stressed adjectives take the ending -ым unless their stem ends in г, к, х, ж, ч, ш, щ (spelling rule number 1), in which case the ending is -им: посещáть музéй с молодым инострáнным (англи́йским) тури́стом, *to visit the museum with a young foreign (English) tourist.*
- All stressed adjectives take the ending -ым: с молоды́м тури́стом, *with a young tourist.*
- All soft adjectives take the ending -им: с пре́жним дире́ктором, *with the former director.*
- All possessive adjectives take the ending -им: с мои́м письмо́м, *with my letter.*

Б If an adjective is describing a feminine noun which is in the instrumental singular, then the adjective should end either in -ой or -ей (just like the instrumental singular noun ending).

- All unstressed adjectives take the ending -ой unless their stem ends in ж, ч, ш, щ, ц (spelling rule number 2), in which case the ending is -ей: фильм с хоро́шей англи́йской актри́сой, *the film with the good English actress.*
- All stressed adjectives take the ending -ой: он рабо́тает с молодо́й англича́нкой, *he works with a young Englishwoman.*
- All soft adjectives take the ending-ей: он рабо́тает с пре́жней учи́тельницей, *he works with a former teacher.*
- All possessive adjectives take the ending -ей: он рабо́тает с мое́й сестро́й, *he works with my sister.*

➤ For spelling rules, see Unit 2, for different categories of adjective, see Units 20–3, for instrumental singular of nouns, see Unit 15, for prepositions with the instrumental case, see Units 84, 88, 89.

1 How are things done? Complete the sentence by putting the adjective in brackets into the instrumental singular (remember: because you are describing the 'instrument by which an action is performed' you don't need the preposition c).

1 Я éду _____ (рáнний) пóездом. *I travel by the early train.*
2 Я пишý _____ (дешёвая) рýчкой. *I write with a cheap pen.*
3 Нáдо мыть посýду _____ (горячая) водóй. *It is necessary to do the washing up with hot water.*
4 Я открывáю дверь _____ (мой) ключóм. *I open the door with my key.*
5 Он глáдит рубáшку _____ (нóвый) утюгóм. *He irons the shirt with the new iron*

2 Make sentences explaining who wants to go to the theatre with whom (remember: because you are describing 'in the company of' you do need the preposition c).

e.g. Зóя/нóвый друг → Зóя хóчет пойти в теáтр с нóвым дрýгом. *Zoya wants to go to the theatre with (her) new boyfriend.*

1 Врач/красивая медсестрá   *Doctor/beautiful nurse*
2 Ивáн/английский турист   *Ivan/English tourist*
3 Журналист/извéстный политик   *Journalist/famous politician*
4 Евгéний/моя сестрá   *Evgeny/my sister*
5 Муж/молодáя женá   *Husband/young wife*

3 Explain what kind of sandwiches you want by putting each phrase into the instrumental singular.

e.g. францýзский сыр → Я хочý бутербрóд с францýзским сыром. *I want a sandwich with French cheese.*

1 свéжая ветчинá   *fresh ham*
2 копчёная рыба   *smoked fish*
3 зелёный огурéц   *green cucumber*
4 дорогóй майонéз   *expensive mayonnaise*

4 Explain what you want to drink with your sandwich by putting the phrase in brackets into the instrumental singular.

1 Кóфе с _____ (холóдное молокó)   *coffee with cold milk*
2 Чай со _____ (свéжий лимóн)   *tea with fresh lemon*

An adjective must always agree with the noun it is describing; if the noun has to be in the instrumental plural, so must the adjective describing it. There are only two instrumental plural adjective endings (irrespective of gender).

A The two possible endings for instrumental plural adjectives are -ыми and -ими. These endings are used for all three genders.

Б Stressed and unstressed adjectives always take the ending -ыми (unless their stem ends in г, к, х, ж, ч, ш, щ (spelling rule 1)).

Examples of the ending -ыми

гид в музе́е с молоды́ми тури́стами
the guide is at the museum with the young tourists

гид посеща́ет теа́тр с иностра́нными актри́сами
the guide visits the theatre with foreign actresses

секрета́рь вошёл с ва́жными пи́сьмами
the secretary came in with important letters

В The instrumental plural adjective ending is -ими if:
• the adjective's stem ends in г, к, х, ж, ч, ш, щ (spelling rule 1)
• the adjective is soft (e.g. си́ний, *dark blue*)
• the adjective is possessive (e.g. мой)

Examples of the ending -ими

The adjective's stem ends in г, к, х, ж, ч, ш, щ:
гид в музе́е с англи́йскими тури́стами
the guide is in the museum with the English tourists

The adjective is soft:
он рабо́тает с пре́жними поли́тиками
he works with former politicans

The adjective is possessive:
мы отдыха́ем с на́шими друзья́ми
we are on holiday with our friends

➤ **For spelling rules, see Unit 2, for different categories of adjective, see Units 20–3, for instrumental plural of nouns, see Unit 16, for prepositions with the instrumental case, see Units 84 and 89.**

1 **What's on the menu? Match the two halves of each phrase, using the English translation as a guideline.**

1 сала́т с
2 суп со
3 ку́рица с
4 моро́женое с

a ру́сскими гриба́ми
b вку́сными абрико́сами
c све́жими овоща́ми
d италья́нскими помидо́рами

Italian tomato salad
Fresh vegetable soup
Chicken with Russian mushrooms
Ice cream with delicious apricots

2 **Explain who Aleksandr was at the theatre with on the different days of the week. Put the words in brackets into the instrumental plural.**

1 В понеде́льник Алекса́ндр был в теа́тре с ____ ____
   (но́вый друг).
2 Во вто́рник Алекса́ндр был в теа́тре с ____ ____
   (францу́зский гость).
3 В сре́ду Алекса́ндр был в теа́тре с ____ ____
   (ва́жный клие́нт).
4 В четве́рг Алекса́ндр был в теа́тре с ____ ____
   (молодо́й ребёнок).
5 В пя́тницу Алекса́ндр был в теа́тре с ____ ____
   (ру́сский студе́нт).
6 В суббо́ту Алекса́ндр был в теа́тре со ____ ____
   (ста́рый пенсионе́р).
7 В воскресе́нье Алекса́ндр был в теа́тре с ____ ____
   (наш брат).

3 **Who is busy with what? Give the Russian for the phrases in brackets in order to complete each sentence.**

e.g. Балери́на занима́ется _____ (new dances) →
Балери́на занима́ется но́выми та́нцами.

1 Писа́тель занима́ется _____ (interesting books).
2 Врач занима́ется _____ (sick patients).
3 Профе́ссор занима́ется _____ (new students).
4 Журнали́ст занима́ется _____ (good newspapers).
5 Программи́ст занима́ется _____ (Russian computers).

An adjective must always agree with the noun it is describing; if you put the noun in the prepositional singular, you must put the adjective describing it in the prepositional singular too. There are special prepositional singular adjective endings for each gender.

A If an adjective is describing a masculine noun which is in the prepositional singular, then the adjective should end either in -ом or -ем:

- All unstressed adjectives take the ending -ом unless their stem ends in ж,ч, ш, щ, ц (spelling rule number 2), in which case the ending is -ем: в но́вом (хоро́шем) рестора́не, *in a new (good) restaurant.*
- All stressed adjectives take the ending -ом: в Большо́м Теа́тре, *in the Bolshoi Theatre.*
- All soft adjectives take the ending-ем: в си́нем пиджаке́, *in a dark blue jacket.*
- All possessive adjectives take the ending -ем or -ём: в моём (твоём, своём, на́шем, ва́шем) до́ме, *in my (your, one's own, our, your) house.*

Б If an adjective is describing a feminine noun which is in the prepositional singular, then the adjective should end either in -ой or -ей.

- All unstressed adjectives take the ending -ой unless their stem ends in ж, ч, ш, щ, ц (spelling rule number 2), in which case the ending is -ей: в но́вой (хоро́шей) гости́нице, *in a new (good) hotel.*
- All stressed adjectives take the ending -ой: в большо́й гости́нице, *in a big hotel.*
- All soft adjectives take the ending-ей: в си́ней руба́шке, *in a dark blue shirt.*
- All possessive adjectives take the ending -ей: в мое́й кварти́ре, *in my flat.*

В If an adjective is describing a neuter noun which is in the prepositional singular, then the adjective should end either in -ом or -ем (just like masculine adjectives).

- All unstressed adjectives take the ending -ом unless their stem ends in ж, ч, ш, щ, ц (spelling rule number 2), in which case the ending is -ем: в ма́леньком по́ле, *in the small field.*
- All stressed adjectives take the ending -ом: в большо́м зда́нии, *in the big building.*
- All soft adjectives take the ending-ем: на си́нем дива́не, *on the dark blue sofa.*
- All possessive adjectives take the ending -ем: в на́шем зда́нии, *in our building.*

➤ For spelling rules, see Unit 2, for different categories of adjective, see Units 20–3, for prepositional singular of nouns, see Unit 17, for prepositions taking the prepositional case, see Units 83 and 89.

1 **Complete the phrases by choosing the appropriate ending from the box below:**

e.g. Врач рабо́тает в но́в____ больни́це → Врач рабо́тает в но́вой больни́це.

```
-ом   -ем   -ой   -ей
```

1 Ба́бушка живёт в ста́р ___ до́ме.   *Granny lives in an old house.*
2 Зо́я живёт в дре́вн ___ кварти́ре.   *Zoya lives in an ancient flat.*
3 Светла́на живёт в шу́мн___ го́роде.   *Svetlana lives in a noisy town.*
4 Андре́й живёт в краси́в___ дере́вне.   *Andrei lives in a beautiful village.*
5 Са́ша живёт в хоро́ш___ го́роде.   *Sasha lives in a nice town.*

2 **Who works where? Match the two halves of the sentences, using the English translation as a guide.**

1 Мой брат рабо́тает   **a** в большо́й больни́це
2 Мой дя́дя рабо́тает   **b** в краси́вом па́рке
3 Моя́ жена́ рабо́тает   **c** в ма́ленькой апте́ке
4 Моя́ тётя рабо́тает   **d** в сосе́днем зда́нии
5 Мой муж рабо́тает   **e** в хоро́шей шко́ле

My brother works at a good school.
My uncle works in a big hospital.
My wife works in the neighbouring building.
My aunt works in a small chemist's.
My husband works in a beautiful park.

3 **Put the phrases that follow into the prepositional singular.**

1 зелёный парк   *green park*
2 Кра́сная Пло́щадь   *Red Square*
3 чёрный портфе́ль   *black briefcase*
4 жёлтая ю́бка   *yellow skirt*
5 си́нее не́бо   *blue sky*

An adjective must always agree with the noun it is describing; if the noun has to be in the prepositional plural, so must the adjective describing it. There are only two prepositional plural adjective endings (irrespective of gender).

A The two possible endings for prepositional plural adjectives are -ых and -их (i.e. just like the endings for genitive plural adjectives). These endings are used for all three genders.

Б Stressed and unstressed adjectives always take the ending -ых (unless their stem ends in г, к, х, ж, ч, ш, щ (Spelling Rule 1)).

Examples of the ending -ых
картины в больших интересных музеях *the pictures are in big interesting museums*
в иностранных школах *in foreign schools*
в важных письмах *in important letters*

В The prepositional plural adjective ending is -их if:
- the adjective's stem ends in г, к, х, ж, ч, ш, щ (spelling rule 1)
- the adjective is soft (e.g. синий, *dark blue*)
- the adjective is possessive (eg мой)

Examples of the ending -их
The adjective's stem ends in г, к, х, ж, ч, ш, щ: в английских гостиницах *in English hotels*
The adjective is soft: в утренних газетах *in the morning papers*
The adjective is possessive: в наших номерах *in our hotel rooms*

> **➤ For spelling rules, see Unit 2, for different categories of adjective see Units 20–3, for prepositional plural of nouns, see Unit 18, for prepositions with the prepositional case, see Units 83, 87, 89.**

1 Describe where and how you spent your holidays by matching up the two halves of each sentence. Use the English translations as a guide.

1 мы лежа́ли	a в си́них бассе́йнах
2 мы де́лали поку́пки	b на жёлтых пля́жах
3 мы обе́дали	c на прекра́сных ко́ртах
4 мы смотре́ли карти́ны	d в больши́х музе́ях
5 мы пла́вали	e в хоро́ших рестора́нах
6 мы игра́ли в те́ннис	f больши́х конце́ртных за́лах
7 мы пи́ли кокте́йли	g в шика́рных магази́нах
8 мы слу́шали конце́рты	h в прия́тных ба́рах

We lay on yellow beaches.
We did shopping in stylish shops.
We had lunch in good restaurants.
We looked at pictures in big museums.
We swam in blue pools.
We played tennis on splendid courts.
We drank cocktails in pleasant bars.
We listened to concerts in big concert halls.

2 Put the following phrases into the prepositional plural.

1 краси́вое зда́ние	*beautiful building*
2 ру́сский го́род	*Russian town*
3 ночно́й клуб	*night club*
4 после́дний авто́бус	*last bus*
5 высо́кое де́рево	*tall tree*

3 Build sentences from the following vocabulary, using the prepositional plural.

e.g. Они́/отдыха́ть/в/прия́тный/куро́рт → Они́ отдыха́ют в прия́тных куро́ртах. *They holiday (rest) in pleasant resorts.*

1 Он/рабо́тать/на/шу́мный/завóд — *He works in noisy factories.*

2 Онá/де́лать поку́пки/в/дорого́й/магази́н — *She does her shopping in expensive shops.*

3 Мы/чита́ть нóвости/в/вече́рняя/газе́та — *We read the news in the evening papers.*

4 Вы/обе́дать/в/ма́ленький/рестора́н — *You have lunch in small restaurants.*

5 Они́/отдыха́ть/в/краси́вый/парк — *They rest in beautiful parks.*

Most Russian adjectives have two sorts of ending: the long form (discussed in Units 20–33) and the short form. The short form exists in the nominative case only (when you are talking about the subject of the sentence) and is usually found at the end of a phrase or sentence. It is much less common than the long form.

A The long form is used 'attributively' – i.e. in front of a noun: Изве́стный актёр живёт в Москве́. *The famous actor lives in Moscow.* The short form is used 'predicatively' – i.e. after the noun: Кли́мат суро́в, *The climate is harsh.*

In modern conversational Russian, the long form is very often used everywhere and the short form hardly ever. However, sometimes the short form **must** be used in order to convey the correct message.

Б Short forms are formed by shortening the long form of the adjective.

Long form	Masculine short form	Feminine short form	Neuter short form	Plural (all genders)
краси́вый	краси́в	краси́ва	краси́во	краси́вы

For some adjectives, this will mean that a 'cluster of consonants' (i.e. more than one) is left together at the end of the masculine short form, and the vowel e (or sometimes o or ё) has to be inserted, for example: изве́стный, *famous, well known* – Э́тот факт изве́стен, *This fact is well known.*

В Some Russian adjectives have no short form (e.g. colour, nationality, substance – *wooden, metal* – ordinal numerals, *first, second* etc. and soft adjectives). But NB, the adjective рад (*glad, happy*) exists *only* in the short form.

Г If the adjective comes before the noun or needs to be in a case other than the nominative, you must use the long form. Otherwise, in most instances you may use either the long or the short form. So '*the town is beautiful*' could be either: Го́род краси́вый or Го́род краси́в. However, there are some adjectives when you should always use the short form in the 'predicative' (i.e. after the noun) position, because to use the long form would imply something different (e.g. the adjective for 'ill' in the long form implies chronically sick, as opposed to the short form, which is used when you want to indicate 'not too well at the moment'). For example: больно́й, *ill* (short form: бо́лен, больна́, бо́льно, больны́); за́нятый, *occupied* (short form: за́нят, занята́, за́нято, за́няты); свобо́дный, *free, vacant* (short form: свобо́ден, свобо́дна, свобо́дно, свобо́дны).

1 In the following English passage underline the adjectives which are in the 'short' (predicative) position (clue: there are five).

Svetlana walks into the house and notices that all the doors and windows are open. The new curtains are blowing about in the wind. The door, however, is shut. On the table a cat lies, howling. It is clearly glad to see her. She is furious when she realizes that her son has gone out without feeding the cat. 'He is so unreliable!' she thinks.

2 The adjectives in brackets are in the masculine singular long form. Put them into the short form.

e.g. Моя́ ко́шка _____ (голо́дный) → Моя́ ко́шка голодна́.
My cat is hungry.

1 Э́то ме́сто _____ (свобо́дный). *This seat is free.*
2 Его́ автомоби́ль _____ (но́вый). *His car is new.*
3 На́ши де́ти _____ (здоро́вый). *Our children are well.*
4 Все о́кна _____ (откры́тый). *All the windows are open.*
5 Ка́ша _____ (вку́сный). *The porridge is delicious.*

3 Match the two halves of each sentence, using the English translations as a guide.

1 Как жаль! Рестора́н   **a** согла́сна
2 Как хорошо́! Ка́тя   **b** ра́ды
3 Как жаль! Врач   **c** откры́та
4 Он прие́хал? Мы   **d** закры́т
5 Хо́лодно, потому́ что дверь **e** за́нят

What a shame! The restaurant is closed.
How nice! Katya agrees (is in agreement).
What a shame! The doctor is busy.
He has arrived? We are glad.
It's cold because the door is open.

4 Look again at the adjectives a–e in Exercise 3.

1 Which is the only one you would never see in the long form?
2 Work out what the masculine singular long forms would be of the other adjectives in the list.

35 long form comparative

If we say that something is 'more interesting' or 'less interesting', we are using the comparative.

A In English we can form the comparative by using the words *more* and *less*, or if the English adjective is very short, we can add *-er* to the end of the adjective (*it is cheaper*). Russian uses the words бо́лее (*more*) or ме́нее (*less*) in front of the long form of the adjective. This is called the compound comparative.

Б The words бо́лее and ме́нее never change (i.e. in their endings) but the long adjective which follows them must agree with the adjective it is describing:

Э́то бо́лее (ме́нее) интере́сный   *This is a more (less) interesting*
   го́род.   *town.*
Она́ живёт в бо́лее (ме́нее)   *She lives in a more (less)*
   интере́сном го́роде.   *interesting town.*

В Some adjectives do not form compound comparatives. They have a long form comparative of their own. Here are the first four:

	Long form adjective	Long form comparative
большо́й *big*	бо́льший (**NB** the stress is on the stem!), *bigger*	
ма́ленький *small*	ме́ньший, *lesser, smaller*	
хоро́ший *good*	лу́чший, *better*	
плохо́й *bad*	ху́дший, *worse*	

The adjectives for *old* and *young* cannot form compound comparatives if you are talking about animate nouns or groups – they have their own long form comparative.

| ста́рый *old* | ста́рший *older, senior* | Моя́ ста́ршая сестра́. *My older sister.* |
| молодо́й *young* | мла́дший *younger* | Мла́дший класс. *The junior class.* |

You can, however, say Э́то бо́лее ста́рое зда́ние, *it is an older building.*

The adjectives for *high* and *low* cannot form compound comparatives if you are using them in the sense which means *superior* and *inferior*:

| высо́кий *high* | вы́сший *superior, higher* | вы́сшее образова́ние *higher education* |
| ни́зкий *low* | ни́зший *inferior, lower* | ни́зший бал *lower (bottom) mark* |

You can, however, say Э́то бо́лее высо́кое зда́ние, *it is a taller building.*

➤ For short form comparatives see Unit 36; for constructions with the comparative, see Unit 37.

1 Underline the adjectives in this passage for which you would need the compound comparative. Circle the ones which have their own long form comparative in Russian.

My younger sister, Masha, really likes shopping. Yesterday she bought a bigger bag, a newer car, a more expensive radio, a more interesting book and a smaller mobile telephone.

2 Complete a translation of this passage giving the Russian for the adjective in brackets.

Моя _____ (*younger*) сестра́, Ма́ша, о́чень лю́бит де́лать поку́пки. Вчера́ она́ купи́ла _____ (*bigger*) су́мку, _____ (*newer*) автомоби́ль, _____ (*more expensive*) ра́дио, _____ (*more interesting*) кни́гу _____ и (*smaller*) со́товый телефо́н.

3 Pair up the words on the left and the right using the English translations as a guide:

1	мла́дший	a	письмо́
2	ста́ршая	b	иде́я
3	бо́лее прия́тный	c	ситуа́ция
4	ме́нее интере́сное	d	шко́ла
5	ни́зший	e	гру́ппа
6	лу́чшая	f	карти́на
7	ху́дшая	g	сын
8	ме́нее краси́вая	h	бал
9	бо́лее шу́мная	i	дом
10	бо́льшая	j	дочь

1 *younger son*
2 *elder daughter*
3 *a more pleasant house*
4 *a less interesting letter*
5 *a lower (bottom) mark*
6 *better idea*
7 *worse situation*
8 *a less beautiful picture*
9 *a more noisy (noisier) group*
10 *a bigger school*

If you are using a comparative adjective 'predicatively' – i.e. after the noun it is describing (*the book is more interesting*), then you can use the short form comparative. This sort of comparative can only be used to mean *more . . .* (*interesting, beautiful* etc.)

A The first really important thing to remember is that you can only use the short form comparative when the person or thing you are describing is in the nominative case.

Б The short comparative is formed by adding the ending -ee to the stem of the adjective. This ending is the same for all genders and is invariable (it never changes):

дом прия́тнее	*the house is more pleasant*
соба́ка краси́вее	*the dog is more beautiful*
письмо́ интере́снее	*the letter is more interesting*
цветы́ прекра́снее	*the flowers are more splendid*

Note that it is more common to use this form of the comparative when you are saying *A=B* (*the house=pleasant*) than it would be to say дом бо́лее прия́тный.

В Some very common adjectives make their comparative short form irregularly. Here are some common ones:

near	бли́зкий	→ бли́же
high	высо́кий	→ вы́ше
loud	гро́мкий	→ гро́мче
hot	жа́ркий	→ жа́рче
far	далёкий	→ да́льше
cheap	дешёвый	→ деше́вле
expensive, dear	дорого́й	→ доро́же
short	коро́ткий	→ коро́че
small	ма́ленький	→ ме́ньше
young	молодо́й	→ моло́же
low	ни́зкий	→ ни́же
bad	плохо́й	→ ху́же
simple	просто́й	→ про́ще
old	ста́рый	→ ста́рше
quiet	ти́хий	→ ти́ше
fat	то́лстый	→ то́лще
good	хоро́ший	→ лу́чше
frequent	ча́стый	→ ча́ще

Г Some adjectives have no short form comparative: adjectives of colour, of substance (e.g. wooden, silk).

➤ **For nominative case, see Units 4-6, for long form comparative, see Unit 35, for constructions with the comparative, see Unit 37.**

1 In which of the following sentences would you be able to use the short form comparative in Russian?

1 *My brother is cleverer.*
2 *This book is less boring.*
3 *His car is cheaper.*
4 *We have bought a newer car.*
5 *Do you know where the more comfortable chair is?*
6 *It is simpler.*
7 *It is further to Moscow.*
8 *We have received a more important letter.*
9 *This letter is shorter.*
10 *This radio is more expensive.*

2 Now complete the Russian versions of these sentences by giving the appropriate comparative form of the adjectives in brackets:

1 Мой брат _____ (ýмный).
2 Эта кни́га _____ (скýчный).
3 Его маши́на _____ (дешёвый).
4 Мы купи́ли _____ (но́вый) дом.
5 Вы не зна́ете, где _____ (удо́бный) стул?
6 Это _____ (просто́й).
7 До Москвы́ _____ (далёкий).
8 Мы получи́ли _____ (ва́жный) письмо́.
9 Это письмо́ _____ (коро́ткий).
10 Это ра́дио _____ (дорого́й).

3 Look at the two pictures and then answer the questions.

ИВА́Н

ВАДИ́М

1 Кто то́лще?
2 Кто моло́же?

In English we form the second part of the comparative by using the word *than* (*he has a more beautiful car than you*). In Russian this part of the sentence is formed either by using the word чем (*than*) or by using the genitive.

А When we are using the long form comparative in Russian, we must form the second part of the comparative by using the word чем:

У него бо́лее краси́вый автомоби́ль, чем у вас.
He has a more beautiful car than you.

The word чем must also be used if the words его, её, их feature in the second part of the comparison:

Э́то бо́лее краси́вый автомоби́ль, чем его́.
It's a more beautiful car than his.

Б If you are using the short form of the comparative, there are two ways in which you can deal with the second part of your comparison (*than* . . .). Either use чем:

Мой дом прия́тнее, чем твой.
My house is pleasanter than yours.

Or use the genitive of the second part of your comparison:

Мой дом прия́тнее твоего́.
My house is pleasanter than yours.

В If you want to 'intensify' your comparative (*it is much more interesting*), simply add the words гора́здо or намно́го:

Мой дом гора́здо прия́тнее твоего́.
My house is much pleasanter than yours.
Э́та кни́га намно́го интере́снее.
This book is much more interesting

Г If you want to say how much taller/shorter, younger/older someone is, use the preposition на:

Она́ моло́же его́ на шесть лет.
She is six years younger than him.

➤ For genitive case, see Units 10–12, for long form of comparative, see Unit 35, for short form, see Unit 36.

1 Match the phrases on the left with those on the right, using the English translations as a guide:

1 Его соба́ка непослу́шнее   a на́шего
2 Э́тот со́товый телефо́н бо́льше   b мое́й
3 Их сад краси́вее   c ва́ших
4 Ва́ше письмо́ интере́снее   d твоего́
5 Мои иде́и лу́чше   e моего́

1 *His dog is naughtier than mine.*
2 *This mobile phone is bigger than yours.*
3 *Their garden is more beautiful than ours.*
4 *Your letter is more interesting than mine.*
5 *My ideas are better than yours.*

2 Big differences! Use the comparative with намно́го and the genitive of comparison to build sentences from the following words. Use the English translation as a guide.

e.g. Вади́м/ста́рый/Ива́н → Вади́м намно́го ста́рше Ива́на. *Vadim is much older than Ivan.*

1 О́льга/до́брый/Ири́на   *Olga is much kinder than Irina.*
2 Андре́й/серьёзный/   *Andrei is much more serious*
   Константи́н   *than Konstantin.*
3 Он/энерги́чный/я   *He is much more energetic than me.*
4 Мой брат/лени́вый/моя́   *My brother is much lazier than*
   сестра́   *my sister.*
5 Ба́бушка/молодо́й/де́душка   *Grandmother is much younger*
                             than grandfather.

3 Translate the following sentences into Russian (decide whether to use чем or the genitive of comparison for the second part of each sentence).

1 This is a more serious problem than his.
2 Moscow is a bigger city than Novgorod.
3 He is older than me.
4 Your television is better than mine.
5 I like the more energetic dog.

If we say something is the *most interesting, smallest, best* we are using the superlative form of the adjective.

A The superlative is very easy to form. Simply put the adjective са́мый in front of the the adjective and noun you are describing. There is no short form of the superlative (so it can be used predicatively and attributively – before or after the noun):

са́мый серьёзный фильм	*the most serious film*
э́тот фильм са́мый серьёзный	*this film is the most serious*

Б Make sure that the adjective са́мый agrees in number, gender and case with its adjective and noun:

Я изуча́ю са́мый краси́вый язы́к.	*I am studying the most beautiful language.*
Я чита́ю са́мую серьёзную кни́гу.	*I am reading the most serious book.*
Мы живём в са́мом прия́тном райо́не.	*We leave in the pleasantest region.*

В Са́мый can be used with the comparatives лу́чший and ху́дший to mean *best* and *worst*, or they can just be used as superlatives in their own right, so: э́то лу́чшая иде́я and э́то са́мая лу́чшая иде́я both mean *it's the best idea.* The same applies to мла́дший (*younger/youngest*) and ста́рший (*older/oldest*).

Г To say '*the most... of*' (e.g. *one of the most interesting books*), use the preposition из:

одна́ из са́мых интере́сных книг
one of the most interesting books

Д A very small number of adjectives form their superlative with the ending -айший or -ейший. The most useful are in phrases such as:

У меня́ нет ни мале́йшей иде́и.	*I haven't the slightest idea.*
Чисте́йший вздор!	*Utter rubbish!*
Ближа́йшая ста́нция метро́.	*The nearest metro station.*

➤ For long and short forms of adjective, see Units 34, for long and short forms of comparative adjectives, see Units 35–7, for uses of из, see Unit 85.

1 Turn the adjective in each sentence into the superlative. (remember agreements).

e.g. Ири́на (лени́вый) → Ири́на са́мая лени́вая. *Irina is the laziest.*

1 Это _____ (краси́вый) парк. *This is the most beautiful park.*

2 Ива́н _____ (хоро́ший) футболи́ст. *Ivan is the best footballer.*

3 Вот _____ (энерги́чный) медсестра́. *Here is the most energetic nurse.*

4 Я чита́ю_____ (интере́сный) кни́гу. *I am reading the most interesting book.*

5 Он живёт в_____ (ма́ленький) кварти́ра. *He lives in the smallest flat.*

2 Complete the sentences with an appropriate superlative adjective, using the English translations as a guide.

1 Он оди́н из _____ гитари́стов. *He is one of the best guitarists.*

2 Это са́мый _____ пляж. *It is the most beautiful beach.*

3 _____ вздор! *Utter rubbish!*

4 Где _____ остано́вка авто́буса? *Where is the nearest bus stop?*

5 Это _____проблéма. *It is the most serious problem.*

3 Choose a suitable adjective from the box and then make the superlative form to complete each sentence:

жа́ркий красси́вый крéпкий холо́дный

1 Зи́ма _____ вре́мя го́да. *Winter is the coldest time of year.*

2 _____ кли́мат. *The hottest climate.*

3 Во́дка _____ напи́ток. *Vodka is the strongest drink.*

4 Это _____ кварти́ра. *It is the most beautiful flat.*

39 adverbs (1)

Adverbs describe how things are done (*she writes slowly*). In English most end in *-ly*. In Russian most adverbs are identical with the neuter short form adjective.

A The most common form of adverb describes how the action of a verb is carried out:

Она́ ме́дленно пи́шет.	*She writes slowly.*
Он бы́стро бе́гает.	*He runs quickly.*

Note that the adverb is usually placed before the verb. Sometimes it is not 'obvious' that there is a verb being described – i.e. the verb *to be* does not exist in the present tense; but phrases describing the weather, for example, rely on adverbs: Сего́дня тепло́ (*it is warm today*) – тепло́ is 'describing' how *it is*.

Б The adverbs ме́дленно and бы́стро are the short neuter forms of the adjectives ме́дленный and бы́стрый. Most adverbs, therefore, end in о. Some adverbs will end in -е (because of the second spelling rule) and if an adjective is soft, its adverb will end in -е:

блестя́щий	→ блестя́ще	*brilliantly*
и́скренний	→ и́скренне	*sincerely*

В Look out for stress changes between some adjectives and adverbs:

тёплый	(*warm*)	→ тепло́	(*it is warm*)
хоро́ший	(*good*)	→ хорошо́	(*well*)

Г Adjectives which end in -ский have adverbs ending in -ски: практи́чески *practically (almost)*. 'Adverbial phrases' which indicate nationality are formed from по and adjectives ending in -ский: мы говори́м по-ру́сски *we speak Russian*.

Д Although the vast majority of adverbs in Russian are formed from adjectives, adverbs which tell us about time and place are not. Here are the most common:

Time	Place
когда́ *when*	где *where*
тогда́ *then, at that time*	здесь *here*
уже́ *already*	там *there*
ещё *still, yet*	куда́ *where to**
до́лго *for a long time*	сюда́ *here (to here)**
давно́ *a long time ago*	туда́ *there (to there)**
неда́вно *recently*	отку́да *from where*
	отсю́да *from here*
	отту́да *from there*

* Note that these indicate motion towards: Куда́ вы идёте? *(To) where are you going?*

> **For short forms of adjective, see Unit 34, for use of prepositions with the accusative to express motion towards, see Units 83 and 84, for second spelling rule, see Unit 2.**

1 **Form adverbs from the following adjectives.**

1	глу́пый	*stupid*
2	прия́тный	*pleasant*
3	хоро́ший	*good*
4	тёплый	*warm*
5	логи́ческий	*logical*
6	го́рдый	*proud*
7	впечатля́ющий	*impressive*
8	саркасти́чный	*sarcastic*
9	эгоисти́ческий	*selfish*
10	ще́дрый	*generous*
11	ти́хий	*quiet*
12	шу́мный	*noisy*

2 **Answer using an adverb which means the opposite of the adverb in the first statement.**

e.g. Ири́на пло́хо поёт? Нет! Она́ хорошо́ поёт.
   Does Irina sing badly? No! She sings well

1	Сего́дня хо́лодно?	(*No, today it is warm*).
2	Пиани́ст пло́хо игра́ет?	(*No, brilliantly*).
3	Студе́нт бы́стро рабо́тает?	(*No, slowly*).
4	Де́ти шу́мно игра́ют?	(*No, quietly*).
5	Брат лени́во игра́ет?	(*No, energetically*).

3 **Work out which language is spoken by whom.**

e.g. Италья́нец → Италья́нец говори́т по-италья́нски.

1	Испа́нец	*Spaniard*
2	Ру́сский	*Russian*
3	Англича́нин	*Englishman*
4	Япо́нец	*Japanese*

40 adverbs (2)

Adverbs, like adjectives, have comparative and superlative forms (e.g. *he runs more quickly* and *he runs the most quickly*).

A The comparative adverb is identical to the short form comparative adjective: so, for example: быстре́е, *more quickly*, ме́дленнее, *more slowly*, лу́чше, *better*:

Он всегда́ рабо́тает быстре́е, чем я.
He always works more quickly than I do.

Adverbs ending in -и form their comparative with бо́лее:

Он всегда́ рабо́тает бо́лее логи́чески, чем я.
He always works more logically than I do.

Б To say, for example, *less quickly, less logically*, use ме́нее with the adverb:

Он всегда́ ду́мает ме́нее логи́чески, чем я.
He always thinks less logically than I do.

В Да́льше (*further*) and ра́ньше (*earlier, previously*) come from adjectives, but are used only as comparative adverbs.

Г Like comparative adjectives, comparative adverbs can form constructions with both чем and with the genitive of comparison:

Ви́ктор рабо́тает усе́рднее,   *Viktor works harder than*
чем Валенти́н.   *Valentin.*

Ви́ктор рабо́тает усе́рднее   *Viktor works harder than*
Валенти́на.   *Valentin.*

The words гора́здо or намно́го (*much*) can also be used with comparative adverbs:

Он рабо́тает гора́здо быстре́е, чем я.
He works much more quickly than I do.

Ещё can be used with a comparative adverb to mean *even*: он рабо́тает ещё быстре́е, *he works even more quickly*.

Д The short form of the comparative adverb is very useful in expressions such as: чем бо́льше, тем веселе́е, *the more the merrier*, как мо́жно скоре́е, *as quickly/soon as possible*, всё ча́ще, *more (and more) often*.

Е To make the superlative of an adverb, simply add всего́ or всех: if you want to say '*best of all*' be careful to check whether you mean '*better than anything else*' or '*better than anyone else*':

Она́ игра́ет на гита́ре лу́чше   *She plays the guitar best of all*
всего́.   (i.e. better than she does anything else).

Она́ игра́ет на гита́ре лу́чше   *She plays the guitar best of all*
всех.   (i.e. better than anyone else).

➤ **For short forms of comparative adjective, see Unit 36, for comparative constructions, see Unit 37.**

1 **Match the phrases on the left with their translations on the right:**

1 чем скоре́е, тем лу́чше   a *as cheaply as possible*
2 как мо́жно про́ще   b *the sooner the better*
3 всё бли́же   c *worse and worse*
4 как мо́жно деше́вле   d *nearer and nearer*
5 всё ху́же   e *as simply as possible*

2 **How are the various sportsmen performing? Build sentences using comparative adverbs.**

e.g. Андре́й бы́стро бе́гает/И́горь → Андре́й бы́стро бе́гает, но И́горь бе́гает ещё быстре́е. *Andrei runs quickly, but Igor runs even more quickly.*

1 Пиани́ст хорошо́ игра́ет /гитари́ст
2 Мой брат лени́во игра́ет/твой брат
3 Тенниси́ст энерги́чно игра́ет /футболи́ст
4 Баскетболи́ст глу́по игра́ет /хоккеи́ст
5 Игро́к в гольф ме́дленно игра́ет/ игро́к в кри́кет

3 **Translate into Russian:**

1 *Katya speaks more quietly than her sister.*
2 *Igor works much harder than Valentin.*
3 *Tatyana sings even worse than Zoya.*
4 *The earlier the better.*
5 *As soon as possible.*

4 **Complete the sentences below with either лу́чше всего́ or лу́чше всех:**

1 Мой брат говори́т по-италья́нски _____ (*better than anyone else*).
2 Он игра́ет в ша́хматы _____ (*best of all; better than any other game*).
3 Я зна́ю врача́ _____ (*better than I know anyone else*).

41 cardinal numerals (1)

Numbers like two, twenty-three, forty-six, ninety etc. are called cardinal numerals – they express a definite quantity.

A Here are the cardinal numerals in Russian from 1 to 20:

1 один	11 одиннадцать
2 два	12 двенадцать
3 три	13 тринадцать
4 четы́ре	14 четы́рнадцать
5 пять	15 пятнадцать
6 шесть	16 шестнадцать
7 семь	17 семнадцать
8 во́семь	18 восемнадцать
9 де́вять	19 девятнадцать
10 де́сять	20 два́дцать

Б Numbers above 20 are formed quite simply in Russian – just place them one after another: 24 = два́дцать четы́ре, 55 = пятьдеся́т пять, 103 = сто три.
Here are the numbers from 30 to 1000:

30 три́дцать	300 три́ста
40 со́рок	400 четы́реста
50 пятьдеся́т	500 пятьсо́т
60 шестьдеся́т	600 шестьсо́т
70 се́мьдесят	700 семьсо́т
80 во́семьдесят	800 восемьсо́т
90 девяно́сто	900 девятьсо́т
100 сто	1 000 ты́сяча
200 две́сти	

В The numeral 'one' has three forms in Russian. It behaves like an adjective: оди́н дом, *one house*; одна́ кварти́ра, *one flat*; одно́ ме́сто, *one place (seat)*.

Г The numeral 'two' has two forms in Russian: два for when it is used with masculine and neuter nouns and две for when it is used with feminine nouns: два бра́та и две сестры́, *I have two brothers and two sisters.*

➢ For declension of numerals, see Unit 42, for use of adjectives with numerals and of cases with numerals, see Unit 43, for genitive singular and plural, see Units 10–12.

1 **Write out these sums as you would say them.**

+ плюс	– ми́нус	= бу́дет

e.g. 46 + 6 = ? со́рок шесть плюс шесть бу́дет пятьдеся́т два
1 100 – 20 = ?
2 2 + 16 = ?
3 33 + 102 = ?
4 29 – 15 = ?
5 85 – 54 = ?

2 **Match up the numbers in words on the left with the figures on the right:**

1	девяно́сто два	**a**	10
2	семьсо́т два́дцать два	**b**	92
3	оди́ннадцать	**c**	722
4	де́сять	**d**	212
5	две́сти двена́дцать	**e**	11

3 **Here are some telephone numbers. Write them out and practise saying them:**

e.g. 25–27–70 два́дцать два – два́дцать семь – се́мьдесят
1 42–93–12
2 84–53–55
3 20–30–40
4 36–62–73
5 18–11–26

4 **Look at this Russian proverb. Which numeral is involved and what is the advice being given?**

НЕ ИМЕ́Й СТО РУБЛЕ́Й, А ИМЕ́Й СТО ДРУЗЕ́Й

42 cardinal numerals (2)

Like nouns, numerals have six cases. In this unit we look just at the case endings of numerals; the use of numerals in their six cases is explained in Unit 43.

А 1 functions like an adjective (* = animate accusative):

	Masculine	Feminine	Neuter
Nom.	оди́н	одна́	одно́
Acc.	оди́н/одного́*	одну́	одно́/одного́*
Gen.	одного́	одно́й	одного́
Dat.	одному́	одно́й	одному́
Instr.	одни́м	одно́й	одни́м
Prep.	одно́м	одно́й	одно́м

Б 2, 3 and 4 are the trickiest numerals in terms of case endings.

	2	3	4
Nom.	два/две	три	четы́ре
Acc.	два/две/двух*	три/трёх*	четы́ре/ четырёх*
Gen.	двух	трёх	четырёх
Dat.	двум	трём	четырём
Instr.	двумя́	тремя́	четырьмя́
Prep.	двух	трёх	четырёх

В Numerals which end in a soft sign (e.g. пять) are feminine nouns. Numerals with a soft sign in the middle change in the middle and at the end. 40 and 100 are much more straightforward (90 works like 100):

Nom.	пять	пятьдеся́т	со́рок	сто
Acc.	пять	пятьдеся́т	со́рок	сто
Gen.	пяти́	пяти́десяти	сорока́	ста
Dat.	пяти́	пяти́десяти	сорока́	ста
Instr.	пятью́	пятью́десятью	сорока́	ста
Prep.	пяти́	пяти́десяти	сорока́	ста

NB In the genitive, dative and prepositional во́семь becomes восьми́.

Г The 'hundreds' base their declension on the first digit, for example:

Nom.	две́сти	пятьсо́т	Dat.	двумста́м	пятиста́м
Acc.	две́сти	пятьсо́т	Instr.	двумяста́ми	пятиста́ми
Gen.	двухсо́т	пятьсо́т	Prep.	двухста́х	пятиста́ми

➤ **For use of numerals in different cases, and for adjectives with numerals, see Unit 43.**

1 Buried in the following passage are six numerals written out as words, but in all sorts of different cases. Can you recognize them? A translation of the passage is given in the Key.

Бори́с неда́вно был в двух кни́жных магази́нах и купи́л три кни́ги. Вчера́ он чита́л свою́ но́вую кни́гу по хи́мии. Он чита́л о шестиста́х ра́зных эксперим́ентах в тридцати́ двух стра́нах. Девяно́сто шесть хи́миков получи́ли результа́ты, но в сорока́ четырёх лаборато́риях произошли́ ава́рии.

2 Give the genitive of the following numerals.
1 4
2 60
3 23
4 92
5 110

3 Give the dative of the following numerals.
1 40
2 18
3 73
4 300
5 600

4 Give the instrumental of the following numerals.
1 3
2 10
3 200
4 20
5 5

5 Give the prepositional of the following numerals.
1 12
2 86
3 45
4 11
5 100

In this unit we look at how to deal with numerals and adjectives and how to use numerals in their different cases.

A The number 1 works like an adjective: Он рабо́тает в одно́м прия́тном ме́сте, *He works in one pleasant place.* However big a compound number is, if the last digit is '1', then the noun remains in the singular: Сто одна́ серьёзная пробле́ма, *101 serious problems.* The numbers 2, 3 and 4 (and their compounds, e.g. 23, 34, 52) are followed by the genitive singular of nouns: У меня́ два о́фиса и два́дцать три рабо́тника. *I have 2 offices and 23 employees.* Numbers above 5 (other than compounds of 2, 3 and 4) are followed by the genitive plural of nouns: У меня́ пять о́фисов, *I have 5 offices* (but watch out for челове́к (*person*), which behaves like this: три челове́ка, пять челове́к).

Б The rules for using 2, 3 and 4 + adjective + noun are different for different genders:
Masculine and neuter: when the numeral is the subject, use the genitive *plural* of the adjective and the genitive *singular* of the noun which follow it: два больши́х стола́, *2 big tables,* два больши́х о́кна, *2 big windows.*
Feminine: use *either* the nominative plural *or* the genitive plural of the adjective and the genitive singular of the noun: три краси́вые (краси́вых) сестёр *3 beautiful sisters.*

В If numbers 5 and above are the subject (again, not compounds of 1, 2, 3 and 4, which follow their own rules) they are followed by the genitive plural of both the *noun* and the *adjective.* This applies to all genders:

пять дороги́х биле́тов	*5 expensive tickets*
два́дцать пять дороги́х биле́тов	*25 expensive tickets*
NB два́дцать два дороги́х биле́та	*22 expensive tickets.*

Г These rules apply if a numeral is in the position of subject or an inanimate object. If a numeral needs to be in a case (e.g. after a preposition), the whole numeral and its adjective and noun need to be in the same case, and the noun will be in the plural (unless it follows the numeral 1):

Я ви́жу оди́н большо́й стол и две карти́ны.	*I see one big table and two pictures.*
Биле́ты для тридцати́ пяти́ ру́сских тури́стов и одного́ англи́йского ги́да.	*Tickets for five Russian tourists and one English guide.*

The animate accusative with numerals is used only for 1, 2, 3, 4 on their own (not in compounds!) So, *I see 2 students, 22 professors and 5 guides* will be: Я ви́жу двух студе́нтов (both in the animate accusative!), два́дцать два профе́ссора (for compounds of 2, 3, 4, no change for animate accusative!) и пять ги́дов (for numbers 5 + (apart from compounds of 2, 3, 4) just use the genitive plural).

1 Write out the numerals in words and put the nouns in brackets into the appropriate case (genitive singular or genitive plural?):

1 Два _____ (журна́л)
2 Шесть _____ (неде́ля)
3 Со́рок _____ (челове́к)
4 Два́дцать три _____ (ко́шка)
5 Оди́ннадцать _____ (час)
6 Сто _____ (рубль)
7 Девятна́дцать _____ (киломе́тр)
8 Ты́сяча _____ (кни́га)
9 Сто четы́ре _____ (ма́льчик)
10 Сто пять _____ (де́вушка)

2 Using sections A, Б, B opposite to help you, translate the following into Russian:

1 two big dogs
2 three small theatres
3 one hundred and ten new students
4 five old houses
5 thirty two energetic boys

3 The preposition к is always followed by the dative. Explain who the policeman is walking towards by putting the following phrases into the dative.

e.g. Милиционе́р/три/англи́йский тури́ст → Милиционе́р идёт к трём англи́йским тури́стам. *The policeman is walking towards three English tourists.*

1 пять/ста́рый профе́ссор   *five old professors*
2 два́дцать/серди́тый клие́нт   *twenty cross customers*
3 оди́ннадцать/шу́мный хулига́н   *eleven noisy hooligans*

4 Look at the following phrases, then look again at section Г opposite and explain which endings are being used and why.

1 Он говори́л с пятью́ но́выми студе́нтами.   *He spoke with five new students.*
2 Вы не ви́дели три́дцать два студе́нта?   *Did you not see the 32 students?*
3 Вы не ви́дели трёх студе́нтов?   *Did you not see the three students?*
4 Он говори́л о пяти́ но́вых студе́нтах   *He spoke about the 5 new students.*
5 Мы купи́ли две но́вые кни́ги.   *We bought two new books.*

Ordinal numerals (*first, second, third* etc.) indicate position in an order or series. In Russian ordinal numerals are adjectives.

1st	пе́рвый	11th	оди́ннадцатый	30th	тридца́тый
2nd	второ́й	12th	двена́дцатый	40th	сороково́й
3rd	тре́тий	13th	трина́дцатый	50th	пятидеся́тый
4th	четвёртый	14th	четы́рнадцатый	60th	шестидеся́тый
5th	пя́тый	15th	пятна́дцатый	70th	семидеся́тый
6th	шесто́й	16th	шестна́дцатый	80th	восьмидеся́тый
7th	седьмо́й	17th	семна́дцатый	90th	девяно́стый
8th	восьмо́й	18th	восемна́дцатый	100th	со́тый
9th	девя́тый	19th	девятна́дцатый	1000th	ты́сячный
10th	деся́тый	20th	двадца́тый	1,000,000th	миллио́нный

А All the ordinal numerals are unstressed or stressed adjectives (i.e. they behave like но́вый and большо́й) except for тре́тий (*third*) which is irregular (* = animate accusative).

	Masculine	Feminine	Neuter	Plural
Nom.	тре́тий	тре́тья	тре́тье	тре́тьи
Acc.	тре́тий/тре́тьего*	тре́тью	тре́тье	тре́тьи/тре́тьих*
Gen.	тре́тьего	тре́тьей	тре́тьего	тре́тьих
Dat.	тре́тьему	тре́тьей	тре́тьему	тре́тьим
Instr.	тре́тьим	тре́тьей	тре́тьим	тре́тьими
Prep.	тре́тьем	тре́тьей	тре́тьем	тре́тьих

Б When making an ordinal adjective from a compound numeral, only the last digit is in the form of an ordinal, so, for example:

Пятьдеся́т втора́я неде́ля го́да *the 52nd week of the year*

В If you need to put a compound numeral in a case other than the nominative, only the last digit changes its case endings:

Дни пятьдеся́т второ́й неде́ли *the days of the 52nd week*

Г In abbreviations the final letter of the ordinal adjective ending is used, for example:

52-я неде́ля   *the 52nd week*

Note that the last two letters of the ordinal adjective must be used if the penultimate letter is a consonant: покупки сто шестьдеся́т восьмо́го клие́нта → покупки 168-го клие́нта.

Д Russian uses Roman numerals for centuries and monarchs:

XXI век   *21st century*   Пётр I   *Peter the First (the Great)*

➤ **For use of ordinal numerals in time phrases, see Unit 45 and for dates, see Unit 46.**

A Answer the questions about the months of the year.

e.g. Февра́ль – второ́й ме́сяц го́да. *February is the second month of the year.*
1 Апре́ль
2 Ноя́брь
3 А́вгуст
4 Май
5 Ию́ль

2 Who has bought which size shoes? Build sentences with the information given.

e.g. Ива́н/46 → Ива́н купи́л ту́фли со́рок шесто́го разме́ра.
1 Вади́м/38
2 Татья́на/30
3 А́нна/ 32
4 Андре́й/43
5 Еле́на/36

3 Explain which floor each department is on.

e.g. Оде́жда – эта́ж 1 → Оде́жда на пе́рвом этаже́. *Clothes are on the first floor.*
1 Бага́ж – эта́ж 2
2 Фотоаппара́ты – эта́ж 3
3 Ту́фли – эта́ж 4
4 Кни́ги – эта́ж 5
5 Сувени́ры – эта́ж 6

4 Explain which photograph is on which page (write out the numbers in words).

e.g. Фотогра́фия го́рода/стр. 14 → Фотогра́фия го́рода на страни́це четы́рнадцатой. *The photograph of the town is on page 14 (on page the 14th).*
1 Фотогра́фия шко́лы/стр. 52
2 Фотогра́фия теа́тра/стр. 229
3 Фотогра́фия у́лицы/стр. 87
4 Фотогра́фия актёра/стр. 61
5 Фотогра́фия актри́сы/стр. 10

Both cardinal and ordinal numerals are needed when telling the time.

A To answer the question *What time is it?* (Который час? or Сколько времени?) by stating an hour: give the cardinal number followed by the word for hour (genitive singular after 2, 3, 4; genitive plural for 5 and above):

три часа́	3 o'clock
шесть часо́в	6 o'clock

Б To give the time on the 'right-hand side' of the clock (i.e. between the hour and the half-hour), you need to use the ordinal numbers. You also need to think ahead, because the way of saying 4.10, for example, is to say *ten minutes of the fifth hour*:

де́сять мину́т пя́того	*4.10*
два́дцать пять мину́т пя́того	*4.25*

To express the half hour, use either полови́на or its abbreviation пол-:

полови́на пя́того	*4.30*
полпя́того	*4.30*

В To give the time on the left-hand side of the clock (i.e. after the half-hour), the preposition без (*without*) is needed. This preposition is followed by the genitive case.

без десяти́ (мину́т) шесть	*5.50 (without ten minutes six; the word* мину́т *is optional*)
без че́тверти шесть	*5.45 (without quarter six)*

Г По́лдень means *mid-day* and по́лночь means *midnight;* в по́лночь means *at midnight.*

Д To answer the question *At what time?* (В кото́ром часу́? Во ско́лько?), use the preposition в + *accusative* for the right-hand side of the clock:

в де́сять мину́т пя́того	*at 4.10*

For the half hour, use в + *prepositional*:

в полови́не пя́того	*at 4.30*

For the left-hand side of the clock, в is not needed:

без че́тверти шесть	*at 5.45*

Е You can also state the time by just using cardinal numerals (i.e. by using the twenty-four hour clock):

Ско́лько вре́мени? Оди́ннадцать три́дцать	*What time is it? 11.30*
В кото́ром часу́? В восемна́дцать пятна́дцать	*At what time? At 18.15*

➤ **For genitive singular, see Unit 10, for без, see Unit 89.**

1 Say what time it is using the twelve-hour clock:

e.g. Кото́рый час? 2.10 → де́сять мину́т тре́тьего

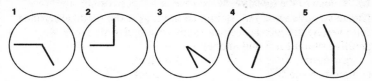

2 Say when the trains leave using the twenty-four hour clock.

e.g. Пермь 18.30 → По́езд в Пермь отхо́дит в восемна́дцать три́дцать. *The train for Perm leaves at 18.30.*

1 Новосиби́рск – 07.15
2 Тверь – 14.55
3 Я́лта – 21.35
4 Воро́неж – 19.30
5 Ки́ров – 17.10

3 Complete the statements on the left by inserting the appropriate times in words, using the information given on the right. Use the twelve-hour clock.

1 Он встаёт в_____   *He gets up at 7.00.*
2 Он за́втракает в _____   *He has breakfast at 7.15.*
3 Его́ рабо́чий день   *His working day begins at 8.45.*
   начина́ется _____
4 Он обе́дает в _____   *He has lunch at 1.35.*
5 Его́ рабо́чий день   *His working day finishes at 5.30.*
   конча́ется в_____

46 dates

Dates, months, and years: how to use cardinal and ordinal numerals to answer the questions *What is the date today? On what date? In which year?*

The months of the year are written with a small initial letter. They are all masculine.

янва́рь	апре́ль	ию́ль	октя́брь
февра́ль	май	а́вгуст	ноя́брь
март	ию́нь	сентя́брь	дека́брь

А To answer the question Како́е сего́дня число́? (*What is the date today?*), the neuter form of the ordinal numeral is used (to agree with число́, *date*) followed by the genitive case of the month:

Сего́дня пе́рвое ма́я. *Today it is the 1st of May.*

Note that in the case of compound numerals, only the last digit is in the ordinal form:

Сего́дня два́дцать седьмо́е февраля́. *Today it is the 27th of February.*

Б To answer the question Како́го числа́? (*On which date?*), the ordinal numeral must be put into the genitive case: День рожде́ния моего́ му́жа тре́тьего октября́. *My husband's birthday is on the 3rd of October.*

В To answer the question Како́й год? (*Which year?*), Russian uses the following formula:

1999 = *the one thousand nine hundred and ninety-ninth year*
ты́сяча де́вятьсот девяно́сто девя́тый год = 1999г.

i.e. the last digit is an ordinal numeral.

2000 = *the 2000th year* = двухты́сячный год = 2000г.

2001 = *the two thousand and first year* = две ты́сячи пе́рвый год = 2001г.

Note that the letter г. (for год) usually follows the year when it is written in figures.

Г To answer the question В како́м году́? (*in which year?*), the ordinal numeral must be put into the prepositional case:

В ты́сяча девятьсо́т пятьдеся́т тре́тьем году́.   *In 1953.*

If details of dates and months are given before the year, then the ordinal numeral must be put into the genitive case:

Она́ родила́сь три́дцать пе́рвого ма́рта ты́сяча девятьсо́т четы́рнадцатого го́да. *She was born on 31st March 1914.*

➤ **For the prepositional singular of adjectives, see Unit 32, for ordinal numerals and abbreviation of ordinal numerals, see Unit 44.**

1 **Write out the dates in words.**

e.g. 2/5   Сего́дня второ́е ма́я.

1 6/11	**4** 3/10	**7** 25/6
2 25/8	**5** 29/2	**8** 1/9
3 7/1	**6** 16/4	**9** 31/12

2 **Explain where you will be on which dates.**

e.g. 01/8 Пари́ж → Пе́рвого а́вгуста я бу́ду в Пари́же. *On the 1st of August I will be in Paris.*

1 10/8 Вене́ция

2 16/8 Берли́н

3 20/8 Москва́

4 25/8 Ки́ров

5 30/8 Но́вгород

3 **Complete the sentences on the left and match them with their meanings on the right.**

1 Я пое́ду во Фра́нцию _____.

a *Her birthday is on 7th March.*

2 Мы получи́ли письмо́ _____.

b *I am going to France on 18th August.*

3 Он позвони́л мне _____.

c *They left Germany on 22nd November.*

4 Её день рожде́ния _____.

d *We received the letter on 3rd April.*

5 Они́ уе́хали из Герма́нии _____.

e *He rang me on 30th January.*

4 **Write out in words the years in which these Russian poets were born.**

1 Пу́шкин роди́лся в 1799г.

2 Ле́рмонтов роди́лся в 1814г.

3 Блок роди́лся в 1880г.

4 Ахма́това родила́сь в 1889г.

5 Пастерна́к роди́лся в 1890г.

6 Цвета́ева родила́сь в 1892г.

47 quantities

In Russian quantities of currency are measured in roubles and kopeks, weights in grams and kilograms and distances in metres and kilometres.

The rules governing use of cardinal numerals are important when dealing with prices, weights and measurements (adjectival agreements with the numeral 1; genitive singular after 2, 3, 4 and compounds of 2, 3, 4; genitive plural after quantities more than 5).

A Russian exchange rates have varied dramatically in recent years; when inflation was at its highest the kopek (копейка) disappeared, but normally the main unit of currency, the rouble (рубль), consists of 100 kopeks:

один рубль	одна копейка
два рубля	две копейки
пять рублей	пять копеек
двадцать один рубль	двадцать одна копейка
двадцать два рубля	двадцать две копейки
двадцать пять рублей	двадцать пять копеек

Note that the abbreviations for рубль and копейка are: р. and к.: 11р.22к. *11 roubles 22 kopeks*

Б The dative case is used to express age, with the word for *year* (год), which has the genitive plural лет: Сколько ему лет? (literally: *how many to him of years?*): Ему 15 лет (21 год, 22 года, 25 лет), *He is 15 (21, 22, 25).*

В The words *litre*, *gram* and *kilogram* have passed straight into Russian as литр, грамм, килограмм (often shortened to кило). The prefix пол- is used to indicate half a litre or half a kilogram. Note that the word грамм has two acceptable forms of the genitive plural: either грамм or граммов:

его вес – семьдесят килограммов	*his weight is 70 kilos*
полкило апельсинов	*half a kilo of oranges*
двести грамм(ов) сыра	*200 grams of cheese*
литр молока	*a litre of milk*

The abbreviation for килограмм is кг.

Г Distance in Russian is measured in metres and kilometres (метр and километр).

Его рост в два метра.	*His height is 2 metres.*
От города до дачи – двадцать километров.	*From the town to the dacha it is 20 kilometres.*
Мы живём в двадцати километрах от дачи.	*We live 20 kilometres from the dacha.*

The abbreviation for километр is км.

➤ **For use of cardinal numerals, see Units 41–3, for the dative case, see Units 13, 14, 28, 29 and 49.**

1 Ask the question and give the answer, indicating the price of each item.

e.g. зубная паста/11р. → Сколько стоит зубная паста? Одиннадцать рублей. *How much is the toothpaste? Eleven roubles.*

1 деревянный стол/1250р. *wooden table*
2 японский телевизор/3000р. *Japanese television*
3 конверт/3р.20к   *envelope*
4 красная ручка/15р.50к. *red pen*
5 бутылка красного вина/40р. *bottle of red wine*

2 Explain how old each member of the family is.

e.g. Дедушка /88 → Дедушке восемьдесят восемь лет. *Grandfather is 88 years old.*

1 Бабушка/81   *grandmother*
2 Мать/55   *mother*
3 Отец/54   *father*
4 Сын/32   *son*
5 Дочь/30   *daughter*
6 Внук/16   *grandson*

3 What quantities have been bought?

e.g. Два килограмма бананов

2кг.

1 хлеб/4кг.   *bread*
2 мясо/½ кг.   *meat*
3 сахар/5кг.   *sugar*
4 помидор/3кг. *tomato*
5 апельсин/6 кг. *orange*

48 personal pronouns (1)

Personal pronouns (*I, you, he, she, it* etc.) can stand in place of a noun to indicate who or what is involved in an action.

A In the following table the personal pronouns are in the nominative case.

Singular	Grammatical name	Plural	Grammatical name
я, *I*	first person singular	мы, *we*	first person plural
ты, *you*	second person singular	вы, *you*	second person plural
он, *he, it*	third person singular	они́, *they*	third person plural
она́, *she, it*	third person singular		
оно́, *it*	third person singular		

Б In the nominative case, the personal pronoun stands in front of the verb in both statement and question:

Вы рабо́таете в Москве́?   *Do you work in Moscow?*
Да, я рабо́таю в Москве́   *Yes, I work in Moscow.*

В *You:* The second person singular ты is used to address people you know very well and for children and pets. Вы is the formal way of addressing one person and it is also the only way of addressing more than one person (whether you know them well or not). Вы is usually written with a capital letter if you are writing to someone.

Г *He, she, it, they:* Он is used when you are dealing with a masculine singular noun:

Телеви́зор не рабо́тает → Он не рабо́тает
The television isn't working → It isn't working
Врач не рабо́тает → Он не рабо́тает
The doctor isn't working → He isn't working

Она́ is used in the place of feminine nouns (*she, it*) and оно́ with neuter nouns (*it*):

О́льга рабо́тает? → Она́ рабо́тает?
Is Olga working? → Is she working?
Ра́дио рабо́тает? → Оно́ рабо́тает?
Is the radio working? → Is it working?

Они́ is the only word for *they*, irrespective of gender:

О́льга и врач рабо́тают? → Они́ рабо́тают?
Are Olga and the doctor working? Are they working?

Д The personal pronoun is not left out in written Russian, but is sometimes omitted in conversational language:

Хо́чешь чай? Да, хочу́.   *Do you want some tea? Yes, I do (want some).*

> **For declension of subject pronouns, see Unit 49.**

1 **Replace the people underlined with a personal pronoun.**

e.g. Татья́на в шко́ле → Она́ в шко́ле. *Tatyana is in school →*
She is in school.
1 Мой брат в о́фисе.
2 Медсестра́ и врач в больни́це
3 Ба́бушка и ты в теа́тре
4 Сестра́ и я в Москве́.
5 Вади́м и Андре́й в Сиби́ри

2 **Replace the nouns underlined with a personal pronoun.**

e.g. Ра́дио на столе́ → Оно́ на столе́. *The radio is on the table*
→ It is on the table.

1 Нож на столе́	*The knife is on the table.*
2 Метро́ в Москве́	*The metro is in Moscow.*
3 Ви́за в су́мке	*The visa is in the bag.*
4 Велосипе́д и мотоци́кл на у́лице	*The bicycle and the motorbike are in the street.*
5 Я́блоки в магази́не	*The apples are in the shop.*

3 **Which of the following people would you address as вы and which as ты?**

1 муж	*husband*
2 сын	*son*
3 соба́ка	*dog*
4 нача́льник	*boss*
5 но́вый клие́нт	*new customer*

4 **Match the sentences on the left with those on the right.**

1 Я не зна́ю, где они́ живу́т.	**a** *You live in town.*
2 Мы живём в дере́вне.	**b** *They know where he is.*
3 Они́ зна́ют, где он.	**c** *She doesn't know where you are.*
4 Ты живёшь в го́роде.	**d** *We live in a village.*
5 Она́ не зна́ет, где вы.	**e** *I don't know where they live.*

There is no special word order for pronouns within a sentence, but they do have different forms for the accusative, genitive, dative, instrumental and prepositional cases.

A

Nom.	я	ты	он/оно́	она́	мы	вы	они́
Acc.	меня́	тебя́	его́	её	нас	вас	их
Gen.	меня́	тебя́	его́	её	нас	вас	их
Dat.	мне	тебе́	ему́	ей	нам	вам	им
Instr.	мной	тобо́й	им	ей	на́ми	ва́ми	и́ми
Prep.	мне	тебе́	нём	ней	нас	вас	них

Б Note that the cases of он are identical to those of оно́.

В The accusative/genitive form of он/оно́ (его́) is pronounced *yevo* (i.e. the letter г is pronounced as a *v*).

Г If you are using the nominative, genitive, dative, instrumental or prepositional case of он/оно́/она́/они́ after a preposition, add an н to the front of the pronoun:

Я игра́ю в те́ннис с ним.   *I play tennis with him.*

(The prepositional case always involves the use of a preposition and this is why the prepositional case of он/оно́/она́/они́ in the table above starts with the letter н).

Д Phrases which include ... *and I* (e.g. *you and I*) start with мы in Russian:

мы с ва́ми   *you and I* (lit.: *we with you*)
мы с ней   *she and I* (lit.: *we with her*)

If you want to say *about me* note that the preposition о becomes обо:
обо мне   *about me*

If you want to say *with me* note that the preposition с becomes со:
со мной   *with me*

Е Russian prefers to use the personal pronoun (rather than the possessive adjective) when talking about parts of the body:

У меня́ боли́т голова́.   *My head aches.*

Ж Russian can use the personal pronoun instead of the possessive adjective when talking about place:

У меня́ в ко́мнате   *In my room*

➤ For use of prepositions, see Units 83–90.

1 Match the phrases on the left and the right, using the English translations as a guide.

1 Я рабо́таю	**a** с ней
2 Он рабо́тает	**b** с ним
3 Ты рабо́таешь	**c** с ва́ми
4 Они́ рабо́тают	**d** с на́ми
5 Вы рабо́таете	**e** со мной

1 *I work with him.*
2 *He works with you (polite).*
3 *You (familiar) work with me.*
4 *They work with her.*
5 *You (formal) work with us.*

2 The verb звони́т; (*to ring, telephone*) takes the dative case. Explain who is ringing whom today.

e.g. Ива́н/я → Сего́дня Ива́н звони́т мне

1 я/ты
2 О́льга/мы
3 Он/вы
4 Са́ша/она́
5 Ты/он

3 Who has a headache? Complete the following sentences by giving the genitive of the personal pronouns in brackets.

У него́ боли́т голова́

1 У _____ (ты) боли́т голова́
2 У _____ (она́) боли́т голова́
3 У _____ (вы) боли́т голова́

4 Explain who is invited to your party by putting the personal pronouns in brackets into the accusative case.

e.g. Я приглаша́ю _____ (ты) на вечери́нку → Я приглаша́ю тебя́ на вечери́нку. *I invite you to a party.*

1 Я приглаша́ю _____ (он) на вечери́нку.
2 Я приглаша́ю _____ (они́) на вечери́нку.
3 Я приглаша́ю _____ (вы) на вечери́нку.

The possessive pronoun (*mine, yours, his* etc.) is formed in exactly the same way as the possessive adjective, but remember that it replaces the adjective and the noun: *Is this your book? Yes, it's mine.*

A If you are indicating possession by *me, you, us* then the possessive pronoun must agree in number, gender and case with what is possessed (not with the possessor). Here are the forms of the possessive pronouns *mine, yours, ours* in the nominative case:

	Masculine	Feminine	Neuter	Plural
mine	мой	моя́	моё	мои́
yours *belonging to* ты	твой	твоя́	твоё	твои́
ours	наш	на́ша	на́ше	на́ши
yours *belonging to* вы	ваш	ва́ша	ва́ше	ва́ши

Э́то твоя́ кни́га Вади́м? Да, моя́.
Is this your book, Vadim? Yes, it's mine.
Э́то твой журна́л, Ка́тя? Да, мой.
Is this your magazine, Katya? Yes it's mine.

Б The possessive pronouns for *his, hers, its, theirs* are invariable (i.e. they never change):

belonging to он: его́	*belonging to* она́: её	*belonging to* оно́: его́	*belonging to* они́: их

Э́то кни́га Вади́ма? Да, его́.
Is this Vadim's book? Yes, it's his.
Э́то журна́л Ка́ти? Да, её.
Is this Katya's magazine? Yes, it's hers.

➤ For possessive adjectives, see Unit 22.

1 Make questions from the following items and give the answer using possessive pronouns.

e.g. она́/маши́на → Это её маши́на? Да, её. *Is it her car? Yes, it's hers.*

1 он/дом	*house*
2 они́/ соба́ка	*dog*
3 вы/ па́спорт	*passport*
4 я/письмо́	*letter*
5 мы/ фотогра́фия	*photograph*

2 A mix-up! Explain to Vadim that he's giving lost property out to the wrong people. Use the English translations as a guideline.

e.g. Па́вел/ру́чка/*mine* Па́вел, вот твоя́ ру́чка. Нет, э́то не моя́. *Pavel, here's your pen. No, it's not mine.*

1 Ка́тя/письмо́/ *mine*	*Katya, here's your letter. No, it's not mine*
2 Ви́ктор/сви́тер/*mine*	*Viktor, here's your sweater. No, it's not mine.*
3 Са́ша и Аня/кни́ги/*ours*	*Sasha and Anya, here are your books. No, they're not ours.*
4 Светла́на и Та́ня/ фотогра́фии/*ours*	*Svetlana and Tanya, here are your photographs. No, they're not ours.*
5 Андре́й/руба́шка/*mine*	*Andrei, here's your shirt. No, it's not mine.*

3 Match the phrases on the right and left, using the English translation as a guide.

1 Паспорта́ в тво́ей су́мке?	**a**	Да, твоё
2 Ключи́ в её маши́не?	**b**	Да, их
3 Письмо́ о на́ших биле́тах?	**c**	Да, её
4 Это моё вино́?	**d**	Да, в мое́й
5 Это их а́дрес?	**e**	Да, о на́ших

1 *Are the passports in your bag? Yes, they're in mine.*
2 *Are the keys in her car? Yes, they're in hers.*
3 *Is the letter about our tickets? Yes, ours.*
4 *Is this my wine? Yes, it's yours.*
5 *Is this their address? Yes, it's theirs.*

If you want to ask the questions *What? Who? Which/what sort of? Whose?* then you need to use interrogative pronouns.

A Что (*what*) is needed when you are asking about the identity of something:

Что это? Рисунок или фотография?   *What is it? A drawing or a photograh?*

The phrase что это такое? means *what is that?*

Что can also be used in its different case forms to make questions:

Nom.	что	Dat.	чему
Acc.	что	Instr.	чем
Gen.	чего	Prep.	чём

e.g. О чём вы говорите? *What are you talking about?*

Б Кто is used when you want to find out the identity of a person:

Кто это? Это новый директор?   *Who is that? Is it the new director?*

Кто can also be used in its different case forms to make questions:

Nom.	кто	Dat.	кому
Acc.	кто	Instr.	кем
Gen.	кого	Prep.	ком

e.g. О ком вы говорите? *Who are you talking about?*
Note that Russian always uses кто when referring to people, unlike English which sometimes uses *what*, for example:

Кем вы хотите быть?   *What do you want to be?* (lit.: *As whom do you want to be?*)

В Какой means *which/what/what sort of* when you are requesting specific detail about something. It is a stressed adjective (and so works in the same way, e.g., as молодой – *young*):

Какой у них дом?   *What sort of house have they got?*
В каких городах вы были?   *Which cities did you visit?* (lit.: *were you in?*)

Г Чей means *whose*, used when you are trying to find out what belongs to whom. It must agree with the noun it precedes:

Masculine singular	Чей это паспорт?	*Whose passport is this?*
Feminine singular	Чья это виза?	*Whose visa is this?*
Neuter singular	Чьё это место?	*Whose place is this?*
Plural	Чьи это билеты?	*Whose tickets are these?*

➤ **For stressed adjectives, see Unit 21.**

1 Match the phrases on the left with the translations on the right:

1 О чём она́ ду́мает?   a Who is he going to the
                                            theatre with?
2 Чем он занима́ется?   b Who do you know?
3 С кем он идёт в теа́тр?   c What is she thinking about?
4 Кем ты хо́чешь быть?   d What do you want to be?
5 Кого́ вы зна́ете?   e What is he busy with?

2 Find out about someone's purchases by making questions from the information below and using the interrogative pronoun **како́й**.

e.g. газе́та → Каку́ю газе́ту вы покупа́ете? *Which/what sort of newspaper are you buying?*

1 кварти́ра   *flat*
2 автомоби́ль   *car*
3 окно́   *window*
4 велосипе́д   *bicycle*
5 кни́ги   *books*

3 Ask what belongs to whom, using the interrogative pronoun **чей**.

e.g. ту́фли → чьи э́то ту́фли? *Whose are these shoes?*

1 га́лстук   *tie*
2 чемода́н   *suitcase*
3 ю́бка   *skirt*
4 пла́тье   *dress*
5 носки́   *socks*

4 Translate these sentences into Russian.

1 *Which newspaper are you reading?*
2 *What are you thinking about?*
3 *Who are you going to the shop with?*
4 *What is this? A book or a magazine?*
5 *Whose are these children?*

To indicate *this, that, such* you need to use the demonstrative pronouns э́тот, тот, тако́й

А Э́тот means *this* (something close by) and тот means *that* (something not so close):

Вы предпочита́ете э́тот   *Do your prefer this tie or that one?*
   га́лстук и́ли тот?

Э́тот and тот have case endings which are very similar to those of adjectives:

	Masculine and Neuter	Feminine	Plural
Nom.	э́тот/тот	э́та/та	э́ти/те
Acc.	э́тот (э́того*)/тот (того́*)	э́ту/ту	э́ти (э́тих*)/те (тех*)
Gen.	э́того/того́	э́той/той	э́тих/тех
Dat.	э́тому/тому́	э́той/той	э́тим/тем
Instr.	э́тим/тем	э́той/той	э́тими/те́ми
Prep.	э́том/том	э́той/той	э́тих/тех

*= animate accusative

Б Note that э́то also has the meanings *this is, that is, these are, those are*. In this meaning, its ending never changes:

Э́то мой муж *This is my*   Э́то мои́ де́ти *These are*
         husband.   *my children.*

В Тот also has the meanings of *the latter* and *the* same (when used with же):

Она́ получи́ла пода́рки от Бори́са и Серге́я. Тот подари́л ей духи́.
She received presents from Boris and Sergei. The latter gave her perfume.

Она́ получи́ла тот же пода́рок от меня́.
She received the same present from me.

The phrase тот же can also be used with са́мый to mean *the very same*:

Она́ получи́ла те же са́мые духи́ от меня́.
She received the very same perfume from me.

Г The demonstrative pronoun тако́й means *such* and is used in combination with long adjectives. It declines like stressed adjectives such as молодо́й, *young*:

Така́я краси́вая карти́на в тако́м интере́сном музе́е.
Such a beautiful picture in such an interesting museum.

➤ **For stressed adjectives, see Unit 21.**

1 Ask about preference by using the demonstrative pronouns э́тот and тот.

e.g. дом → Вы предпочита́ете э́тот дом и́ли тот дом, вон там? *Do you prefer this house or that house over there?*

1 пальто́   *coat*
2 ша́пка   *hat*
3 шарф   *scarf*
4 руба́шка   *shirt*
5 ту́фли   *shoes*

2 Complete the sentences by giving the Russian for the word in brackets.

1 Кто _____ (*is it*)? _____ наш врач.
2 Они́ живу́т в _____ (*this*) до́ме.
3 Вчера́ мы бы́ли в теа́тре с Бори́сом и Серге́ем. _____ (*the latter*) рабо́тает врачо́м.
4 Вы уже́ зна́ете об _____ (*this*) пробле́ме?
5 Вот _____ (*the same*) кни́га!
6 Он получи́л _____ (*the very same*) га́лстук.
7 Мы чита́ем _____ (*the same*) газе́ту.
8 Они́ рабо́тают на _____ (*these*) заво́дах.
9 Я иду́ в теа́тр с _____ (*such*) интере́сными друзья́ми.
10 Лу́чшие магази́ны на _____ (*this*) у́лице.

3 Choose the appropriate word from the box to complete the following sentences.

э́то   каку́ю   така́я   како́м

1 В _____ го́роде ты живёшь?
2 Кто_____?
3 Э́то_____ краси́вая фотогра́фия.
4 _____ша́пку ты предпочита́ешь?

53 determinative pronouns

Determinative pronouns make it clear who or what is involved; in Russian they are: весь (*all*), ка́ждый (*every*), любо́й (*any*), весь (*...self*) and сам (*the very*).

A The pronoun весь indicates *all, the whole*:

Он рабо́тал весь день.   *He worked all day.*
Мы приглаша́ем всю гру́ппу.   *We invite the whole group.*

Весь declines as follows:

	Masculine	Feminine	Neuter	Plural
Nom.	весь	вся	весь	все
Acc.	весь/ всего́*	всю	весь/всего́*	все/всех*
Gen.	всего́	всей	всего́	всех
Dat.	всему́	всей	всему́	всем
Instr.	всем	всей	всем	все́ми
Prep.	всём	всей	всём	всех

* = animate accusative

Б Ка́ждый means *every* and declines like an unstressed adjective (i.e. it declines like но́вый):

Он рабо́тает ка́ждое у́тро.   *He works every morning.*

В Любо́й means *any* and declines like a stressed adjective (i.e. it declines like молодо́й, *young*):

Позвони́те мне в любо́е   *Ring me at any time.*
время́

Г Сам (*himself*) declines like э́тот (so, for example сама́ means *herself*) and it must agree with the noun it defines:

Мы пригласи́ли самого́   *We invited the president himself.*
президе́нта.

Д Са́мый declines like an unstressed adjective (i.e. it declines like но́вый). It makes the location of something very specific:

В са́мом це́нтре го́рода.   *Right in the centre (in the very centre) of town.*

➤ For unstressed adjectives, see Unit 20, for stressed adjectives, see Unit 21.

1 Match the phrases on the left with their translations on the right:

1 Я пишу́ ей ка́ждый день.   **a** *The teacher himself said this.*
2 Приходи́ в любо́й день.   **b** *I write to her every day.*
3 Мы бы́ли в о́фисе весь ве́чер. **c** *Come on any day.*
4 Сам учи́тель сказа́л э́то.   **d** *I will wait for you right by the entrance.*
5 Я подожду́ тебя́ у са́мого вхо́да.   **e** *We were in the office all evening.*

2 Choose the appropriate word from the box below to complete each sentence. Use the English translations which follow as a guide.

> всей   ка́ждого   любо́м   сам   самому́

1 Мо́жно купи́ть ма́рки в _____ магази́не.
2 _____ компози́тор идёт на конце́рт.
3 Есть таки́е города́ по _____ А́нглии.
4 У меня́ пода́рки для _____ ребёнка.
5 Он идёт к_____ дире́ктору.

1 *It is possible to buy stamps in any shop.*
2 *The composer himself is going to the concert.*
3 *There are such towns throughout England.*
4 *I have presents for every child.*
5 *He is going to see the director himself.*

3 Translate into Russian.
1 We work every day.
2 The actress herself is going to the theatre.
3 I will wait right by the library.
4 All our friends are going to the concert.
5 Which tickets do you want? Any.

4 Answer the questions according to the instruction in English.
1 Где мо́жно купи́ть чай?   *in any shop*
2 Где мо́жно купи́ть ко́фе?   *in every shop*
3 Где мо́жно купи́ть молоко́?   *in all shops*
4 Где мо́жно купи́ть вино́?   *in the centre itself (right in the centre)*

The reflexive pronoun себя means *self* and it must refer back to the subject of the verb; it is used when *self* would be either stated or implied.

A In English we might say *He is bringing the camera with him* (in other words, we don't actually say *with himself*, but this is what is implied). In Russian this would require the use of the reflexive pronoun себя: Он берёт с собой фотоаппарáт.

Б The pronoun себя declines as follows:

Accusative	себя
Genitive	себя
Dative	себе
Instrumental	собóй
Prepositional	себé

Note that is used for all persons (*myself, yourself, himself, herself, itself, ourselves, yourselves, themselves*) and that it does not exist in the nominative.

В Себя is often required after prepositions in contexts where we would not state the word *self* in English, for example:

Он вѝдит пéред собóй   *He sees a big dog in front of*
большýю собáку.   *him(self)*
Мы закрьіли за собóй   *We closed the door behind us*
дверь.   *(ourselves)*
Он купѝл шоколáд для себя. *He bought the chocolate for*
                                himself.

Г Note the useful phrase самó собóй разумéется (*it stands to reason*). The reflexive pronoun is also used to make certain common verbs, e.g.:

вестѝ себя   *to behave*
представлять себé   *to imagine*
чýвствовáть себя   *to feel*

1 Put an asterisk by the words which would have to be followed by a reflexive pronoun in Russian (hint: there are five).

The tourist came into his room and shut the door behind him. He saw in front of him a large room with a bed, a chair and a washbasin, but no towels. He was glad he had brought some with him. As he was feeling rather tired, he decided to have a wash and a sleep, although he imagined that the bed would not be very comfortable.

2 Match the phrases on the left with their translations on the right.

1 Как вы себя чувствуете?
2 Как он ведёт себя?

3 Вы берёте с собой деньги?

4 Что вы видите перед собой?
5 Вы думаете только о себе!

a *How is he behaving?*
b *Are you bringing the money with you?*
c *You only think about yourself!*
d *How are you feeling?*
e *What can you see in front of you?*

3 Choose the appropriate word from the box in order to complete the following sentences, using the English translation as a guide.

себя   себе   собой

1 Он хорошо ведёт_____.
2 Я представляю _____, что это трудно.
3 Закрой за _____ дверь!
4 Я плохо чувствую_____.
5 Мы купили шампанское для_____.

1 *He is behaving well.*
2 *I imagine that it is difficult.*
3 *Close the door behind you!*
4 *I feel ill.*
5 *We bought the champagne for ourselves.*

4 Translate into Russian.
1 *What did you buy for yourself?*
2 *He thinks only about himself.*
3 *I am bringing the wine with me.*
4 *We are bringing the dog with us.*

Кото́рый is a relative pronoun which is used after nouns to mean *who, which, that*.

A Russian uses the adjective кото́рый as a linking word between parts of the sentence to indicate *who, which, that*. For example: *The young man is skiing. The young man is the former world champion.*
→ *The young man who is skiing is the former world champion.*

Молодо́й челове́к, кото́рый ката́ется на лы́жах, экс-чемпио́н ми́ра.

Кото́рый refers to both people and things:
Маши́на, кото́рую он купи́л, о́чень ма́ленькая.
The car which he has bought is very small.
Note that the phrase including кото́рый is enclosed by commas.

Б Кото́рый is an adjective, so it has masculine, feminine, neuter and plural endings for all six cases. In order to work out the gender and the number, first look at the noun which it follows; in order to work out the case, work out what 'job' кото́рый is doing in the second part of the sentence. For example, is it a subject or an object?:
Актри́са, кото́рая (*subject*) игра́ет роль О́льги, о́чень тала́нтливая.
The actress who is playing the role of Olga is very talented.
Актри́са, кото́рую (*object, therefore accusative*) вы лю́бите, о́чень тала́нтливая.
The actress whom you like is very talented.

В If the кото́рый part of the sentence involves a preposition, that preposition must always come in front of кото́рый.
О́фис, в кото́ром мы рабо́таем, не о́чень большо́й.
The office in which (prepositional case after в*) we work is not very big.*
Друзья́, с кото́рыми мы отдыха́ли, живу́т в Ло́ндоне.
The friends with whom (instrumental case after с*) we were on holiday live in London.*

NB Кото́рый is only for use after nouns; to say *'that'* after verbs, don't use кото́рый, use что:
Я ду́маю, что они́ прие́дут.
I think that they will come.

➤ **For use of что, кто as relative pronouns, see Unit 56.**

1 Make sentences about the following people's jobs, with который referring to the subject in the nominative case.

e.g. Влади́мир/Ки́ев/врач → Влади́мир, кото́рый живёт в Ки́еве, врач.

1 О́льга/Ки́ров/продавщи́ца

2 На́ши друзья́/Можа́йск/учителя́

3 Ви́ктор/Москва́/перево́дчик

4 Са́ша/Воро́неж/юри́ст

5 А́ня/Я́лта/медсестра́

6 Вади́м/О́бнинск/гид

2 Describe what Olga has just bought, with который referring to the object in the accusative case:

e.g. апельси́ны/вку́сные → Апельси́ны, кото́рые О́льга купи́ла, вку́сные.

1 велосипе́д/большо́й   *bicycle/big*

2 джи́нсы/мо́дные   *jeans/fashionable*

3 цветы́/краси́вые   *flowers/beautiful*

4 ю́бка/коро́ткая   *skirt/short*

3 Complete the sentences using the preposition and the relative pronoun который. The case is given in brackets at the end of the sentence.

e.g.   Стол, под _____ сиди́т ко́шка, в углу́. (под + *instr.*)
→ Стол, под кото́рым сиди́т ко́шка, в углу́. *The chair, under which the cat is sitting, is in the corner.*

1 Друг, к _____ мы идём, музыка́нт.

(к + *dat.*)

2 Зда́ния, в _____ они́ рабо́тают, о́чень больши́е.

(в + *prep.*)

3 Врач, с _____ она́ говори́ла, о́чень до́брый.

(с + *instr.*)

4 Фильм, о _____ вы говори́те, не о́чень хоро́ший.

(о + *prep.*)

5 Студе́нты, от ____ мы получи́ли письмо́, рабо́тают
в А́фрике.   (от + *gen.*)

4 Use который to make one sentence in Russian out of two using the English sentence as a guide:

e.g. Мой дя́дя инжене́р. Ты говори́л с ним вчера́. *My uncle, with whom you spoke yesterday, is an engineer.* → Мой дя́дя, с кото́рым вы говори́ли вчера́, инжене́р.

1 Соба́ка о́чень ста́рая. Ты   *The dog which you*
сфотографи́ровал её.   *photographed is very old.*

2 Шко́ла о́чень хоро́шая.   *The school about which you are*
Ты говори́шь о ней.   *speaking is very good.*

As well as being interrogative pronouns, что (*what*) and кто (*who*) are also used as relative pronouns.

А Что is used as:

* a relative pronoun to всё (*all, everything*): У меня всё, что надо, *I have everything (that) I need*
* It is also used with то (*that*) to link two parts of a sentence. Notice that both то and что must decline according to the context:

  Я расскажу вам о том, что я знаю.
  I'll tell you about (that which) what I know.
  Мы начнём с того, чем мы занимались вчера.
  We'll start with what (literally 'from that which') we were busy with yesterday.

* It is used to 'sum up' a previous part of the sentence (i.e. it links up to the whole of the preceding clause):

  Он рассказывал нам о своей поездке в Африку, что было очень интересно.
  He told us about his trip to Africa, which was very interesting.

Б Кто is used as a relative pronoun

* after тот (*the one...*):

  Тот, кто хочет прийти на вечеринку.
  Whoever (literally 'the one who') wants to come to the party.

* after все (*everyone*)

  Я приглашаю всех, кто хочет прийти на вечеринку.
  I invite all who want to come to the party.

Notice that кто is always followed by a singular verb (as it is in English).

➤ For use of что and кто as interrogative pronouns, see Unit 51.

1 **Match each Russian phrase with its translation.**

1 Я дам вам всё, что на́до.
2 Мы интересу́емся тем, что вы говори́те.
3 Тот, кто не хо́чет танцева́ть, мо́жет отдыха́ть.
4 Э́ти места́ для тех, кто уже́ купи́л биле́ты.
5 Я расскажу́ вам обо всём, что случи́лось.

a *These places are for those who have already bought their tickets.*
b *Whoever (the one who) does not want to dance can rest.*
c *I will tell you about everything that (all that which) happened.*
d *I will give you everything (all that) you need.*
e *We are interested in what (that which) you say.*

2 **Choose the appropriate word from the box below to complete each sentence. English translations are given as a guide:**

кто	что

1 Все, _____ смотре́л фильм, говоря́т, что хоро́ший.
2 Он зна́ет всех, _____ придёт на вечери́нку.
3 Они́ забы́ли биле́ты, _____ бы́ло о́чень пло́хо.
4 Я начну́ с того́, _____ он сказа́л мне.
5 Он сказа́л мне всё, _____ он знал.
6 Они́ смо́трят телеви́зор ка́ждый ве́чер, _____ о́чень пло́хо.

1 *Everyone (all) who watched the film says that it is good.*
2 *He knows everyone (all) who is (are) coming to the party.*
3 *They have forgotten the tickets, which is very bad.*
4 *I will start with what (that which) he told me.*
5 *He told me everything (that) he knows.*
6 *They watch television every evening, which is bad.*

57 indefinite pronouns

The particles -то and -нибудь can be added to the pronouns кто, что, какой to give the Russian for *someone, something, some... or other*.

A If we add the particle -то to the Russian word for *who* we get the Russian for *someone*:

Кто-то позвонил, когда вы были на работе.
Someone rang while you were at work.
Борис говорил кому-то, когда зазвонил телефон.
Boris was talking to someone when the telephone rang.

Кто-то indicates a particular person, who definitely was involved or is involved in an action, but the identity of that one particular person is not known.

The particle -то has the same specific force if it is added to что or какой:

Врач дал ей что-то от кашля.
The doctor gave her something for her cough.
Врач дал ей какое-то лекарство.
The doctor gave her some medicine or other.

B If we add the particle -нибудь to the Russian word for *who* we get another way of saying *someone*, but this time in a vague sense, not implying one specific person:

Если кто-нибудь позвонит, запишите их номер телефона.
If someone (anyone) rings, write down their telephone number.
Дайте билеты кому-нибудь в офисе.
Give the tickets to someone (anyone) in the office.

The particle -нибудь has the same vague force if it is added to что or какой:

Расскажи нам что-нибудь о России.
Tell us something (anything at all) about Russia.
Купите какие-нибудь таблетки.
Buy some tablets or other (any tablets).

B Note that these particles can also be used with adverbs of time and place.

-то *(specific)*	-нибудь *(vague)*
где-то *somewhere*	где-нибудь *somewhere/anywhere*
куда-то *somewhere (direction)*	куда-нибудь *somewhere/anywhere (direction)*
когда-то *once, at one time*	когда-нибудь *at any time, ever*
как-то *somehow*	как-нибудь *somehow, anyhow*
почему-то *for some reason*	почему-нибудь *for some/any reason*

➤ **For declensions of кто and что, see Unit 51.**

1 Underline the words in the following passage where you would choose to use the particle -то and put a circle round the words where you would choose to use the particle -нибудь in Russian.

Someone called you this morning. He said something about a meeting tomorrow. For some reason he didn't want to talk to me. He just said that if you can't be on time you should ring anyone in the office.

2 Now complete the Russian version of this passage with the appropriate phrases:

_____позвони́л тебе́ сего́дня у́тром. Он сказа́л _____ о совеща́нии за́втра. Он _____не хоте́л говори́ть со мной. Он сказа́л то́лько, что е́сли вы не смо́жете прие́хать во́-время, на́до позвони́ть _____ в о́фисе.

3 Complete each sentence by choosing the appropriate phrase from the box, using the English translations as a guide.

> где́-нибудь   како́м-то   когда́-нибудь   кого́-то
> что́-нибудь   что́-то

1 Гид _____ сказа́л об экску́рсии в музе́й.
2 Вы бы́ли _____ в Москве́?
3 Напиши́те _____о ва́шей семье́!
4 Они́ хотя́т отдыха́ть _____ на ю́ге.
5 Она́ уже́ зна́ет _____ в орке́стре.
6 Я ра́ньше рабо́тал в _____ о́фисе в Ки́рове.

1 *The guide said something about an excursion to a museum.*
2 *Have you ever been to Moscow?*
3 *Write something (anything at all) about your family!*
4 *They want to go on holiday somewhere or other in the south.*
5 *She already knows someone in the orchestra.*
6 *Previously I worked in some office or other in Kirov.*

A present tense verb describes an action or a state that is taking place now, or that is ongoing. A large group of verbs follow a regular pattern of present tense endings: -ю, -ешь, -ет, -ете, -ют.

A To make the present tense, we must first of all look at the infinitive (the *to do* part of the verb). Verbs whose infinitive ends in the letters -ать usually belong to the *'first conjugation'* – i.e. a group of verbs that form their present tense according to the same pattern. In Russian there is only one form of the present tense, so я рабо́таю is the only way of saying *I work, I do work, I am working.*

Б In order to make the present tense of a verb ending in -ать the first thing to do is to remove the last two letters (ть), and then add the endings, which are different for each *person* of the verb. Here is the verb for *to work* (рабо́тать); the endings added to make the present tense are underlined:

я рабо́та<u>ю</u>	*I work*
ты рабо́та<u>ешь</u>	*you work*
он, она́, оно́ рабо́та<u>ет</u>	*he, she, it works*
мы рабо́та<u>ем</u>	*we work*
вы рабо́та<u>ете</u>	*you work*
они́ рабо́та<u>ют</u>	*they work*

В Occasionally, first conjugation infinitives end in -ять, as in the case of the verbs *to cough* (ка́шлять) and *to stroll* (гуля́ть). Their present tense is made in just the same way as for verbs ending in -ать:

я гуля́<u>ю</u>	*I stroll*
ты гуля́<u>ешь</u>	*you stroll*
он, она́, оно́ гуля́<u>ет</u>	*he, she, it strolls*
мы гуля́<u>ем</u>	*we stroll*
вы гуля́<u>ете</u>	*you stroll*
они́ гуля́<u>ют</u>	*they stroll*

Г Occasionally first conjugation infinitives end in -еть, as in the case of the verbs *to know how to* (уме́ть). Their present tense is made in just the same way as for verbs ending in -ать:

я уме́<u>ю</u>	*I know how to*
ты уме́<u>ешь</u>	*you know how to*
он, она́, оно́ уме́<u>ет</u>	*he, she, it knows how to*
мы уме́<u>ем</u>	*we know how to*
вы уме́<u>ете</u>	*you know how to*
они́ уме́<u>ют</u>	*they know how to*

➤ **For personal pronouns and persons of the veb, see Unit 48.**

1 **Put the infinitives of these first conjugation verbs into the present tense to agree with their subject.**

e.g. игра́ть/он → он игра́ет, *he is playing*
1	знать/вы	*to know*
2	понима́ть/ты	*to understand*
3	ка́шлять/я	*to cough*
4	рабо́тать/она́	*to work*
5	отвеча́ть/они́	*to answer*
6	спра́шивать/мы	*to ask*
7	покупа́ть/он	*to buy*
8	гуля́ть/мы	*to stroll*
9	слу́шать/вы	*to listen*
10	уме́ть/ты	*to know how to*

2 **Complete the sentences by filling in the correct verb endings.**

e.g. Он _____ (чита́ть) газе́ту. → Он чита́ет газе́ту.
He is reading a newspaper.

1 Вы _____ (слу́шать) ра́дио. *You are listening to the radio.*

2 Мы _____ (игра́ть) в те́ннис. *We are playing tennis.*

3 Ты _____ (покупа́ть) чай. *You are buying tea.*

4 Она́ _____ (понима́ть) вопро́с? *Does she understand the question?*

5 Я _____ (знать) дире́ктора. *I know the director.*

3 **Complete each sentence with an appropriate verb from the box.**

гуля́ют игра́ешь отвеча́ет покупа́ю понима́ем

1 Я _____ но́вый компью́тер.
2 Он _____ на вопро́с.
3 Мы _____ ва́шу пробле́му.
4 Ты_____ в футбо́л?
5 Они́ ча́сто _____ в па́рке.

59 regular present tense (2)

A present tense verb describes an action or a state that is taking place now, or that is ongoing. A large group of verbs follow a regular pattern of present tense endings: -ю (-у), -ишь, -ит, -им, -ите, -ят -(ат).

A To make the present tense, we must first of all look at the infinitive (the *to do* part of the verb). Verbs whose infinitive ends in the letters -ить belong to the '*second conjugation*' – i.e. a group of verbs which all form their present tense according to the same pattern. In Russian there is only one form of the present tense, so я говорю is the only way of saying *I speak, I do speak, I am speaking*. (Notice that the ending for *I* is -ю and the ending for *they* is -я; because of the first spelling rule sometimes we need to change these endings to -у and -а).

Б In order to make the present tense of a verb ending in -ить the first thing to do is to remove the last three letters (ить) to give the *stem*, and then add the endings, which are different for each *person* of the verb. Here is the verb *to speak* (говорить) with the endings added to make the present tense underlined:

я говор**ю**	*I speak*	мы говор**им**	*we speak*
ты говор**ишь**	*you speak*	вы говор**ите**	*you speak*
он, она́, оно́ говор**и́т**	*he, she, it speaks*	они́ говор**я́т**	*they speak*

В Sometimes second conjugation infinitives end in -ять or -еть as in the case of the verbs *to stand* (стоя́ть) and *to look/watch* (смотре́ть). Their present tense is made in just the same way as for verbs ending in -ить:

я сто**ю́**	*I stand*		я смотр**ю́**	*I look*
ты сто**и́шь**	*you stand*		ты смо́тр**ишь**	*you look*
он, она́, оно́ сто**и́т**	*he, she, it stands*		он, она́, оно́ смо́тр**ит**	*he, she it looks*
мы сто**и́м**	*we stand*		мы смо́тр**им**	*we look*
вы сто**и́те**	*you stand*		вы смо́тр**ите**	*you look*
они́ сто**я́т**	*they stand*		они́ смо́тр**ят**	*they look*

Г Occasionally second conjugation infinitives end in -ать, as in the case of the verbs *to shout* (крича́ть). Their present tense is made in just the same way as for verbs ending in -ить:

я крич**у́**	*I shout*	мы крич**и́м**	*we shout*
ты крич**и́шь**	*you shout*	вы крич**и́те**	*you shout*
он, она́, оно́ крич**и́т**	*he, she, it shouts*	они́ крич**а́т**	*they shout*

➤ For personal pronouns and persons of the verb, see Unit 48; for first spelling rule, Unit 2.

1 Put the infinitives of these second conjugation verbs into the present tense to agree with their subject.

e.g. говори́ть/мы → мы говори́м, *we are speaking*

1 смотре́ть/я	*to look, watch*
2 стро́ить/ты	*to build*
3 сто́ить/оно́	*to cost*
4 кури́ть/вы	*to smoke*
5 ва́рить/они́	*to cook*
6 гото́вить/мы	*to prepare*
7 лежа́ть/я	*to lie (be lying down)*
8 стоя́ть/она́	*to stand*
9 слы́шать/вы	*to hear*
10 говори́ть/ты	*to speak*

2 Complete the sentences by filling in the correct verb endings.

e.g. Он _____ (гото́вить) обед → Он гото́вит обе́д.
He is preparing lunch.

1 Вы _____ (слы́шать) ра́дио.	*You (can) hear the radio.*
2 Мы _____ (стоя́ть) у окна́.	*We stand by the window.*
3 Они́ _____ (стро́ить) дом.	*They are building a house.*
4 Она́ _____ (смотре́ть) фильм?	*Is she watching the film?*
5 Ты _____ (звони́ть) дире́ктору.	*You are ringing the director.*

3 Complete each sentence with an appropriate verb from the box.

звоню́   слы́шите   смо́тришь   сто́ит   стоя́т

1 Я ча́сто _____ мои́м друзья́м.
2 Вы _____ звоно́к телефо́на?
3 Ко́фе _____10 рубле́й.
4 Ты _____ футбо́л?
5 Они́ _____ у вхо́да.

60 consonant changes

Some second conjugation verbs change the final consonant of the stem in the first person singular only (i.e. in the *I* form of the present tense) before adding the endings -ю (-у), -ишь, -ит, -им, -ите, -ят (-ат). Note that the ending for *I* is -ю and the ending for *they* is -я; because of the first spelling rule sometimes we need to change these endings to -у and -а.

A If the stem of a second conjugation verb ends in -д, in the first person singular the д changes to ж, as in the verb *to see*:

ви́деть я ви́жу ты ви́дишь он ви́дит мы ви́дим вы ви́дите они́ ви́дят

Б If the stem of a second conjugation verb ends in -з, in the first person singular the з changes to ж, as in the verb *to take (by transport)*:

вози́ть я вожу́ ты во́зишь он во́зит мы во́зим вы во́зите они́ во́зят

В If the stem of a second conjugation verb ends in -с, in the first person singular the с changes to ш, as in the verb *to carry*:

носи́ть я ношу́ ты но́сишь он но́сит мы но́сим вы но́сите они́ но́сят

Г If the stem of a second conjugation verb ends in -ст, in the first person singular, the ст changes to щ, as in the verb *to whistle*:

свисте́ть я свищу́ ты свисти́шь он свисти́т мы свисти́м вы свисти́те они́ свистя́т

Д If the stem of a second conjugation verb ends in -т, in the first person singular the т changes to ч, as in the verb *to fly*:

лете́ть я лечу́ ты лети́шь он лети́т мы лети́м вы лети́те они́ летя́т

Е If the stem of a second conjugation verb ends in б, в, м, п, ф, then in the first person singular an extra л is added, as in the verb *to prepare*:

гото́вить я гото́влю ты гото́вишь он гото́вит мы гото́вим вы гото́вите они́ гото́вят

Ж Here is a summary of consonant changes (*remember: they are only for the я form of the present tense*):

д	→ ж	ст	→ щ
з	→ ж	т	→ ч
с	→ ш	б, в, м, п, ф	→ бл, вл, мл, пл, фл

1 All the verbs in the following list are second conjugation. Give the first person singular (я form) of the present tense of each one. (Hint: some need a consonant change and some don't.)

1	люби́ть	*to like/love*
2	спать	*to sleep*
3	говори́ть	*to speak*
4	сиде́ть	*to sit*
5	ла́зить	*to climb*
6	стоя́ть	*to stand*
7	проси́ть	*to ask*
8	смотре́ть	*to look/watch*
9	корми́ть	*to feed*
10	звони́ть	*to ring/telephone*

2 Complete the sentences with an appropriate verb from the box.

во́зит гото́влю лети́те ношу́ сиди́т

1 О́льга _____ у телеви́зора.
2 Я _____ обе́д.
3 Авто́бус _____ пассажи́ров.
4 Я _____ пи́сьма на по́чту.
5 Сего́дня вы _____ на самолёте.

3 Match the phrases on the left and right, using the English translation as a guide

1	Фе́рмер	a	сиди́м у са́мого экра́на.
2	Вы	b	ко́рмит свои́х коро́в.
3	Мы	c	гото́влю у́жин на ку́хне.
4	Я	d	кричи́т он.
5	Ура́!	e	спи́те всю ночь.

1 *The farmer feeds his cows.*
2 *You sleep all night.*
3 *We sit right by the screen.*
4 *I prepare supper in the kitchen.*
5 *Hurrah! he shouts.*

Not all verbs follow the regular patterns of the first and second conjugations, but most irregular verbs do follow a pattern of their own. The important thing is to know the *stem* and the *first* and *second persons* of an irregular verb.

A Most verbs which do not follow the pattern of the regular verbs described in Units 58 and 59 still have an infinitive ending ть; a few have infinitives ending in -ти or -чь. In this unit we will look at verbs with the irregular present tense endings:

-у	-ём
-ёшь	-ёте
-ёт	-ут

i.e. the я and они forms both feature the letter у and all the other forms have the letter ё.

Б These endings are added to the *stem* of the verb. Each time you come across an irregular verb, it is important to learn the stem. Here are some common examples.

Infin.	Stem	я	ты	он, она́, оно́	мы	вы	они́
брать *to take*	бер-	беру́	берёшь	берёт	берём	берёте	беру́т
ждать *to wait*	жд-	жду	ждёшь	ждёт	ждём	ждёте	ждут
жить *to live*	жив-	живу́	живёшь	живёт	живём	живёте	живу́т
идти́* *to walk, go on foot*	ид-	иду́	идёшь	идёт	идём	идёте	иду́т
класть *to put*	клад-	кладу́	кладёшь	кладёт	кладём	кладёте	кладу́т

* Note that other verbs ending in -ти follow this pattern (e.g. расти́, *to grow*).

Some other irregular verbs work in almost the same way, but have -ю and -ют as their first person singular and third person plural endings:

Infin.	Stem	я	ты	он, она́, оно́	мы	вы	они́
лить *to pour*	ль-	лью	льёшь	льёт	льём	льёте	льют
петь *to sing*	по-	пою́	поёшь	поёт	поём	поёте	пою́т
пить *to drink*	пь-	пью	пьёшь	пьёт	пьём	пьёте	пьют

1 Make the present tense by choosing the appropriate ending from the box.

-у	-ю	-ёшь	-ёт	-ём	-ёте	-ут	-ют

e.g. ждать/ты → ты ждёшь
1 брать/мы
2 жить/я
3 пить/вы
4 класть/они́
5 идти́/он
6 петь/ты
7 лить/я
8 ждать/они́
9 пить/я
10 жить/мы

2 Insert the correct subject to match the verb.
1 _____ жду
2 _____ иду́т
3 _____ поём
4 _____ живёшь
5 _____ пьют
6 _____ берёте
7 _____ кладёт

3 Look at the pictures of Ivan and Vadim and answer the question.
Кто поёт и кто пьёт?

ВАДИМ　　　　　　　ИВАН

4 Translate into Russian.
1 *Ivan drinks vodka.*
2 *Olga lives in a flat.*
3 *He is waiting at the theatre.*
4 *We are taking the tickets.*
5 *They are singing this evening.*

In this unit we look at some more irregular present tense verbs. Although they do not follow the patterns of the first and second conjugations, they do have recognizable patterns of their own.

A In this unit we will look at irregular verbs with the endings:

-у (or -ю)	-ем
-ешь	-ете
-ет	-ут (or -ют)

i.e. the я and они forms both feature the letter у (or -ю) and all the other forms have the letter е.

Б These endings are added to the *stem* of the verb. Each time you come across an irregular verb, it is important to learn the stem. Here are some common examples.

Infin.	Stem	я	ты	он, она́, оно́	мы	вы	они́
éхать *to go by transport, travel, drive*	éд-	éду	éдешь	éдет	éдем	éдете	éдут
иска́ть *to look for*	ищ-	ищу́	и́щешь	и́щет	и́щем	и́щете	и́щут
мыть *to wash*	мó-	мóю	мóешь	мóет	мóем	мóете	мóют
писа́ть *to write*	пиш-	пишу́	пи́шешь	пи́шет	пи́шем	пи́шете	пи́шут
пла́кать *to cry*	плач-	плачу́	пла́чешь	пла́чет	пла́чем	пла́чете	пла́чут

В The verbs *to be able* and *to want* have a less regular pattern in the present tense, in the sense that their stem changes during the present tense:

мочь *to be able (can)*
я могу́
ты мо́жешь
он мо́жет
мы мо́жем
вы мо́жете
они́ мо́гут

хоте́ть *to want*
я хочу́
ты хо́чешь
он хо́чет
мы хоти́м
вы хоти́те
они́ хотя́т

1 Complete the following sentences with the present tense of the appropriate verb. Use the English translations as a guide.

e.g. Он _____отдыха́ть в Крыму́ → Он хо́чет отдыха́ть в Крыму́. *He wants to have a holiday in the Crimea.*

1 Я ча́сто _____моему́ другу́.
2 Сего́дня мы _____ в центр го́рода.
3 Он не _____прийти́ в теа́тр.
4 Вы не о́чень ча́сто _____посу́ду.
5 Почему́ ты_____?
6 Они́ _____свои́ паспорта́.
7 Тури́ст не _____ смотре́ть фильм.
8 Кому́ вы_____?
9 Вы _____в музе́й и́ли в цирк?
10 Нет, спаси́бо, я не _____ ко́фе.

1 *I often write to my friend.*
2 *Today we are travelling into the centre of town.*
3 *He can't come to the theatre.*
4 *You don't very often wash the dishes.*
5 *Why are you crying?*
6 *They are looking for their passports.*
7 *The tourist doesn't want to watch the film.*
8 *Who are you writing to?*
9 *Are you going to the museum or the circus?*
10 *No, thank you, I don't want any coffee.*

2 Choose the appropriate personal pronoun from the box to complete each sentence (you will need to use some of them more than once).

Я	ТЫ	ОН	МЫ	ВЫ	ОНИ́

1 _____ и́щут ги́да.
2 _____ не хо́чет рабо́тать.
3 _____ почему́-то пла́чут.
4 _____ хочу́ чита́ть газе́ту.
5 _____ е́дешь в го́род.
6 _____ и́щет свой биле́т.
7 _____ мо́ют посу́ду.
8 _____ мо́жете прийти́ на конце́рт.
9 _____ е́дем в Москву́.
10 _____ пи́шешь письмо́.

63 irregular present tense (3)

In this unit we look at irregular present tense verbs whose infinitive ends in -авать, -овать or -евать. We also find out how to say *I am* and *I have* in Russian.

A Дава́ть, the verb for *to give*, is an example of a present tense of verbs whose infinitive ends in -авать. Its present tense is formed like this:

я даю́	*I give*	мы даём	*we give*
ты даёшь	*you give*	вы даёте	*you give*
он даёт	*he gives*	они́ даю́т	*they give*

NB the verb *to swim*, пла́вать, has the present tense пла́ваю, пла́ваешь (i.e. like a first conjugation verb).

Б Путеше́ствовать, the verb *to travel*, is an example of a verb whose infinitive ends in -овать, and танцева́ть, the verb *to dance*, is an example of the -евать infinitive ending. The present tense of these verbs is:

я путеше́ствую	*I travel*	я танцу́ю	*I dance*
ты путеше́ствуешь	*you travel*	ты танцу́ешь	*you dance*
он путеше́ствует	*he travels*	он танцу́ет	*he dances*
мы путеше́ствуем	*we travel*	мы танцу́ем	*we dance*
вы путеше́ствуете	*you travel*	вы танцу́ете	*you dance*
они́ путеше́ствуют	*they travel*	они́ танцу́ют	*they dance*

В Russian has an infinitive for the verb *to be* (быть), but there is no present tense. So, if you want to make a statement using the present tense of the verb *to be*, you need to use one of the following methods:

- use a dash if you are defining a noun: Áня – врач, *Anya is a doctor.*
- use nothing at all, other than the word (usually an adverb) you wish to state: Хо́лодно, *it is cold,* интере́сно, *it is interesting.*
- use the word есть: В го́роде есть апте́ка, *There is a chemist's in town.*
- or, if you want to say *there isn't, there aren't*, use нет followed by the genitive case: Здесь нет кио́ска, *There's no kiosk here.*

Г To say *has/have* use the preposition у with the genitive case of the 'owner' and the nominative of the thing owned: У нас дом, *We have a house* (lit.: *by us house*); у Áни соба́ка, *Anya has a dog* (lit.: *by Anya dog*). Есть can be used to give added emphasis: У вас есть дом?, *Do you have a house?* To use this construction in the negative, use нет and the genitive of the thing not owned: У нас нет до́ма, *We haven't got a house.*

➤ For present tense of first conjugation verbs, see Unit 58, for genitive case, see Units–10–12.

1 **Put the infinitive into the correct form of the present tense.**

1	я/танцева́ть	*to dance*
2	ты/дать	*to give*
3	он/рекомендова́ть	*to recommend*
4	мы/встава́ть	*to get up*
5	вы/советова́ть	*to advise*
6	они́/рискова́ть	*to risk*
7	она́/узнава́ть	*to find out, recognize*
8	я/испо́льзовать	*to use*
9	мы/тре́бовать	*to demand, require*
10	они́/путеше́ствовать	*to travel*

2 **Translate into Russian.**

1 My brother is an engineer.
2 It is cold today.
3 There is a key on the table.
4 There aren't any shops in the village.

3 **Explain who has got what.**

e.g. Ка́тя/сын ✔   У Ка́ти есть сын.
     А́ня /сын ✘ →   У А́ни нет сы́на.

Вади́м	дом	✔
Бори́с	автомоби́ль (м)	✘
Та́ня	телеви́зор	✔
Зо́я	кварти́ра	✔
И́горь	ко́шка	✘
Серге́й	компью́тер	✘

4 **Match the phrases.**

1	У врача́	a	мно́го книг
2	У профе́ссора	b	мно́го раке́ток
3	У библиоте́каря	c	мно́го пи́сем
4	У почтальо́на	d	мно́го студе́нтов
5	У тенниси́ста	e	мно́го пацие́нтов

64 reflexive verbs: present tense

Reflexive verbs express an action that reflects back to the subject. The infinitive ends in -ся or -сь.

A A reflexive verb is the sort of verb which in English is followed by ... *self* or where ... *self* can be understood, for example *to wash* (*oneself*). The ending -ся (or sometimes -сь) is what identifies a reflexive verb in the infinitive and these endings appear in the present tense as follows:

умыва́ть*ся to wash oneself, get washed*	
я умыва́ю*сь*	мы умыва́ем*ся*
ты умыва́ешь*ся*	вы умыва́ете*сь*
он умыва́ет*ся*	они́ умыва́ют*ся*

Some common examples of reflexive verbs where ... *self* is stated or implied are:

гото́виться	*to prepare oneself, get ready*
купа́ться	*to bathe, take a bath*
ложи́ться спать	*to go to bed* (lit.: *to lie down to sleep*)
одева́ться	*to dress oneself, get dressed*
причёсываться	*to do one's hair*
раздева́ться	*to get undressed, take one's coat off*

Б Some verbs which are reflexive in Russian would not state or even imply the word ... *self* in English; these reflexive verbs often involve the idea of 'to be...' and are *intransitive* verbs (i.e. they have no object). For example, the Russian verb *to be situated* is находи́ться: Наш дом нахо́дится в го́роде. *Our house is situated in the town.* Other common 'intransitive' reflexive verbs are *to begin* (i.e. *to be started*) and *to end* (i.e. *to be finished*).

to begin, start:

начина́ться Фильм начина́ется в 9 часо́в *the film starts at 9 o'clock*

to end, finish:

конча́ться Фильм конча́ется в 11 часо́в *the film ends at 11 o'clock*

В Another group of reflexive verbs whose English versions would not state or imply ... *self* are concerned with feelings. Here are some common examples:

беспоко́иться	*to worry, be anxious*
боя́ться	*to fear, be afraid*
горди́ться	*to be proud*
наде́яться	*to hope*
смея́ться	*to laugh*
улыба́ться	*to smile*

1 Fill in the missing words.

Она <u>одева́ется</u> в 7 часо́в

1 Я _____ в 8 часо́в.

2 Он _____.

2 Match the phrases on the left with their translations on the right.

1 Врач беспоко́ится о пацие́нте.

2 Конце́рт начина́ется в 7 часо́в.

3 Он всегда́ ра́но ложи́тся спать.

4 Я наде́юсь, что всё бу́дет хорошо́.

5 Он ча́сто купа́ется в реке́.

6 Во ско́лько вы умыва́етесь?

7 Архите́ктор горди́тся но́вым зда́нием.

8 Когда́ начина́ется фильм?

9 Мы мно́го смеёмся.

10 О чём ты беспоко́ишься?

a *The concert starts at seven.*

b *At what time do you get washed?*

c *The doctor is worried about the patient.*

d *He often bathes in the river.*

e *When does the film start?*

f *He always goes to bed early.*

g *What are you worried about?*

h *The architect is proud of the new building.*

i *We laugh a lot.*

j *I hope everything will be all right.*

3 Translate into Russian.

1 *I get dressed at 8 o'clock.*
2 *He gets washed at 7 o'clock.*
3 *They get undressed at 10 o'clock.*
4 *The concert ends at 10 o'clock.*
5 *You go to bed at 11 o'clock.*

65 aspects

Most Russian verbs have two infinitives: *imperfective aspect* and *perfective aspect*. English has no equivalent of the Russian system of aspects. A small minority of verbs have only one infinitive, while verbs of motion (*to run, to swim* etc.) have three.

A When you look up a Russian verb in a dictionary you will usually be given two infinitives, for example писа́ть/написа́ть (*to write*). The first of these is called the *imperfective* and the second is the *perfective*. The imperfective infinitive is used to make:
• the present tense • the compound future • the imperfective past.
The imperfective is always associated with the process of an incomplete, unspecific, ongoing action or a frequently occurring action.
The perfective infinitive is used to make:
• the simple future • the perfective past tense.
The perfective is always associated with result, successful completion.

Б Imperfective and perfective '*pairs*' are usually related to each other in one of the following ways:
• писа́ть/написа́ть (*to write*) i.e. the perfective = imperfective + prefix (i.e. small addition to the front of the infinitive). Other common examples of this sort of pair are: ви́деть/уви́деть (*to see*); чита́ть/прочита́ть (*to read*).
• реша́ть/реши́ть (*to decide*) i.e. the imperfective is 1st conjugation and the perfective is 2nd conjugation. Other common examples of this sort are: получа́ть/получи́ть (*to receive*).
• Sometimes there is a really striking difference between the two infinitives: говори́ть/сказа́ть (*to talk, speak, say*); возвраща́ться/верну́ться (*to return*); сади́ться/сесть (*to sit down*).
Unfortunately, there is no simple way of predicting what the perfective might be.

В Even when using the infinitive itself, we must be careful to select either the imperfective or the perfective according to the golden rule of: *imperfective = process/frequent/unspecific and perfective = result/completion.* For example: Я уме́ю писа́ть, *I know how to write.* Here the imperfective for *to write* has been chosen because we are describing an ongoing situation, a habitual state of affairs. In contrast, Он обеща́л написа́ть письмо́ дире́ктору сего́дня (*He promised to write to the director today*) requires the perfective of *to write*, since it refers to a specific occasion.

Г Certain verbs are always followed by an imperfective infinitive in Russian: конча́ть/ко́нчить, *to finish*, начина́ть/нача́ть, *to begin*, продолжа́ть, *to continue*, перестава́ть/переста́ть, *to cease, stop* (e.g. *He stopped playing*).

➤ **For verbs of motion, see Units 70–1.**

1 In the following sentences, which of the infinitives (*to...*) and verbs ending in *-ing* would be imperfective in Russian and which would be perfective?

1 *The guide continued speaking.*
2 *I want to write the letter to Boris tomorrow.*
3 *I prefer to read newspapers.*
4 *They stopped playing at 9 o'clock.*
5 *He decided to return on Tuesday.*

2 Now complete the translations of these sentences by filling in the appropriate infinitive in Russian.

1 Гид продолжа́л _____ .
2 Я хочу́ _____ письмо́ Бори́су за́втра.
3 Я предпочита́ю _____ газе́ты.
4 Они́ переста́ли _____ в де́вять часо́в.
5 Он реши́л _____ во вто́рник.

3 Translate the following sentences and phrases into Russian; the imperfective/perfective pair of infinitives is given on the right.

1 He prefers to read newspapers.   чита́ть/прочита́ть
2 I want to send this letter today.   посыла́ть/посла́ть
3 The actor starts speaking at 7.   говори́ть/сказа́ть
4 We continue watching television.   смотре́ть/посмотре́ть
5 They like to relax on the beach.   отдыха́ть/отдохну́ть
6 I want to take the book now.   брать/взять
7 We want to buy this dog.   покупа́ть/купи́ть
8 Do you prefer to listen to the radio?   слу́шать/прослу́шать
9 Do you want to return today?   возвраща́ться/верну́ться

66 compound future

The future tense is used to talk about what will or is going to happen. In Russian, the compound future is used to describe actions in the future which are incomplete, unspecific, repeated or continuing: e.g. *I will write to you every day; tomorrow I will write a few letters and do some gardening.*

A The compound future, as its name suggests, is made up of two parts, the future tense of the verb *to be* + an infinitive.

Б Although the verb *to be*, быть, has no present tense of its own, it does have a future:

я бу́ду	*I will be*	мы бу́дем	*we will be*
ты бу́дешь	*you will be*	вы бу́дете	*you will be*
он бу́дет	*he will be*	они́ бу́дут	*they will be*

This can be used in its own right, as well as being part of the compound future, for example За́втра мы бу́дем в Москве́, *Tomorrow we will be in Moscow.*

В The second component of the compound future is the imperfective infinitive or aspect, because the compound future is associated with the process of an incomplete, unspecific, ongoing action or a frequently occurring action in the future:

Я бу́ду писа́ть тебе́ ка́ждый день. *I will write to you every day.*

Here the compound future is describing a repeated action in the future.

За́втра мы бу́дем смотре́ть телеви́зор и рабо́тать в саду́. *Tomorrow we will watch television and work in the garden.*

Here the compound future is needed because the action described is not concerned with any result or completion and there is no specific time at which the events will happen.

Г In Russian if the future is implied it must be used:

Когда́ мы бу́дем в А́встрии, мы бу́дем ката́ться на лы́жах. *When we are* (i.e. when we will be) *in Austria we will ski.*

Когда́ я бу́ду в Росси́и, я ча́сто бу́ду посеща́ть теа́тр. *When I am* (i.e. will be) *in Russia I will visit the theatre often.*

➤ **For simple future, see Unit 67, for imperfective and perfective aspects, see Units 65.**

1 Underline the verbs in the following passage which would be in the compound future in Russian (hint: there are four).

On Saturday I fly to Saint Petersburg at 10am. While I am there I will have meetings with Russian representatives of the company, but I hope that I will also visit some museums and theatres. I promise that I will ring you as regularly as I can during my stay, or else I will use e-mail at the hotel.

2 Build sentences using the compound future, to give the meanings indicated on the right.

e.g. Я/де́лать/поку́пки на ры́нке → Я бу́ду де́лать поку́пки на ры́нке. *I will do the shopping at the market.*

1 Он ча́сто/звони́ть/дру́гу.	He will ring his friend often.
2 Ба́бушка/отдыха́ть/до́ма.	Granny will be resting at home.
3 Мы/игра́ть/ в гольф ка́ждый день.	We will play golf every day.
4 За́втра я/занима́ться/уро́ками.	I will be busy with lessons tomorrow.
5 В университе́те он/изуча́ть/ исто́рию.	At university he will study history.

3 Match the phrases on the left with those on the right, using the English translation as a guide.

1 За́втра мы	**a** бу́дете в Росси́и, вы бу́дете звони́ть мне ка́ждый день?
2 Сего́дня ве́чером ты	**b** бу́дем игра́ть в кри́кет.
3 В ма́е они́	**c** бу́дут отдыха́ть в Ита́лии.
4 Когда́ вы	**d** бу́ду рабо́тать в саду́.
5 По́сле обе́да я	**e** бу́дешь писа́ть мно́го пи́сем.

1 *Tomorrow we will play cricket.*
2 *This evening you will write a lot of letters.*
3 *In May they will go on holiday (rest) in Italy.*
4 *When you are (will be) in Russia, will you ring me every day?*
5 *After lunch I will work in the garden.*

67 simple future

The future tense is used to talk about what will or is going to happen. In Russian, the simple future is used to describe actions in the future which are single, specific, complete; they are concerned with result and successful completion (rather than process).

A The simple future is formed from the perfective infinitive. There are no new endings to learn, since it is formed in exactly the same way as the present tense, but from the perfective infinitive. So, for example, the difference between *I am doing* and *I will do*: я де́лаю (*I am doing*) is formed from the imperfective infinitive де́лать and я сде́лаю (*I will do*) is formed from the perfective infinitive сде́лать.

написа́ть	я напишу́	*I will write*
пообе́дать	ты пообе́даешь	*you will have lunch*
объясни́ть	он объясни́т	*he will explain*
получи́ть	мы полу́чим	*we will receive*
реши́ть	вы реши́те	*you will decide*

B Although the perfective infinitive for most verbs is formed by the addition of a prefix to the imperfective or a change to the second conjugation for the perfective, some common verbs have irregular verbs for their perfective:

Meaning	Imperfective infin.	Perfective infin.	Simple future
to get up	встава́ть	встать	я вста́ну, ты вста́нешь, он вста́нет, мы вста́нем, вы вста́нете, они́ вста́нут
to give	дава́ть	дать	я дам, ты дашь, он даст, мы дади́м, вы дади́те, они́ даду́т
to lie down	ложи́ться	лечь	я ля́гу, ты ля́жешь, он ля́жет, мы ля́жем, вы ля́жете, они́ ля́гут
to sit down	сади́ться	сесть	я ся́ду, ты ся́дешь, он ся́дет, мы ся́дем, вы ся́дете, они́ ся́дут
to say	говори́ть	сказа́ть	я скажу́, ты ска́жешь, он ска́жет, мы ска́жем, вы ска́жете, они́ ска́жут (**NB** other verbs ending in -казать conjugate in the same way)
to be able, can	мочь	смочь	я смогу́, ты смо́жешь, он смо́жет, мы смо́жем, вы смо́жете, они́ смо́гут

B If the future tense is implied, the future tense must be used:
Éсли он придёт во́время, мы ся́дем в авто́бус.
If it arrives on time, we will catch ('sit on') a bus.

> **For compound future, see Unit 66, for imperfective and perfective aspects see Unit 65, for formation of present tense verbs, see Units 58–64.**

1 Underline the verbs in the following passage which would be in the simple future in Russian (hint: there are four).

I will ring you tomorrow at 10am, then I will write a letter to the director. As far as I know, he will be visiting lots of offices in England, but he has promised that he will visit our office on Tuesday. He will be considering all our proposals before his departure. Hopefully, he will sign the contract on Tuesday.

2 What will you achieve while your friend is watching television? Build sentences using the simple future:

e.g. Пока́ ты бу́дешь смотре́ть телеви́зор ____ написа́ть письмо́ → я напишу́ письмо́ Бори́су. *Whilst you're watching television I'll write the letter to Boris.*

1 позвони́ть дру́гу   *I'll ring a friend.*
2 накорми́ть соба́ку   *I'll feed the dog.*
3 пообе́дать на ку́хне   *I'll have lunch in the kitchen.*
4 купи́ть молоко́   *I'll buy some milk.*
5 вы́учить но́вые слова́   *I'll learn some new words.*

3 Here is a page from your diary, with just the briefest of notes. Make up sentences to describe your plans for each day. Monday has been done for you:

ПОНЕДЕЛЬНИК	встре́тить Са́шу	*meet Sasha*
ВТОРНИК	купи́ть пода́рки	*buy presents*
СРЕДА	позвони́ть ма́ме	*ring Mother*
ЧЕТВЕРГ	написа́ть письмо́ бра́ту	*write letter to brother*
ПЯТНИЦА	вы́учить грамма́тику	*learn grammar*
СУББОТА	отремонти́ровать маши́ну	*repair the car*
ВОСКРЕСЕНЬЕ	заказа́ть биле́ты	*book tickets*

e.g. В понеде́льник я встре́чу Са́шу.

68 past tense (1): imperfective

The imperfective past is used to describe actions which were repeated, continuing or incomplete. It is made from the imperfective infinitive.

A The imperfective past tense would be needed in Russian to express repeated, incomplete, interrupted actions in the past, e.g.:

> *I always used to play squash on Saturdays; He was playing squash when he fell; We played squash yesterday; We played squash for two hours yesterday.*

The final example includes the length of time the activity continued and when this is the case the imperfective will always be required. The imperfective past is also used when describing weather, colour, mood, appearance etc.: *It was cold when we were playing squash.*

Б To form the imperfective past tense, remove the last two letters (ть) from the imperfective infinitive, then add the endings (reflexive endings on the right):

- if the subject of the verb is masculine singular   add -л   -лся
- if the subject of the verb is feminine singular   add -ла   -лась
- if the subject of the verb is neuter singular   add -ло   -лось
- if the subject is plural (any gender)   add -ли   -лись

In other words, the endings have to agree in number and gender in the singular with the subject of the verb. For вы, the past tense ending will always be -ли whether вы is being used to refer politely to one person or in the plural to apply to more than one person; for я and ты the ending will depend on the identity of the person (Игорь, ты за́втракал? Катя, ты за́втракала? *Igor/Katya, were you having breakfast?*)

игра́ть   → Вчера́ мы игра́ли в сквош   *Yesterday we played squash.*

одева́ться → Они́ всегда́ одева́лись   *They always used*
 в шесть часо́в   *to get dressed at 6 o'clock.*

В Irregular verbs form their past tense in the same way (e.g. жить → мы жи́ли *we lived*), apart from verbs whose infinitive does not end in -ть:

везти́ (*to take by transport*) → вёз, везла́, везло́, везли́
вести́ (*to take on foot, lead*) → вёл, вела́, вело́, вели́
есть (*to eat*) → ел, е́ла, е́ло, е́ли
идти́ (*to go on foot, walk*) → шёл, шла, шло, шли
мочь (*to be able, can*) → мог, могла́, могло́, могли́
нести́ (*to carry*) → нёс, несла́, несло́, несли́

Г The verb *to be* (быть) exists only in the imperfective. This occurs very frequently in descriptions of weather, colour, mood, appearance etc.: e.g. Вчера́ он был в плохо́м настрое́нии. *Yesterday he was in a bad mood.*

1 **Police enquiry: explain who was doing what when the telephone rang.**

e.g. Когда́ зазвони́л телефо́н/Вади́м/спать → Вади́м спал.
When the telephone rang Vadim was sleeping.

1	Óльга/за́втракать	*Olga was having breakfast.*
2	Меня́ зову́т Еле́на, я/мыть посу́ду	*I (Elena) was washing up.*
3	Он/игра́ть в ка́рты	*He was playing cards.*
4	Мы смотре́ть/телеви́зор	*We were watching television.*
5	Вы/возвраща́ться в о́фис	*You were returning to the office.*
6	Они́/писа́ть пи́сьма	*They were writing letters.*
7	Бори́с и Светла́на/гото́вить обе́д	*Boris and Svetlana were preparing lunch.*

2 **Underline the verbs in the passage below which would be in the imperfective in past tense in Russian (hint: there are six).**

When we used to live in a flat it was impossible to have a dog, but when we moved into a house with a garden, we bought one. He was a large black mongrel and he loved to play in the garden. One day he was barking by the gate when the postman arrived. He thought the dog was aggressive and refused to come in.

3 **Explain why the underlined verbs in the following sentences are in the imperfective past tense.**

1 Вчера́ он <u>рабо́тал</u> в библиоте́ке два часа́.
Yesterday he worked in the library for 2 hours.

2 Она́ <u>игра́ла</u> в те́ннис, когда́ она́ уви́дела Бори́са.
She was playing tennis when she saw Boris.

3 В ма́рте мы <u>бы́ли</u> в Ита́лии.
In March we were in Italy.

4 Они́ <u>шли</u> в центр, когда́ заме́тили авто́бус.
They were walking to the centre when they noticed the bus.

5 Вы всегда́ <u>де́лали</u> поку́пки в на́шем магази́не.
You always used to do your shopping in our shop.

69 past tense (2): perfective

The perfective past is used to describe completed actions in the past; the emphasis is on result (not process).

A The perfective past tense would be needed in Russian to express ideas such as:

Вчера́ он купи́л автомоби́ль.	*Yesterday he bought a car.*
Она́ позвони́ла Вади́му в де́сять часо́в.	*She rang Vadim at 10 o'clock*

Б The perfective past tense is very simple to form. Remove the last two letters (ть) from the imperfective infinitive. The endings are as follows (reflexive endings on the right):

- if the subject of the verb is masculine singular: add -л -лся
- if the subject of the verb is feminine singular: add -ла -лась
- if the subject of the verb is neuter singular: add -ло -лось
- if the subject is plural (any gender): add -ли -лись

In other words, the endings are rather like those of an adjective, in that they have to agree in number and gender in the singular with the subject of the verb. If the subject of the verb is вы, then the past tense ending will always be -ли whether вы is being used to refer politely to one person or in the plural to apply to more than one person; for я and ты the ending will depend on the identity of the person (Игорь, ты поза́втракал? Ка́тя, ты поза́втракала? *Igor/Katya, have you had breakfast?*)

написа́ть	→ Вчера́ вы написа́ли ва́жное письмо́.	*Yesterday you wrote an important letter.*
сказа́ть	→ «Да,» сказа́л он.	*'Yes,' he said.*
оде́ться	→ Сего́дня они́ оде́лись в семь часо́в.	*Today they got dressed at 7 o'clock.*

В Irregular verbs form their perfective past tense in the same way; here are some examples of those whose infinitives do not end in -ть:

лечь (*to lie down*)	→ лёг, легла́, легло́, легли́
съесть (*to eat*)	→ съел, съе́ла, съе́ло, съе́ли
пойти́ (*to go on foot, walk*)	→ пошёл, пошла́, пошло́, пошли́
смочь (*to be able, can*)	→ смог, смогла́, смогло́, смогли́
понести́ (*to carry*)	→ понёс, понесла́, понесло́, понесли́

Г Russian has no *pluperfect* tense (*I had written the letter*); the perfective past is used for all of the following: *I wrote, I have written, I had written*. The golden rule is that if the action was completed in the past, the perfective must be used:

Он пообе́дал в два часа́.	*He had lunch at 2 o'clock.*
Да, он уже́ пообе́дал.	*Yes, he has already had lunch.*
Он уже́ пообе́дал, когда́ Ве́ра верну́лась.	*He had already had lunch when Vera returned.*

> **➤ For imperfective and perfective aspects, see Unit 65, for imperfective past, see Unit 68.**

1 **What has already been done? Look at the rota below and explain who has done what. The first one has been done for you:**

Óльга	пропылесо́сить	to hoover	✓
Вади́м	вы́мыть посу́ду	to do the washing up	✓
Вы	пригото́вить обе́д	to prepare the lunch	✓
Они́	сде́лать поку́пки	to do the shopping	✓
На́дя	накорми́ть соба́ку	to feed the dog	✓
И́горь	вы́стирать бельё	to do the washing	✓

e.g. Хорошо́! Óльга уже́ пропылесо́сила. *Good! Olga has already done the hoovering.*

2 **Underline the verbs in the following passage which you would translate by the perfective past (hint: there are 10).**
She had already finished the book when the phone rang. It was Boris, inviting her to the theatre. She refused politely, because she had already agreed to go to the cinema with Sergei. While she was speaking to Boris, her brother rang the doorbell. She hung up quickly and rushed to the door. Her brother was looking tired. 'I have brought the plants you asked for,' he said.

3 **Igor and Zoya have had a lot of interruptions. Explain what they were doing by translating the following sentences into Russian. NB! Some of the past tenses will be imperfective and some perfective. The vocabulary you need is in brackets.**

1 *Igor and Zoya were repairing the car when Boris rang.*
(ремонти́ровать/отремонти́ровать автомоби́ль, звони́ть/позвони́ть)

2 *Igor and Zoya were doing the washing when the washing machine broke down.*
(стира́ть/вы́стирать бельё, стира́льная маши́на лома́ться/слома́ться)

3 *Igor and Zoya were planting trees in the garden when their son returned.*
(сажа́ть/посади́ть дере́вья в саду́, сын возвраща́ться/верну́ться)

4 *Igor and Zoya were doing the shopping when Zoya lost the money.*
(де́лать/сде́лать поку́пки, теря́ть/потеря́ть де́ньги)

Verbs of motion have two imperfectives and one perfective infinitive; this means that there are two ways of forming the present tense and the imperfective past tense.

A E.g. to go on foot, to walk:

A Imperfective (indefinite)	B Imperfective (definite)	C Perfective
ходить	идти	пойти

From column A we make:
- The present tense which deals with habits and generalizations: Ему два года и он уже ходит везде. *He is 2 and he already walks everywhere.*
- The past tense which deals with habits, generalizations *and* return journeys. Он всегда ходил по городу после обеда, *He always walked around town after lunch.* Он уже ходил в город, *He has already been to town (i.e. there and back).*

From column B we make:
- The present tense which deals with actions in progress, that are happening now: Он идёт в квартиру. *He is walking into the flat.*
- The past tense which deals with an action in progress, in one direction: Он шёл в город, когда он упал. *He was walking into town when he fell.*

From column C we make:
- The simple future: Завтра он пойдёт в город. *Tomorrow he will walk into town.*
- The past tense which means a single completed action (in one direction): Он пошёл в город в 4 часа. *He went (set off) for town at 4 o'clock.*

(Note the use of пошёл in the context of weather: пошёл дождь, *it has started to rain.*)

Here are the three infinitives of other verbs of motion which follow the same pattern:

	A	B	C
to run	бегать	бежать (бегу, бежишь)	побежать
to take, lead (on foot)	водит	вести (веду, ведёшь)	повести
to transport	возить	везти (везу, везёшь)	повезти
to travel, drive, go by transport	ездить (езжу, ездишь)	ехать (еду, едешь)	поехать
to fly	летать	лететь (лечу, летишь)	полететь
to carry	носить	нести (несу несёшь)	понести
to swim, sail	плавать	плыть (плыву, плывёшь)	поплыть

➤ For irregular past tense verbs, see Unit 68.

1 Practise using the Column A verbs in order to complete these sentences.

1 Он ча́сто _____ за грани́цу. *He often travelled (went) abroad.*

2 Ка́ждый день она́ _____ в па́рке. *Every day she runs in the park.*

3 Когда́ он жил на берегу́ мо́ря, он _____ в мо́ре. *When he lived at the seaside he used to swim in the sea.*

4 Мы обы́чно _____ из Хитро́у. *We usually fly from Heathrow.*

5 Она́ уже́ _____ дочь в шко́лу. *She has already taken her daughter to school (by car).*

2 Practise using the Column B verbs in order to complete these sentences.

1 Сего́дня он _____ за грани́цу. *He is travelling (going) abroad today.*

2 Куда́ она́ _____ тепе́рь? *Where is she running to now?*

3 Он _____ к фи́нишу. *He is swimming towards the finishing line.*

4 Мы _____ из Хитро́у, когда́ самолёт слома́лся. *We were flying out of Heathrow when the 'plane broke down.*

5 Она́ _____ в шко́лу, когда́ потеря́ла ключ. *She was taking her daughter to school (by car) when she lost her key.*

3 Practise using the Column C verbs in order to complete these sentences.

1 За́втра он _____ в Гре́цию. *Tomorrow he will go to Greece,*

2 Я сейча́с _____ за врачо́м. *I will run for the doctor now.*

3 Он _____ до фи́ниша. *He will swim as far as the finishing line.*

4 Мы _____ в Москву́ в 3 часа́. *We flew to Moscow at 3 o'clock.*

5 Она́ _____ дочь в шко́лу в 9 часо́в. *She took her daughter to school (by car) at 9 o'clock.*

4 Choose the correct verb from the box to complete the sentences.

нёс понёс несёт

1 Почтальо́н _____ (*is carrying*) пи́сьма на по́чту.
2 Почтальо́н уже́ _____ (*has carried*) пи́сьма на по́чту.
3 Почтальо́н _____ (*was carrying*) пи́сьма на по́чту.

Prefixed verbs of motion are a very useful group of verbs, indicating specific direction. They have only one imperfective and one perfective form.

A It is important to know i) the meaning of each prefix; ii) the imperfective and perfective infinitives to which these prefixes are added; iii) which preposition to use after the prefixed verb. For example: *to walk, to go on foot* makes its prefixed forms by adding to the infinitives -ходить/-йти:

Imperfective and perfective infinitives	Following preposition and case	Example
входить/войти *to enter, walk/go in*	в/на + acc.	Мо́жно войти в теа́тр? *Is it possible to go into the theatre?*
выходить/выйти *to go out of*	из/с + gen.	Он выхо́дит из рестора́на. *He is going out of the restaurant.*
доходить/дойти *to go/walk as far as*	до + gen.	Они́ ча́сто дохо́дят до па́рка. *They often walk as far as the park.*
заходить/зайти *to pop in, call in*	в + acc. (to a place) к + dat. (to see a person)	Я хочу́ зайти́ в апте́ку тепе́рь. *I want to pop into the chemist's now.*
отходить/отойти *to move away from*	от + gen.	Он отошёл от две́ри. *He moved away from the door.*
переходить/ перейти *to cross*	че́рез + acc.	Мы перейдём че́рез у́лицу здесь. *We'll cross the road here.*
подходить/подойти *to approach*	к + dative	Я подхожу́ к окну́. *I approach the window.*
приходить/прийти *to arrive NB perfective drops letter* й – я приду́	в/на + acc.	Он то́лько что пришёл на ле́кцию. *He has only just arrived at the lecture.*
проходить/пройти *to walk past, pass*	ми́мо + gen.	Кто прохо́дит ми́мо окна́? *Who is walking past the window?*
сходить/сойти *to get off, down from*	с + gen.	На́до сойти́ с авто́буса. *It is necessary to get off the bus.*
уходить/уйти *to leave*	из/с + gen.	Он ушёл час наза́д. *He left an hour ago.*

Б The same prefixes may be used by the following pairs:

-бе́гать/-бежа́ть	*run*	-вози́ть/-везти́	*transport*
-води́ть/-вести́	*lead*	-лета́ть/-лете́ть	*fly*
-носи́ть/-нести́	*carry*	-пла́вать/-плыть	*swim, sail*

Note that -езжа́ть/-éхать (*travel, drive*) is the only pair that starts with a vowel, and the only one for which any of the prefixes change in any way (под → подъ, с → съ).

➤ **For restrictions on use of в, see Unit 83.**

1 Complete the passage with the appropriate prefixed verbs of motion. They are all in the present tense and are forms of -ходить/-йти or -езжать/-ехать.

Ка́ждое у́тро я **1**_____ (*go out of*) из до́ма в во́семь часо́в. Я **2**_____ (*approach*) к остано́вке авто́буса. Когда́ авто́бус **3**_____ (*arrives*), я **4**_____ (*get in*). Когда́ я **5**_____ (*arrive*) в го́род, я **6**_____ (*get off*) и **7**_____ (*walk past*) ми́мо библиоте́ки и **8**_____ (*go into*) в о́фис.

2 Choose the appropriate preposition from the box to complete each sentence according to the sense of the English translations.

в из к до с ми́мо от че́рез на

1 О́льга вбежа́ла ___ ко́мнату.   *Olga ran into the room.*
2 Авто́бус подъезжа́ет __ остано́вке.   *The bus is approaching the stop.*
3 Бори́с доплы́л __фи́ниша.   *Boris swam as far as the finishing line.*
4 Тури́сты вы́шли __музе́я.   *The tourists went out of the museum.*
5 Макси́м придёт __ конце́рт за́втра.   *Maksim will (come to) arrive at the concert tomorrow.*
6 Бизнесме́ны вылета́ют __ Хитроу сего́дня.   *The businesmen are flying out of Heathrow today.*
7 Студе́нты прохо́дят ___ университе́та.   *The students are walking past the university.*
8 Ба́бушка сошла́ __ авто́буса. *Grandmother got off the bus.*
9 Актёр отошёл ___ неё.   *The actor moved away from her.*
10 Он всегда́ перехо́дит ____ у́лицу здесь.   *He always crosses the road here.*

3 Translate into Russian.
1 *I am walking into the theatre.*
2 *He is carrying the books into the room.*
3 *We are running out of the park.*
4 *They are leading the dog across the street.*

72 conditions (1): open

An 'open' condition is one which still has a chance of occurring: *If it is fine tomorrow we will go to the beach*. If the condition refers to the future, Russian uses future tense in both parts of the sentence. If the condition refers to an ongoing situation in the present tense, the present is used in both parts: *If you like the food, I am pleased*.

A If the open condition refers to the future, the future tense must appear in both parts of the sentence; i.e. we must say:

If it will be fine tomorrow we will go to the beach.
Éсли за́втра пого́да бу́дет хоро́шая, мы пойдём на пляж.
If you will get up on time, we will be able to catch the bus.
Éсли ты вста́нешь во́время, мы смо́жем сесть в авто́бус.

Б The future tense of *to be* is needed to give the future with words such as на́до (*it is necessary*) and нельзя́ (*it is not possible, one may not*):

За́втра нельзя́ бу́дет смотре́ть телеви́зор.
It won't be possible to watch the television tomorrow.

В If the open condition refers to an ongoing situation in the present, then the present tense must appear in both parts of the sentence:

If you like the food, I am pleased.
Éсли вам нра́вится еда́, я рад (ра́да).

So, the golden rule is: don't try to mix the tenses. First check that the condition is 'open', then work out: *present tense throughout* or *future?*

➤ For closed conditions, see Unit 73, for formation of future, see Units 66–7.

1 First some practice in making the future tense. *Boris won't be allowed to go out tonight unless...* Complete the conditions imposed on him by using the future tense.

Бори́с смо́жет пойти́ на дискоте́ку, но то́лько е́сли он...
Boris will be able to go to the disco tonight, but only if he...
убира́ть/убра́ть в до́ме → уберёт в до́ме *(will tidy) tidies up in the house.*

1 писа́ть/написа́ть письмо́ де́душке	*to write a letter to grandfather*
2 пылесо́сить/пропылесо́сить ковёр	*to hoover the carpet*
3 стира́ть/вы́стирать бельё	*to do the washing*
4 ра́но встава́ть/встать	*to get up early*
5 чи́стить/почи́стить маши́ну	*to wash the car*

2 More practice with the future! Give ten variations on the beginning of a theme by translating the phrases into Russian; the imperfective/perfective verb pair is given for you on the right.

e.g. Я бу́ду рад (ра́да), е́сли он... *I will be glad if he...*

1	*arrives on time*	приезжа́ть/прие́хать
2	*doesn't forget his money*	забыва́ть/забы́ть
3	*rings the professor*	звони́ть/позвони́ть
4	*writes a letter to his brother*	писа́ть/написа́ть
5	*sells his motorbike*	продава́ть/прода́ть
6	*gives me a present*	дава́ть/да́ть
7	*books the tickets*	зака́зывать/заказа́ть
8	*buys a dog*	покупа́ть/купи́ть
9	*does the shopping*	де́лать/ сде́лать
10	*returns early*	возвраща́ться/верну́ться

3 Tick the sentences where you would use the present tense in both parts and put a cross against the sentences where you use the future in both parts.

1 *We are always glad if they send us a card.*
2 *They will not be pleased if you don't send them a card.*
3 *You are never satisfied if the food is cold.*
4 *If you don't ring me tonight I will be furious.*

73 conditions (2): closed

Russian uses **если** and the conditional tense to describe hypothetical or 'closed' conditions, e.g. *If it were fine we would go to the beach today* (or *If it had been fine we would have gone to the beach today*) – i.e. the implication is that it isn't (or wasn't) fine, so the trip to the beach isn't (or wasn't) possible.

A If a condition is no longer possible, or could never happen, or is just a general assumption (hypothesis), then the conditional is needed with если. The conditional tense is formed very simply: take the past tense of the verb (either imperfective or perfective, depending on the usual rules determining choice of aspect) and add the word бы twice: usually after если in the 'if' part of the sentence (the conditional clause) and then after the verb in the 'what would happen' part of the sentence (the main clause).

NB If there is бы in one half of the sentence, it must be matched by a second бы in the other half:

Éсли бы он знал пра́вду, он о́чень рассерди́лся бы.
If he knew the truth he would be very angry.

Alternatively, the *if* clause comes second:

Он о́чень рассерди́лся бы, если бы он знал пра́вду

The implication in this type of condition is that 'he doesn't, so he won't'. Note that the two parts of the sentence are separated by a comma.

Б The good news is that there is no conditional perfect tense in Russian. *He would have been very angry if he had known the truth* would simply be, as above: Он о́чень рассерди́лся бы, если бы он знал пра́вду; i.e. the same form covers *would, would have*.

В Although the position of бы is usually as described in **A**, it can follow any word in the sentence which requires special emphasis:

Éсли бы она́ узна́ла об э́том, она́ бы засмея́лась.
*If she had found out about this, **she** would have laughed.*

Г **NB** Conditions do not always include a если clause; sometimes they simply express a desire: Я о́чень хоте́л(а) бы отдыха́ть в Ита́лии! *I would really like to have a holiday in Italy!*.

➤ **For open conditions, see Unit 72, for imperfective and perfective aspects, see Unit 65, for formation of past tense, see Units 68 and 69.**

1 Match up the two halves of each sentence. Hint: make sure the subject of the verb in one half is the same as the subject in the other (or that it matches the pronoun in the y construction).

e.g. у меня́ → я пошла́ бы

1 Е́сли бы у меня́ бы́ло вре́мя,
2 А́ня купи́ла бы дом,
3 Они́ пла́вали бы в бассе́йне,
4 Вади́м отдыха́л бы в Япо́нии,
5 Е́сли бы у нас бы́ли биле́ты,

a е́сли бы у них бы́ло вре́мя.
b я пошла́ бы на о́перу.
c е́сли бы он говори́л по-япо́нски.
d мы пошли́ бы в теа́тр.
e е́сли бы у неё бы́ли де́ньги.

2 Е́сли бы бы́ли де́ньги... What would they do if they had the money? Build sentences from the information given.

e.g. Та́ня/путеше́ствовать за грани́цей → Е́сли бы у неё бы́ли де́ньги, Та́ня путеше́ствовала бы за грани́цей. *If she had the money, Tanya would travel abroad.*

1 Они́/постро́ить да́чу — to build a house in the country
2 Мы/купи́ть пода́рки для друзе́й — to buy presents for friends
3 Па́вел/сиде́ть до́ма — to stay (sit) at home
4 Ка́тя/купи́ть но́вую оде́жду — to buy new clothes
5 Вы/доста́ть биле́ты в Большо́й Теа́тр — to get tickets for the Bolshoi Theatre

3 Е́сли бы то́лько! *If only!* Complete the sentences by making a main clause from the information given.

e.g. Е́сли бы то́лько он позвони́л, я/переда́ть ему́ но́вости. → Е́сли бы то́лько он позвони́л, я переда́л(а) бы ему́ но́вости. *If only he had rung, I would have given him the news.*

1 Е́сли бы то́лько мы не забы́ли, А́ня не/рассерди́ться на нас. *If only we hadn't forgotten Anya would not be (would not have been) cross with us.*
2 Е́сли бы то́лько она́ зна́ла об э́том, она́/позвони́ть ему́. *If only she had know about this, she would have rung him.*
3 Е́сли бы то́лько мы пришли́ во́время, мы/уви́деть их. *If only we had arrived on time, we would have seen them.*

4 Бы́ло бы лу́чше, е́сли бы... *It would be better if...* Complete the phrase using the information given.

e.g. мы/написа́ть письмо́ ему́ → Бы́ло бы лу́чше, е́сли бы мы написа́ли ему́ письмо́. *It would be better if we wrote him a letter.*

1 она́/согласи́ться на э́то — to agree to this
2 у него́/быть телефа́кс — to have a fax machine
3 я/знать его́ а́дрес — to know his address

The imperative or command form is used to tell people what to do, to make requests and suggestions.

A The imperative can be made from either the present tense (imperfective) or the simple future (perfective). Commands made from the imperfective present refer to things that need to be done habitually and they tend to be more friendly than those made from the perfective future. Negative commands are usually made from the imperfective (but the perfective is used for warnings) and commands with a very specific element from the perfective. Here are some examples:

	Make the imperative from:
Do sit down and make yourself comfortable.	imperfective
'Sit down at once!' said the police officer.	perfective
Always pay your bills on time!	imperfective
Don't open the door!	imperfective

B If you want to give a command to someone you address as ты or вы, then for most verbs, first of all take the ты form of the present tense or simple future and remove the last three letters. If you're left with a vowel, add й (if you're commanding ты) or йте (if you're commanding вы); if you're left with a consonant add и (if you're commanding ты) or ите (if you're commanding вы).

Type of verb	Infinitive	Present: ты form	Command form (ты)	Command form (вы)
1st conjugation	игра́ть	игра́ешь	игра́й! *play!*	игра́йте! *play!*
2nd conjugation	смотре́ть	смо́тришь	смотри́! *look!*	смотри́те! *look!*
Irregular present	писа́ть	пи́шешь	пиши́! *write!*	пиши́те! *write!*
Reflexive	сади́ться	сади́шься	сади́сь! *sit down!*	сади́тесь! *sit down!*

C Some common irregular imperatives: есть *to eat* → ешь! е́шьте! пить *to drink* → пей! пе́йте! быть *to be* → будь! бу́дьте! помо́чь *to help* → помоги́! помоги́те! встава́ть, *to get up* → встава́й! встава́йте!

Requests: in official requests the infinitive may be used. For example: *Please do not disturb,* Про́сьба не беспоко́ить (lit.: *request not to disturb*); *No smoking!* Не кури́ть!; *Suggestions:* Дава́й (дава́йте) is used with the мы form of the verb to mean *let's...*: Дава́йте посмо́трим телеви́зор, *Let's watch television.*

1 **Match the Russian commands with their English versions.**

1 Подожди́те мину́точку!
2 Переда́йте мне во́ду!
3 Иди́ сюда́!
4 Позвони́ мне за́втра!
5 Сади́сь!
6 Дава́й погуля́ем!
7 Про́сьба не говори́ть!
8 Проходи́те в гости́ную!
9 Слу́шайте внима́тельно!
10 Подпиши́те, пожа́луйста!

a *Ring me tomorrow!*
b *Let's go for a walk!*
c *Pass me the water!*
d *Listen carefully!*
e *Sign, please!*
f *Do sit down!*
g *Go through to the sitting room!*
h *Wait a moment!*
i *Quiet, please (no talking)!*
j *Come here!*

2 **Make the ты form of the imperative from the infinitives.**

1 спать — *to sleep*
2 написа́ть — *to write*
3 брать — *to take*
4 купи́ть — *to buy*
5 поблагодари́ть — *to thank*

3 **Make the вы form of the imperative from the infinitives.**

1 забы́ть — *to forget*
2 отдыха́ть — *to rest*
3 слу́шать — *to listen*
4 рабо́тать — *to work*
5 улыба́ться — *to smile*

4 **Translate into Russian.**

1 Don't forget the tickets. (warning)
2 No smoking!
3 Pass me the key, please.
4 Let's ring Tanya.

75 negatives (1)

If you want to explain what is not being done, happening etc., you need the negative. This is formed with **не** before the conjugated verb (i.e. verb in a tense).

А He should be placed immediately before the verb:

Он не рабо́тает.	*He isn't working.*
Мы не зна́ем, когда́ она́ придёт.	*We don't know when she will arrive.*

Б As the verb *to be* has no present tense, the word **нет** is used to mean *there is/are not*; this is always used with the genitive of the thing which is lacking:

У меня́ нет вре́мени.	*I have no time* (lit.: *by me there is not any time*).
Его́ нет до́ма.	*He is not at home* (lit.: *of him there is not at home*).

В The following negative words must always include **не** and a conjugated verb; in English we can say, eg, *nowhere* or *not anywhere*, but Russian has only one way of making such negative phrases:

ничего́ не	*nothing, not... anything*
никогда́ не	*never, not ... ever*
нигде́ не	*nowhere, not ... anywhere* (of position, location)
никуда́ не	*nowhere, not... anywhere* (of direction, movement towards)
никто́ не	*no one, not anyone*

Negative word	Example
ничего́ *nothing*	Я ничего́ не понима́ю. *I don't understand anything.*
никогда́ *never*	Я никогда́ не смотрю́ телеви́зор. *I never watch television.*
нигде́ *nowhere* (of position)	Я нигде́ не ви́жу ключи́. *I can't see the keys anywhere.*
никуда́ *nowhere* (of direction)	Вы никуда́ не идёте сего́дня? *Aren't you going anywhere today?*
никто́ *no one*	Никто́ не понима́ет её. *No one understands her.*

The negatives **ничего́** and **никто́** decline like **что** and **кто**. If they are used with a preposition, then the preposition must follow the **ни** part of the word:

Я никого́ не зна́ю.	*I don't know anyone.*
Я ни о ком не ду́маю.	*I'm not think about anyone.*
Я ничего́ не зна́ю.	*I don't know anything.*
Я ни о чём не ду́маю.	*I'm not thinking about anything.*

➤ **For conjugation of что and кто, see Unit 51, for use of negative and infinitive, see Unit 76, for use of preposition о see Unit 89.**

1 Build negative sentences using the following components.

e.g. Ви́ктор/не/люби́ть/слу́шать му́зыку → Ви́ктор не лю́бит слу́шать му́зыку. *Viktor doesn't like listening to music.*

1 Ви́ктор/никогда́ не/петь пе́сни — *Viktor never sings songs.*

2 Ви́ктор/нигде́ не/слу́шать поп-му́зыку — *Viktor never listens to pop music anywhere.*

3 Ви́ктор /никто́ не/слу́шать поп-му́зыку с — *Viktor doesn't listen to pop music with anyone.*

4 Ви́ктор/ничего́ не/знать о му́зыке — *Viktor knows nothing about music.*

2 Complete the following conversation by giving a negative answer to each question, according to the prompts.

e.g. Вы хоти́те вино́? *I never drink wine* → Я никогда́ не пью вино́.

1 Вы лю́бите фи́льмы? — *I don't like watching films.*

2 Здесь есть кинотеа́тр? — *There isn't a cinema here.*

3 Чем вы занима́етесь в свобо́дное вре́мя? — *I don't do anything (am not busy with anything) in my spare time.*

4 Где вы лю́бите отдыха́ть? — *I don't like to go on holiday (rest) anywhere.*

3 Match the following sentence halves to make full sentences.

1 Я ничего́   a не ду́маешь

2 Мы никогда́   b не понима́ю

3 Вы нигде́   c не посеща́ем теа́тр

4 Они́ никому́   d не отдыха́ете

5 Ты ни о ком   e не пи́шут

76 negatives (2)

In Russian there are negative words which are used with infinitives, not with conjugated verbs (e.g. *there is nothing for me to do*). These negatives begin with the stressed syllable не́.

A The key negative words used with infinitives (with very literal translations into English) are:

не́где	*not where*	Не́где стоя́ть	*There's nowhere to stand.*
не́куда	*not to where*	Не́куда идти́	*There's nowhere to go.*
не́кто	*not who*	Не́кого спроси́ть	*There's no one to ask.*
не́когда	*not when*	Не́когда отдыха́ть	*There's no time to rest.*
не́что	*not what*	Не́чего есть	*There's nothing to eat.*

The negatives не́что and не́кто decline like что and кто; if they are used with a preposition, then the preposition must follow the не́ part of the word:

| Не́чем писа́ть. | *There's nothing to write with.* |
| Не́ на что жа́ловаться. | *There's nothing to complain about.* |

Б If you want to indicate who has nothing to eat, nowhere to rest etc., then you must use the dative case of that person:

| Вам не́ на что жа́ловаться. | *You've got nothing to complain about.* |
| Мне не́чем писа́ть. | *I've got nothing to write with.* |

В These negative and infinitive phrases can be put into a past or future context by using the past and future tenses of быть:

| Мне не́чем бы́ло писа́ть. | *I had nothing to write with.* |
| Вам не́ на что бу́дет жа́ловаться. | *You will have nothing to complain about.* |

Г Не́чего can be used to mean *there's no point*. Не́ за что can be used to mean *don't mention it, you're welcome*.

➤ For conjugation of что and кто, see Unit 51, for use of negative and conjugated verbs, see Unit 75.

1 **Match the Russian phrases with their English translations.**

1 Не́когда чита́ть.
2 Ива́ну не́ с кем говори́ть.
3 Нам не́чего бы́ло пить.
4 Вам не́куда бу́дет идти́.

5 Здесь не́чего чита́ть.
6 Тебе́ не́ о чём беспоко́иться.
7 Не́кого спроси́ть.
8 Не́чего беспоко́иться.
9 Не́ за что.
10 Де́тям не́ с кем бу́дет игра́ть.

a *Ivan has no one to talk to (with).*
b *You will have nowhere to go.*
c *Don't mention it.*
d *The children will have no one to play with.*
e *There is no time to read.*
f *There is no point worrying.*
g *There is nothing to read here.*
h *We had nothing to drink.*
i *There is no one to ask.*
j *You have nothing to worry about.*

2 **Build sentences about the problems of Ivan and Maria.**

e.g. Ива́н и Мари́я/идти́ в теа́тр/не́кто/с → Ива́ну и Мари́и не́ с кем идти́ в теа́тр. *Ivan and Maria have no one to go to the theatre with.*

1 Ива́н и Мари́я/смотре́ть телеви́зор/ не́когда
2 Ива́н и Мари́я/писа́ть пи́сьма/не́что
3 Ива́н и Мари́я/приглаша́ть на обе́д/не́кто
4 Ива́н и Мари́я/пить/не́что
5 Ива́н и Мари́я/звони́ть/не́кто

no time to watch television
nothing to write letters with
no one to invite to lunch
nothing to drink
no one to ring

3 **Translate into Russian.**

1 *You will have nothing to do.*
2 *Boris had no one to talk to.*
3 *There's nothing to eat.*
4 *The doctor had no time to rest.*
5 *We had nothing to read.*

The infinitive is used in phrases to mean *it is possible, it is impossible, it is necessary* and *it is time to*.

A The key words expressing possibility and permission, impossibility and prohibition, necessity are:

мо́жно	*it is possible, one may*
нельзя́	*it is impossible, one may not*
на́до	*it is necessary*
пора́	*it is time to*

These words are all followed by infinitives and are used with the dative of the person being advised of possibility, permission etc.:

Нельзя́ кури́ть!	*No smoking! (it is not possible to smoke)*
Здесь мо́жно фотографи́ровать?	*Is it possible to take photographs here?*
Мне на́до спать	*I need to sleep (for me it is necessary to sleep)*

Б In the case of нельзя́ the choice between imperfective or perfective infinitive affects the meaning:

- *Imperfective*: Вам нельзя́ выходи́ть сего́дня! *You can't go out today!* (i.e. because you are ill, not allowed to).
- *Perfective:* Нельзя́ вы́йти. *You can't go out.* (i.e. it is not possible to go out, e.g. because someone has lost the key).

В Мо́жно is a very useful term in both questions and statements and is often used on its own when you are trying to find out whether something is *possible* or *permitted*. For example, if you want to find out if a seat is free, you would say Мо́жно? If it is in order for you to sit there, the person you have asked will reply Мо́жно. (*May I sit here? Yes, you may.*)

Возмо́жно means *it is possible* and is an alternative to мо́жно only in the sense of possibility (not in the sense of permission).

Г Ну́жно, like на́до, refers to necessity:

Что на́до де́лать?	*What is it necessary to do?*

Д Пора́ means *it is time to* and occurs in phrases such as:

Нам пора́ идти́.	*It's time for us to go.*

This is often abbreviated to Нам пора́ and sometimes just пора́.

Е Use the past and future tenses of быть to put expressions of possibility, permission etc. into past and future contexts:

Что на́до бу́дет де́лать?	*What will it be necessary to do?*
Мне на́до бы́ло спать.	*I needed to sleep.*

1 Choose the appropriate word from the box to give the required sense.

мóжно	нельзя́	нáдо	порá

1 Нам _____ верну́ться домóй.
2 Спортсмéну _____ кури́ть.
3 Где _____ купи́ть морóженое?
4 Почему́ нам _____ читáть э́ту кни́гу?
5 К сожалéнию _____ позвони́ть отсю́да.

1 *It's time for us to return home.*
2 *A sportsman shouldn't/mustn't smoke.*
3 *Where can one buy ice-cream?*
4 *Why must we read this book?*
5 *Unfortunately, it's not possible to ring from here.*

2 Match the piece of advice on the right with the problem on the left:

1 Тáня не лю́бит спорт.   a Ему́ нáдо купи́ть аспири́н.
2 У Бори́са боли́т головá.   b Ей нáдо купи́ть нóвое.
3 Её рáдио не рабóтает.   c Ей нельзя́ купи́ть билéт
                                 на матч.

3 Translate into Russian.

1 *He must rest in hospital.*
2 *It was time for us to go.*
3 *It will be possible to swim.*
4 *No, you can't watch television.*
5 *Yes, you must work.*

Indirect statements are reports of what people have said or asked: *He said he was going to St Petersburg; He asked if I was going to Moscow.*

A In English there is a change of the tense of verb between direct and indirect statement:

In direct speech	*'I <u>am going</u> to St Petersburg,' he said.*
In indirect speech	*He said he <u>was going</u> to St Petersburg.*
In direct speech	*'I <u>will go</u> to St Petersburg,' he said.*
In indirect speech	*He said he <u>would go</u> to St Petersburg.*
In direct speech	*'He <u>has already gone</u> to St Petersburg,' we said.*
In indirect speech	*We said that <u>he had already gone</u> to St Petersburg.*

In Russian the tense in the indirect statement remains the same as it was in the direct statement (although, as in English, there may be some change of the person of the verb):

Direct speech	«Я éду в Санкт-Петербу́рг,» сказа́л он.
Indirect speech	Он сказа́л, что он éдет в Санкт-Петербу́рг.
Direct speech	«Я поéду в Санкт-Петербу́рг,» сказа́л он.
Indirect speech	Он сказал, что он поéдет в Санкт-Петербу́рг.
Direct speech	«Он ужé поéхал в Санкт-Петербу́рг,» сказа́ли мы.
Indirect speech	Мы сказа́ли, что он ужé поéхал в Санкт-Петербу́рг.

Note that Russian always needs the word for *that* (что) in an indirect statement, preceded by a comma.

Б In English we introduce an indirect question with the words *if* or *whether*

Direct question	*'Will you return?' we asked.*
Indirect question	*We asked him whether he would return.*

In Russian, indirect questions must never start with the word éсли (*if*), but always with the word ли (*whether*). As for indirect statements, Russian keeps the tense of the direct question in the indirect version:

Direct question	«Вы вернётесь?» проси́ли мы.
Indirect question	Мы спроси́ли, вернётся ли он.

Notice that the word order is usually:
Verb of asking + comma + verb + ли *+ subject*, i.e. Мы спроси́ли + , + вернётся + ли + он.

Я хочу́ знать, приéдут ли они́ и́ли нет.	*I want to know whether they are coming or not.*

1 Match the sentences with their translations.

1 Профе́ссор сказа́л, что ле́кция начнётся в два часа́.
2 Милиционе́р спроси́л, куда́ мы е́дем.
3 Врач сказа́л, что ему́ ско́ро бу́дет лу́чше.
4 Гид хоте́л знать, что тури́сты хотя́т посеща́ть.
5 Официа́нт спроси́л, хотя́т ли они́ суп.

a *The policeman asked where we were going.*
b *The guide wanted to know what the tourists wanted to visit.*
c *The professor said that the lecture would begin at 2 o'clock.*
d *The waiter asked whether they wanted soup.*
e *The doctor said that he would soon be better.*

2 Report on the questions you asked during a conversation, using the English on the right as a guide.

e.g. Он/купи́ть/биле́ты *I asked if he had bought the tickets.* →
Я спроси́л(а), купи́л ли он биле́ты.

1 Бори́с/прие́хать за́втра — *I asked if Boris would arrive tomorrow.*
2 О́льга/заплати́ть за кни́ги. — *I asked if Olga had paid for the books.*
3 Клие́нты/пожа́ловаться на това́ры — *I asked if the customers were complaining about the goods.*
4 Бори́с/позвони́ть дире́ктору — *I asked if Boris had rung the director.*
5 О́льга/верну́ться — *I asked if Olga would return.*

3 Rewrite the jumbled sentences in the correct order. Use the English as a guide.

e.g. зна́ю ли я не прие́хал он → Я не зна́ю, прие́хал ли он.
I don't know whether he's arrived.

1 мо́жно мы спроси́ли в 8 часо́в поза́втракать ли. — *We asked if it was possible to have breakfast at 8 o'clock.*
2 спроси́л пошёл дискоте́ку он друг ли на. — *He asked if his friend had gone to the disco.*
3 когда́ он нам вернётся сказа́л. — *He told us when he would return.*
4 письмо́ ли она́ ты не получи́ла зна́ешь. — *Do you know whether she's received the letter?*
5 я подпи́шет знать ли хочу́ контра́кт дире́ктор. — *I want to know if the director will sign the contract.*

An indirect command, advice or wish involves more than one subject and verb: Person A wants/commands Person B to do something: *I want him to go home; They ordered him to go home.* In Russian the word что́бы, followed by the past tense (either imperfective or perfective), is used in indirect commands/wishes (this is also known as the subjunctive).

A The imperative is used for direct commands:

Direct command   *Go home!*   Иди́те домо́й!

In the direct statement of a wish, the infinitive is used:

I want to go home   Я хочу́ идти́ домо́й.

In an indirect command or wish, the subject of the first part of the sentence is not the same as the subject of the second part of the sentence (person A wants/commands person B to do something):

Indirect command   Они́ приказа́ли, что́бы он пошёл домо́й.
                   They ordered him to (that he should) go home

Indirect wish   Я хочу́, что́бы он пошёл домо́й
                   I want him (that he should) go home.

Б Что́бы is *never* used with the present or future tenses, only the past.

В Что́бы is always preceded by a comma.

Г Common verbs of commanding, wishing, advising which require the use of что́бы in indirect commands are:

говори́ть/сказа́ть	*to say, tell*
жела́ть/пожела́ть	*to wish*
предлага́ть/предложи́ть	*to suggest*
прика́зывать/приказа́ть	*to order*
рекомендова́ть/отрекомендова́ть	*to recommend*
сове́товать/посове́товать	*to advise*
тре́бовать/потре́бовать	*to demand, require*

Some examples; notice how English sometimes needs *should* in order to get the sense of command/recommendation:

Милиционе́р сказа́л, что́бы они́ отошли́ от две́ри.
The policeman said that they should move away from the door.

Я предлага́ю, что́бы вы всегда́ встава́ли ра́ньше.
I suggest that you (should) always get up earlier.

➤ For imperfective/perfective, see Units 65, 68 and 69.

1 Build sentences to include indirect commands/wishes etc.

e.g. Он не/хотéть/онá/игрáть в тéннис → Он не хóчет, чтóбы онá игрáла в тéннис. *He doesn't want her to play tennis.*

1 Врач/трéбовать/спортсмéн/не курúть.
The doctor demands that the sportsman should not smoke.
2 Гид/рекомéндовать/турúсты/обéдать в ресторáнах.
The guide recommends that the tourists should eat in restaurants.
3 Профéссор/трéбовать/студéнты/прочитáть всю кнúгу.
The professor demands that the students read the whole book.
4 Я/хотéть/мой сын/стать врачóм.
I want my son to become a doctor.
5 Дéти/хотéть/родúтели/купúть дорогúе игрýшки.
The children want their parents to buy expensive toys.

2 Form sentences from the following sentences, using the English as a guide.

1 Я хочý, чтóбы он
2 Начáльник приказáл, чтóбы онú
3 Вы хотúте, чтóбы я

4 Он сказáл, чтóбы

5 Официáнт хотéл, чтóбы клиéнт

a дал емý на чай.
b все зрúтели сéли.
c рабóтал усéрднее.
d вышла из кóмнаты?
e приходúли вóвремя.

1 *I want him to work harder.*
2 *The boss ordered that they (should) arrive on time.*
3 *Do you want me to leave the room?*
4 *He said that all the audience should be seated.*
5 *The waiter wanted the customer to give him a tip.* (lit.: 'for tea')

3 Translate into Russian.

1 *I want you to ring me tomorrow.*
2 *The doctor wants the patient to stay in bed.*
3 *The professor demands that the students work in the library.*
4 *The policeman suggests that you go home.*
5 *I ordered them to sit down.*

80 purpose

A 'purpose clause' is part of a sentence which describes an action undertaken in order to achieve a certain outcome: *I have come (in order) to tell you that dinner is served.* In Russian the word чтобы is used with either the infinitive or a past tense verb in order to produce a purpose clause.

A If the subject of the verb is the same in both parts of the sentence, then чтобы is used with an infinitive. In the following example the person making the telephone call is the same person who is passing on the news about Tamara:

Я звоню́ тебе́, что́бы переда́ть но́вости о Тама́ре.
I'm ringing you to pass on the news about Tamara.

In English this kind of purpose clause is expressed as *(in order) to...*

Б Что́бы is usually omitted after verbs of motion:

Он пришёл переда́ть ей хоро́шие но́вости.
He came to pass on the good news to her.

В If there is a change of subject, then чтобы must be used with the past tense (imperfective or perfective, depending on the usual criteria of choice: process or result?):

Я звоню́ тебе́, что́бы ты по́нял пра́вду.
I'm ringing you so that you should understand the truth.

In English this kind of purpose clause is expressed as *in order that/so that...*

➤ **For imperfective/perfective, see Units 65, 68 and 69.**

1 **Why do people want to do things? Build sentences with чтобы. Use the English translations as a guide.**

e.g. Он/посещáть музéи/картины/посмотрéть → Он хóчет посещáть музéи, чтобы посмотрéть картины. *He wants to visit the museums (in order) to look at the pictures.*

1 Мы/купить телевизор/смотрéть мáтчи
2 Вы/позвонить дрýгу/пригласить егó на концéрт
3 Ты/написáть письмó/передáть нóвости
4 Они/посетить Москвý/видеть интерéсные местá
5 Туристы/ посещáть пляжи/отдыхáть

1 *We want to buy a television in order to watch the matches.*
2 *You want to ring (your) friend in order to invite him to the concert.*
3 *You want to write a letter in order to pass on the news.*
4 *They want to visit Moscow in order to see some interesting places.*
5 *The tourists want to visit the beaches in order to relax (rest).*

2 **Boris has rung for a variety of reasons. Build sentences using чтобы and the past tense.**

e.g. я/объяснить проблéму → Борис позвонил, чтобы я объяснил проблéму. *Boris rang so that I should explain the problem.* (for me to explain the problem).

1 онá/отвéтить на вопрóс — *to answer the question*
2 он/извиниться — *to apologize*
3 мы/обсудить ситуáцию — *to discuss the situation*
4 вы/пригласить егó на обéд — *to invite him to lunch*
5 они/заказáть билéты — *to book tickets*

3 **Choose the appropriate word or phrase from the box to complete each sentence:**

чтобы позвонить позвонить чтобы _____ позвонил

1 Óльга вышла _____ дрýгу.
Olga went out to ring a friend.
2 Óльга искáла автомáт _____ дрýгу.
Olga was looking for a phone box in order to ring a friend.
3 Óльга хотéла, _____ друг _____ ей.
Olga wanted (her) friend to ring her.

In an impersonal construction the verb is used in the third person singular without a definite subject, e.g. мне ка́жется, *it seems to me that*...

A Many impersonal constructions involve the third person singular of the verb and the dative case. Here are some common examples:

Мне ка́жется, что он прав.	*It seems to me that he is right.*
Мне надое́ло рабо́тать.	*I'm fed up of working.*
Нам удало́сь найти́ их дом.	*We managed to find their house.*
Вам нра́вится танцева́ть?	*Do you like dancing?*
Тебе́ хо́чется пить?	*Do you feel like a drink? (=are you thirsty?)*

B Since быть (*to be*) does not exist in the present tense, many impersonal constructions consist only of the dative case and an adverb. Many expressions of *feeling* are made in this way:

Мне хо́лодно.	*I am cold/I feel cold.* (lit.: *to me it is cold*)
Бори́су лу́чше.	*Boris is/feels better.* (lit.: *to Boris it is better*)
Как тебе́ не сты́дно!	*You should be ashamed of yourself!* (lit.: *how to you is it not shameful?*)
Нам бы́ло о́чень интере́сно.	*We found it very interesting.* (lit.: *to us it was very interesting*)

B The verb нра́виться literally means *to please* and it *can* be used with a definite subject:

Мне нра́вится кни́га.	*I like the book* (lit.: *to me the book is pleasing*)
Им нра́вятся кни́ги.	*They like the books.*
Вам понра́вилась экску́рсия?	*Did you like the excursion?* (lit.: *To you did the excursion please?*)

Notice that the object of the English sentence (*book*) is the subject of the Russian sentence (the thing that does the pleasing).

Г The dative case is used with жаль (an impersonal predicate) to mean *sorry*:

Нам жаль ба́бушку.	*We feel sorry for granny.*

Notice that the person you feel sorry for is in the *accusative* case.

➤ **For dative case of nouns, see Units 13 and 14, for adverbs, see Unit 39, for declension of personal pronouns, see Units 48 and 49.**

1 Make sentences from the words in the box which correspond to the translations.

жаль	мне	надоéло✓	нам✓	хóлодно	скýчно
им	хóчется	ей	удалóсь	емý	нрáвится
тебé	пить	вам	собáку	найти ключ	плáвать

e.g. *We're fed up.* → Нам надоéло.

1 *They are bored.*
2 *I am cold.*
3 *She feels sorry for the dog.*
4 *He likes swimming.*
5 *Do you (sing.) feel thirsty?*
6 *Did you (pl.) manage to find the key?*

2 Who feels sorry for whom? Match the phrases on the left with the translations on the right

1	Мне жаль егó.	**a**	*They feel sorry for me.*
2	Нам жаль их.	**b**	*I feel sorry for him.*
3	Тебé жаль её.	**c**	*You feel sorry for her.*
4	Им жаль меня.	**d**	*You feel sorry for us.*
5	Вам жаль нас.	**e**	*We feel sorry for them.*

3 Build sentences explaining who likes what/whom, using the English as a guide.

e.g. Кáтя/нóвая пьéса → Кáте нрáвится нóвая пьéса. *Katya likes the new play.*

1	Он/актрúса	*He likes the actress.*
2	Врач/больнúца	*The doctor likes the hospital.*
3	Профéссор/студéнты	*The professor likes the students.*
4	Вы/экскýрсия	*You liked the excursion.*
5	Я/онá	*I like her.*

4 Some complaints! – Translate them into Russian.

1 *I'm fed up!*
2 *I'm hot!*
3 *I feel worse!*

82 conjunctions

Conjunctions are words which link phrases to make longer phrases or whole sentences (e.g. *and, but, because*).

А И means *and*. It is used to introduce extra information:

Я игра́ю на кла́рнете и на фле́йте. *I play the clarinet and the flute.*

It is not preceded by a comma unless it links phrases with different subjects:

Ма́льчик пла́кал, и никто́ не слы́шал его́.
The boy was crying and no one heard him.

И... и means *both... and*: Он лю́бит и чай и ко́фе. *He likes both tea and coffee.*

А can be translated as *and* or *but*; it gives information which contrasts with other information given, but does not contradict it. It is preceded by a comma.

Я преподаю́ ру́сский язы́к, а он преподаёт биоло́гию.
I teach Russian language but/and he teaches biology.

Но means *but* when the ideas described are not compatible; it has a sense of *despite/however*. It is preceded by a comma.

Она́ не лю́бит духи́, но он дал ей духи́.
She doesn't like perfume, but he gave her perfume.

Она́ обеща́ла позвони́ть, но забы́ла. *She promised to ring, but she forgot.*

To say *or*, use и́ли (no comma!); to say *either... or* use и́ли... и́ли (always a comma between the two parts of the sentence):

Вы хоти́те чай и́ли ко́фе? *Do you want tea or coffee?*

Мы пое́дем и́ли в Гре́цию, и́ли в Ита́лию. *We will either go to Greece or Italy.*

In negative contexts, use ни... ни (always a comma betweeen the two parts of the sentence):

Он не пьёт ни ви́ски, ни вино́. *He drinks neither whisky nor wine.*

Б Что (*that*) is required much more frequently in Russian than in English. It must not be omitted in contexts involving *to say, to think, to believe* etc.:

Я ду́маю, что он в саду́   *I think (that) he is in the garden*
NB что is always preceded by a comma.

В Потому́ что (*because*) is usually preceded by a comma (although you can move the comma to the middle of the phrase if you want to give special emphasis to the clause – *because of the fact that*). A comma always precedes так как (*since*) and appears in the middle of the phrase из-за того́, что (*because*):

Он не прие́дет сего́дня, потому́ что (так как/ из-за того́, что) он бо́лен. *He won't come today because he's ill.*

➤ **For use of что́бы (in order to/that), see Units 79 and 80, for use of е́сли (if), see Units 72 and 73.**

1 Make sentences.

1 Я пью	*both...and*	вино́, во́дку
2 Я не игра́ю	*neither...nor*	кри́кет, футбо́л
3 Я люблю́ о́перу	*and, but*	он, бале́т
4 Я не иду́ на конце́рт	*because*	програ́мма, неинтере́сная
5 Я не зна́ю	*where*	он, рабо́тает

2 Insert commas as necessary.

1 Она́ обеща́ла написа́ть письмо́ но она́ забы́ла.
She promised to write a letter but she forgot.
2 Он изуча́ет матема́тику и фи́зику.
He studies maths and physics.
3 Серге́й печа́лен и никто́ не обраща́ет внима́ния на него́.
Sergei is sad and no one is taking any notice of him.
4 Тури́сты серди́ты потому́ что в гости́нице хо́лодно.
The tourists are angry because the hotel is cold.
5 Дире́ктор ду́мает что клие́нт дово́лен.
The director thinks that the customer is satisfied.

3 Complete the sentences with the appropriate conjunctions from the box.

когда́ где из-за того́, что и́ли ни... ни но а

1 Ма́ма врач, _____ па́па программи́ст.
2 Я переда́м тебе́ письмо́, _____ ты прие́дешь.
3 Что лу́чше, газе́та _____ журна́л?
4 Ситуа́ция серьёзная, _____ тра́нспорта нет.
5 Вы не зна́ете, _____ мо́жно купи́ть моро́женое?
6 Он пригласи́л меня́ в рестора́н, _____ я не хочу́.
7 Де́ти не хотя́т ___ смотре́ть телеви́зор, ___ игра́ть в саду́.

4 Translate into Russian.

1 *I'm glad because he's bought a ticket.*
2 *I want to go to the concert, but there aren't any tickets.*
3 *Do you want two tickets or three?*

Prepositions tell us about the position of things. It is important to know which case is used after each preposition.

A The preposition в means *in* or *at* when it is followed by the prepositional case:

Где он? Он в бáнке	*Where is he? He's at the bank.*
Официáнт рабóтает в ресторáне	*The waiter works in the/at the restaurant.*

Б The preposition в means *into* or *to* when it is followed by the accusative case (i.e. when direction, rather than position, is important):

Кудá он идёт? В банк?	*Where's he going? To the bank?*
Официáнт вхóдит в ресторáн	*The waiter is going into the restaurant.*

В The preposition на means *on* or *at* when it is followed by the prepositional case:

Где ключи́? На столé.	*Where are the keys? On the table.*
Онá на рабóте.	*She's at work.*

Г The preposition на means *on to* or *to* when it is followed by the accusative case (i.e. when direction, rather than position, is important):

Он положи́л ключи́ на стол.	*He put the keys on to the table.*
Онá идёт на рабóту	*She is going to work.*

The following words **cannot** be used with в if you are describing location or motion towards; instead you must use на (even when you want to say *in, into*):

вокзáл	*station*	сéвер	*north*
востóк	*east*	спектáкль	*show*
завóд	*factory*	стадиóн	*stadium*
зáпад	*west*	стáнция	*station*
концéрт	*concert*	у́лица	*street*
лéкция	*lecture*	Урáл	*Urals*
плóщадь	*square*	урóк	*lesson*
пóчта	*post office*	фáбрика	*factory*
рабóта	*work*	экзáмен	*exam*
ры́нок	*market*	юг	*south*

Вчерá мы бы́ли на концéрте.	*Yesterday we were at a concert.*
Лóндон на ю́ге Áнглии.	*London is in the south of England.*

These nouns all combine with the preposition с (+ genitive case) if you want to say *from* (он с Урáла, *he is from the Urals*).

Note that the vowel o is sometimes added to the preposition в when it is followed by a word which starts with a cluster of consonants во Фрáнции *in France*.

➤ **For prepositional case, see Units 17 and 18, for accusative case, see Units 7–9.**

1 **Build sentences to explain where things are.**

e.g. Ключи́/стол → Ключи́ на столе́. *The keys are on the table.*

1	Дом/го́род	*The house is in the town.*
2	Це́рковь/дере́вня	*The church is in the village.*
3	Кни́га/шкаф	*The book is in the cupboard.*
4	Автомоби́ль/у́лица	*The car is in the street.*
5	Компью́тер/о́фис	*The computer is in the office.*
6	Бри́столь/за́пад А́нглии	*Bristol is in the west of England.*
7	По́езд/ста́нция	*The train is at the station.*
8	Тигр/зоопа́рк	*The tiger is in the zoo.*
9	Почтальо́н/по́чта	*The postman is at the post office.*
10	Пиани́ст/конце́рт	*The pianist is at the concert.*

2 **Make sentences to explain who is going where.**

Врач/больни́ца → Врач идёт в больни́цу. *The doctor is going to the hospital.*

1	Секрета́рь/рабо́та	*The secretary is going to work.*
2	Ви́ктор/стадио́н	*Viktor is going to the stadium.*
3	Учи́тель/шко́ла	*The teacher is going to the school.*
4	Студе́нт/ле́кция	*The student is going to the lecture.*
5	Соба́ка/сад	*The dog is going into the garden.*

3 **Put the word in brackets into either the prepositional or the accusative, according to the sense.**

1 Я рабо́таю в _____(шко́ла).
2 Мы живём на _____ (се́вер) А́нглии.
3 Он спеши́т на _____ (рабо́та).
4 Тури́ст на _____ (Кра́сная Пло́щадь).
5 Мы е́дем во _____ (Фра́нция).
6 Пассажи́ры иду́т на _____(вокза́л).
7 Вы отдыха́ете в _____ (Крым).
8 Они́ предпочита́ют пла́вать в _____ (бассе́йн).
9 Сего́дня они́ летя́т в _____ (Москва́).
10 Соба́ка спит в _____ (сад).

Prepositions tell us about the position of things. It is important to know which case is used after each preposition.

А За means *behind* or *beyond*. It is used with the instrumental case to describe location:

За нашим домом большой сад.   *There's a big garden behind our house.*

За полем находится лес.   *Beyond the field there's a forest.*

It is used with the accusative case to describe direction:

Вор спешит за дом.   *The thief hurries behind the house.*

Б Перед means *in front of* and it is used only with the instrumental case:

Автомобиль стоит перед домом.   *The car is standing in front of the house.*

В Между means *between* and it is only used with the instrumental case:

Актёр стоит между актрисой и продюссером.   *The actor is standing between the actress and the producer.*

Г Над means *above* and it is used only with the instrumental case:

Картина висит над камином.   *The picture is hanging above the fireplace.*

Д Под means *under* and it is used with the instrumental if position is being described and accusative if motion is involved:

Кошка сидит под столом.   *The cat is sitting under the table.*

Я кладу ведро под стол.   *I put the bucket under the table.*

Е У means *by* and it is only used with the genitive case:

Вы стоите у двери.   *You are standing by the door.*

Вчера мы были у бабушки.   *Yesterday we were at granny's.*
   (at granny's house; lit.: by granny)

➤ **For prepositional case, see Units 17 and 18, for accusative case, see Units 7–9, for instrumental case, see Units 15 and 16, for use of y in expressions for *to have*, see Unit 63.**

1 Choose the appropriate preposition from the box to complete each sentence. Use the English translation as a guide.

за	между	над	перед	под	у

1 Школа находится _____ церквью и театром.
2 Вчера мы были _____ Виктора.
3 Ключи лежат _____ газетой.
4 Я подожду тебя _____ кинотеатром.
5 Зеркало висит _____ столом.
6 Туалеты находятся _____ зданием.

1 *The school is situated between the church and the theatre.*
2 *Yesterday we were at Viktor's.*
3 *The keys are under the newspaper.*
4 *I will wait for you in front of the cinema*
5 *The mirror hangs above the table.*
6 *The toilets are behind the building.*

2 Olga's not sure where things are... Build sentences explaining where she should look:

e.g.

Ольга/кошка/диван/дверь. → Ольга думает, что кошка под диваном, но она у двери. *Olga thinks the cat is under the sofa, but it is by the door.*

1 Ольга/ручка/книга/телефон
Olga thinks the pen is under the books, but it is by the telephone.

2 Ольга/билеты/зеркало/паспорт
Olga thinks the tickets are behind the mirror, but they are under the passport.

3 Ольга/автомобиль/дом/дом
Olga thinks the car is in front of the house, but it is behind it.

4 Ольга/портрет/камин/стол
Olga thinks the portrait is above the fireplace, but it is above the table.

5 Ольга/холодильник/шкаф/дверь
Olga thinks the fridge is between the cupboards, but it is behind the door.

Prepositions tell us about the position of things. It is important to know which case is used after each preposition.

A До means *as far as*. It is followed by the genitive case:

Идите до парка и вы увидите церковь.	*Walk as far as the park and you will see the church.*

Б Из means *from* in the sense of *from out of* and it is followed by the genitive case:

Врач выходит из больницы.	*The doctor comes out of the hospital.*
Борис из Москвы.	*Boris is from Moscow.*

В К means *towards* or *to the house of* and it is always followed by the dative case:

Милиционер спешит к хулиганам.	*The policeman hurries towards the hooligans.*
Сегодня мы идём к друзьям.	*Today we are going to some friends (to the house of friends/to see friends).*

Г Мимо means *past* and it is always followed by the genitive case:

Студенты проходят мимо университета.	*The students are walking past the university.*

Д От means *from* in the sense of *away from*:

Официант отошёл от стола.	*The waiter moved away from the table.*
Она получила письмо от друга.	*She received a letter from her friend.*

Е По means *along* (or *round*, as in the example) and is followed by the dative case:

Мы идём по главной улице.	*We are walking along the main street.*
Он любит ходить по магазинам.	*He likes to go round the shops.*

It is also found in expressions with *telephone, television, radio, post*:

говорить по телефону	*to speak on the telephone*

Ж Через means *across* (or *through*, as in the example) and it is followed by the accusative case:

Бабушка медленно переходит через улицу.	*Granny walks slowly across the street.*
Можно заказать билеты через гида.	*You can order tickets through the guide.*

➤ **For accusative case, see Units 7–9, for dative case, see Units 13 and 14, for genitive case, see Units 10–12.**

1 Choose the appropriate preposition from the box to complete the sentence. Use the English translations as a guide.

> из   к   мимо   от   по   через

1 Отойди́те _____ две́ри!
2 Спортсме́н бежи́т __ фи́нишу.
3 Тури́сты гуля́ют ___ у́лице.
4 Спортсме́н бежи́т _____ зри́телей.
5 Я ду́маю, что он ____ Ки́ева.
6 Автомоби́ль е́дет____ мост.

1 *Move away from the door!*
2 *The sportsman is running towards the finishing line.*
3 *The tourists are strolling along the street.*
4 *The sportsman is running past the spectators.*
5 *I think he's from Kiev.*
6 *The car is driving over the bridge.*

2 Put the word in brackets into the appropriate case.

1 Здесь на́до переходи́ть че́рез _____ (у́лица).
2 Подходи́те к _____ (ка́сса), пожа́луйста.
3 От _____ (кто) вы получи́ли письмо́?
4 Джиова́нни из _____ (Ита́лия).
5 Проходи́те ми́мо _____ (ка́сса) в теа́тр.

3 Translate into Russian.

1 *She doesn't like walking round the shops.*
2 *The professor is hurrying towards the students.*
3 *The dog is crossing the street.*

In expressions of time from a second to a day, в and the accusative are required in order to say *at* or *on*, but if you want to talk about days (e.g. *on Mondays*) по and the dative are needed.

A B and the accusative are used in expressions with *second, moment, minute, hour*:

В э́тот моме́нт он по́нял, *At that moment he realized that*
что забы́л свой па́спорт. *he had forgotten his passport.*

Note that expressions such as *Just a moment!* are used without the preposition and with the accusative: Мину́точку! *Hang on a minute/Just a minute!*

Б Days of the week are used with в and the accusative when they are singular:

в понеде́льник	*on Monday*
во вто́рник	*on Tuesday*
в сре́ду	*on Wednesday*
в четве́рг	*on Thursday*
в пя́тницу	*on Friday*
в суббо́ту	*on Saturday*
в воскресе́нье	*on Sunday*

Note also:

в э́тот день	*on that day*
в мой день рожде́ния	*on my birthday*

B When days are used in the plural, по and the dative are needed:

по понеде́льникам	*on Mondays*
по вто́рникам	*on Tuesdays*
по сре́дам	*on Wednesdays*
по четверга́м	*on Thursdays*
по пя́тницам	*on Fridays*
по суббо́там	*on Saturdays*
по воскресе́ньям	*on Sundays*

➤ For telling the time according to twelve- and twenty-four hour clocks, see Units 45.

1 Complete the sentences on the left and match them with those on the right.

1 В _____ я игра́ю в гольф.
2 По _____ я рабо́таю в о́фисе.
3 В _____ зазвони́л телефо́н.
4 В _____ мы идём в кинотеа́тр.
5 По _____ я занима́юсь спо́ртом.
6 По _____ я хожу́ в це́рковь.
7 По _____ он пла́вает в бассе́йне.
8 По _____ гид отдыха́ет до́ма.
9 В _____ мы пое́дем в Гре́цию.
10 В _____ вы пое́дете в Санкт-Петербу́рг.

a On Wednesdays I do sport.
b On Friday we are going to the cinema.
c On Sundays I go to church.
d On Thursdays the guide rests at home.
e On Monday I am playing golf.
f On Friday we are going to Greece.
g On Tuesdays I work at the office.
h On Saturday you are going to St Petersburg.
i On Thursdays he swims in the pool.
j At that moment the telephone rang.

2 Look at Olga's diary for the week and then answer the questions that follow.

ПОНЕДЕЛЬНИК	ПЯТНИЦА
Рабо́та	Рабо́та
ВТОРНИК	СУББОТА
Го́род	Рабо́та
СРЕДА	ВОСКРЕСЕНЬЕ
Кинотеа́тр	К друзья́м
ЧЕТВЕРГ	
Бассе́йн	

1 В каки́е дни О́льга рабо́тает?
2 В како́й день О́льга идёт в го́род?
3 В како́й день О́льга идёт к друзья́м?

English does not always use a preposition with time phrases (such as *this week*, *next year*), but Russian always does.

A Weeks are used with на and the prepositional case:

на э́той неде́ле	*this week*
на про́шлой неде́ле	*last week*
на бу́дущей неде́ле	*next week*
на сле́дующей неде́ле	*the following week*

Б Months are used with в and the prepositional:

в январе́	*in January*	в ию́ле	*in July*
в феврале́	*in February*	в а́вгусте	*in August*
в ма́рте	*in March*	в сентябре́	*in September*
в апре́ле	*in April*	в октябре́	*in October*
в ма́е	*in May*	в ноябре́	*in November*
в ию́не	*in June*	в декабре́	*in December*

Note also:

в э́том ме́сяце	*this month*
в про́шлом ме́сяце	*last month*
в бу́дущем ме́сяце	*next month*
в сле́дующем ме́сяце	*the following month*

B Years are used with в and the prepositional:

в э́том году́	*this year*
в про́шлом году́	*last year*
в бу́дущем году́	*next year*
в сле́дующем году́	*the following year*

The same construction is also used for centuries:

в двадца́том ве́ке	*in the twentieth century*
в два́дцать пе́рвом ве́ке	*in the twenty-first century*

➤ **For dates, see Unit 46.**

1 **Explain when you will see each other.**

e.g. Мы уви́димся/янва́рь → Мы уви́димся в январе́. *We will see one another in January.*

1 Мы уви́димся/э́тот год
2 Мы уви́димся/э́та неде́ля
3 Мы уви́димся/март
4 Мы уви́димся/ию́нь
5 Мы уви́димся/бу́дущий год
6 Мы уви́димся/февра́ль
7 Мы уви́димся/э́тот ме́сяц
8 Мы уви́димся/а́вгуст
9 Мы уви́димся/бу́дущая не́деля
10 Мы уви́димся/21-й век

2 **Explain in which month people's birthdays are.**

e.g. День рожде́ния/ба́бушка/2 → День рожде́ния ба́бушки в феврале́.

1 День рожде́ния/Серге́й/3
2 День рожде́ния/А́ня/4
3 День рожде́ния/Татья́на/9
4 День рожде́ния/сестра́/12
5 День рожде́ния/брат/1
6 День рожде́ния/муж/10
7 День рожде́ния/Ка́тя/8
8 День рожде́ния/Вади́м/5
9 День рожде́ния/Зо́я/6
10 День рожде́ния/И́горь/11

3 **Translate into Russian (useful vocabulary on the right).**

1 *In December we like to ski.*   ката́ться на лы́жах
2 *In August we like to lie on the beach.*   лежа́ть на пля́же
3 *In February we like to stay at home.*   сиде́ть до́ма
4 *In July we like to walk in the country.* гуля́ть в дере́вне

This unit covers the time prepositions *during, until, over, after, since, in* and *ago*.

A The phrase во время followed by the genitive case is the Russian way of saying *during*. (**NB** Note that во время is written as two separate words – unlike вовремя, *on time*):

Во время концерта Виктор   *Viktor was sound asleep*
крепко спал.   *during the concert.*

Б As well as meaning *as far as*, до also means *before* and *until*. It is followed by the genitive case:

Мы там были до семи часов. *We were there before/until 7 o'clock.*

В To explain the time over which something is done, use the preposition за with the accusative case (sometimes we would say *in* here, rather than *over*):

Она написала книгу за 4 недели. *She wrote the book in 4 weeks.*

Г После means after and it is followed by the genitive case:

После обеда мы пойдём в город. *After lunch we will go into town.*

Д The preposition с indicates *since* or *from* a certain time. It is followed by the genitive case. Note that it is often used in expressions with the present tense to mean *has been, have been*:

Я работаю с раннего утра. *I have been working since early morning.*

Е As well as meaning *across*, через means *in* of time in the sense of 'after an amount of time has elapsed'. It is followed by the accusative case.

Поезд отходит через десять минут. *The train leaves in ten minutes.*

Ж Назад means *ago*. It is not followed by anything, since it comes at the end of the time phrase:

Они переехали в новый дом *They moved to their new*
два месяца назад. *house two months ago.*

NB Remember that prepositions are for use with nouns, not verbs. To use a time preposition with a verb, introduce an extra phrase between the preposition and the verb, called a compound conjunction, e.g.:

Preposition + noun	Time preposition phrase + verb
До обеда мы лежали на пляже. *Before lunch we lay on the beach.*	До **того, как** мы пошли в ресторан, мы лежали на пляже. *Before we went to the restaurant we lay on the beach.*

1 Choose the appropriate preposition from the box to match the sense of the phrase (hint: you will need some of them more than once).

до после через назад с за во время

1 _____ экску́рсии тури́сты внима́тельно слу́шали.
2 _____ э́то вре́мя, он никого́ не ви́дел.
3 Поса́дка начнётся _____ час.
4 Фильм на́чался 15 мину́т _____.
5 _____ ле́кции мы пошли́ в кафе́.
6 _____ утра́ _____ ве́чера.
7 Он прочита́л всю кни́гу _____ два дня.

1 *During the excursion the tourists listened attentively.*
2 *Over this time he saw no one.*
3 *Boarding will start in an hour.*
4 *The film began 15 minutes ago.*
5 *After the lecture we set off to the cafe.*
6 *From morning till evening.*
7 *He read the whole book in two days.*

2 Complete the sentences on the left and match them with those on the right.

1 _____ вы ушли́, мы поу́жинали.
2 _____ обе́да он ничего́ не ел.
3 Он отремонти́ровал маши́ну _____ час.
4 Авто́бус прие́дет _____ 20 мину́т.
5 Они́ ушли́ два часа́ _____.
6 _____ у́жина мы спа́ли.
7 Я здесь _____ утра́.
8 Вы написа́ли письмо́ _____ час.
9 _____ полёта не кури́ть!
10 _____ фильм на́чался, мы поу́жинали.

a *He repaired the car in an hour.*
b *They left two hours ago.*
c *No smoking during the flight.*
d *During lunch he ate nothing.*
e *Before the film started we had supper.*
f *The bus will arrive in 20 minutes.*
g *After you had left we had supper.*
h *You wrote the letter in an hour.*
i *Before supper we slept.*
j *I have been here since this morning.*

This unit covers the prepositions *without, except, about, according to, opposite/against* and *for*.

А Без means *without* and is followed by the genitive case:

чай без са́хара   *tea without sugar*

Б The preposition кро́ме means *except(for)/apart from* and it is followed by the genitive case:

Кро́ме Ви́ктора, все пришли́   *Except for Viktor everyone*
во́время.   *arrived on time.*

В О means *about* in the sense of *concerning* and it is followed by the prepositional case:

Мы говори́ли о пого́де.   *We talked about the weather.*

Note that those nouns which have the irregular prepositional ending in -ý (саду́, *in the garden*) form their prepositional regularly with the preposition о: он говори́т о са́де, *he is talking about the garden.*

Г The preposition по is used with the dative case and means *according to*:

по стати́стике   *according to the statistics*
по-мо́ему   *in my opinion (according to me)*

Д При is followed by the prepositional case and has several meanings: *by, near, attached to, in the presence of, during the reign of*. For example:

Он сказа́л э́то при мне.   *He said this in my presence.*
При коммуни́зме.   *Under (i.e. during the time of)*
                               communism.

Е Про́тив (sometimes напро́тив) is followed by the genitive case and means *opposite* or *against* (in the sense of *opposed to*):

Шко́ла нахо́дится про́тив   *The school is situated opposite*
теа́тра.   *the theatre.*
Я не про́тив э́того.   *I am not opposed to this.*

Ж За is followed by the accusative case when it means *for* in the sense of *on behalf of, in support of, in response to*:

Спаси́бо за пода́рок.   *Thank you for the present.*
Я за э́то предложе́ние.   *I'm for this suggestion.*

З Для means *for* in the sense of *meant for, intended for*:

Э́тот пода́рок для вас   *This present is for you.*

И На and the accusative and в and the accusative mean *for* in the sense of *to gain admission to* an event or a place:

Я купи́л(а) биле́ты на   *I bought tickets for the*
о́перу/в теа́тр.   *opera/theatre.*

> **For prepositional case (and irregulars), see Unit 17, for use of c and instrumental, see Unit 15.**

1 **Choose the appropriate preposition from the box to match the sense of the phrase.**

без в для за кроме на о по при против

1 Он любит всех композиторов, _____ Бетховена.
2 Это книга _____ меня? Спасибо!
3 Он всегда пьёт кофе _____ молока.
4 _____ нашего дома красивый парк.
5 Вы уже купили билеты ___ музей?
6 _____-моему, это не правда
7 Мы долго говорили ___погоде.
8 Он целовал её ____ всех.
9 Спасибо ____ деньги.
10 Где билеты ___ матч?

1 *He loves all composers except Beethoven.*
2 *Is this book for me? Thank you!*
3 *He always drinks coffee without milk.*
4 *Opposite our house there's a beautiful park.*
5 *Have you already bought the tickets to the museum?*
6 *In my opinion this is not true.*
7 *We talked for a long time about the weather.*
8 *He kissed her in front of (in the presence of) everyone.*
9 *Thank you for the money.*
10 *Where are the tickets for the match?*

2 **The following sentences have been jumbled. Put the words in the correct order and match the sentences with their translations.**

1 мы за поблагодарили подарок её   **a** *They live in a house opposite the hospital.*

2 доме они в напротив живут больницы   **b** *Are you for or against this idea?*

3 или за идей против этой вы   **c** *They went to the disco without me!*

4 все Бориса довольны кроме   **d** *We thanked her for the present.*

5 меня ходили дискотеку они на без   **e** *Apart from Boris everyone iscontent.*

3 **Translate into Russian.**
1 *I have bought some perfume for her.*
2 *Thank you for the suggestion.*
3 *What did you talk about?*

90 verbs + prepositions

This unit summarizes common verbs which must be followed by a preposition.

A The preposition в is used:
- After the verb игра́ть to indicate which *game* or *sport* is being played; the *game* or *sport* must be put into the accusative case: игра́ть в гольф, *to play golf*, игра́ть в ка́рты, *to play cards*.
- After the verb смотре́ть to indicate something looked through or into: смотре́ть в окно́, *to look out of the window*, смотре́ть в зе́ркало, *to look into the mirror*.

Б The preposition за and the accusative case is used with the following verbs:

благодари́ть за (e.g. пода́рок)	*to thank for (e.g. a present)*
нака́зывать за (e.g. оши́бку)	*to punish for (e.g. a mistake)*
плати́ть за (e.g. поку́пки)	*to pay for (e.g. the shopping)*
продава́ть за (e.g. 50 рубле́й)	*to sell for (e.g. 50 roubles)*

В The preposition к and the dative case is used with the following verbs:

гото́виться к (e.g. экза́менам)	*to prepare for (e.g. exams)*
относи́ться к (e.g. други́м)	*to behave towards (e.g. others)*

Г The preposition на and the accusative case is used with the following verbs:

жа́ловаться на (e.g. слу́жбу)	*to complain about (e.g. the service)*
наде́яться на (e.. лу́чшее)	*to hope for (e.g. the best)*
отвеча́ть на (e.g. вопро́с)	*to answer (e.g. a question)*
серди́ться на (e.g. меня́)	*to get cross with (e.g. me)*
смотре́ть на (e.g. ка́рту)	*to look at (e.g. the map)*

Д The preposition на and the prepositional case is used to indicate which musical instrument is played:

игра́ть на кла́рнете	*to play the clarinet*
игра́ть на гита́ре	*to play the guitar*

Е The preposition с is used with the genitive case in the phrase *to begin at*

Дава́йте начнём с нача́ла. *Let's begin at the beginning.*

Ж The preposition у (and the genitive case) is used after verbs of *taking, buying, stealing, requesting* to indicate the person from whom something is *taken, bought, stolen, requested*:

Он взял у меня́ 10 рубле́й. *He took ten roubles from me.*
Мы купи́ли у А́ни буты́лку молока́. *We bought a bottle of milk from Anya.*

➤ **For prepositions used after Verbs of Motion, see Unit 71.**

1 Choose the appropriate preposition from the box to complete the sense, then match each sentence with its translation.

в	за	к	на	с	у

1 Он играет ____ футбол.

2 Мы купили машину ___Бориса.

3 Катя играет ___флейте.

4 Ты поблагодарил нас ___ приглашение.

5 Мы начали ___ первой страницы.

6 Врач очень хорошо относится ___ своим пациентам.

7 Посмотрите ___окно!

8 Посмотрите ___фотографа!

a *Look out of the window!*

b *The doctor behaves very well towards his patients.*

c *He plays football.*

d *Look at the photographer!*

e *Katya plays the flute.*

f *We bought the car from Boris.*

g *We began at the first page.*

h *You thanked us for the invitation.*

2 Look at the drawings and make sentences with the verb играть to describe what they are doing.

1 Борис играет _____ _____

2 Татьяна играет _____ _____

3 Translate into Russian.

1 *We are cross with you.*

2 *We are hoping for the best.*

3 *He is answering my question.*

4 *It is not necessary to complain about the letter.*

5 *Pay for the books at the cash desk.*

6 *They are selling the chair for 200 roubles.*

7 *We are buying the chair from Anya.*

8 *Do you play the guitar?*

9 *Look at the dog!*

10 *We usually start at the first page.*

taking it further

And finally, here are details of books and websites to help you develop your command of the Russian language:

Books

The first of the four books below deals with language to approximately GCSE standard; the others take you to a more advanced level.

Teach Yourself Russian, by Daphne West, Hodder & Stoughton, 2001 (ISBN 0 340 80156 5)

A Comprehensive Russian Grammar, by Terence Wade, Blackwell, 1996 (ISBN 0 631 17502 4)

Tranzit, by Daphne West and Michael Ransome, Bramcote Press, 1996 (ISBN 1 900405 00 8)

Kompas, by Michael Ransome, Daphne West and Rachel Smith, Bramcote Press, 2002 (ISBN 1 900405 08 3)

Websites

The following are all 'megasites' with many links to web pages on a huge range of topics related to Russia:

Reesweb: http://www.ucis.pitt.edu/reesweb

Russophilia: http://www.russophilia.co.au/flash.html

Sher's Russian Index: http://www.websher.net

Slavophilia: http://www.slavophilia.net/

key to exercises

Unit 1

1 1 e, 2 a, 3 b, 4 d, 5 c **2** 1 у, 2 т, 3 ж, 4 н, 5 р 6 а, 7 ф, 8 к, 9 е 10 ó **3** 1 11.30, 2 1 (ОРТ)

Unit 2

1 1 актри́са   2 балери́на   3 банки́р   4 до́ктор
5 журнали́ст   6 компью́тер   7 ме́неджер   8 но́вый
9 пиани́ст   10 программи́ст   11 профе́ссор   12 соба́ка
13 студе́нт   14 тури́ст   15 хорошо́
2 Ваня наконец спрашивает Маш<u>ю</u> (*never* ю *after* ш! *write* у *instead!*)   «Где собак<u>ы</u>?» (*never* ы *after* к! *Write* и *instead!*)   «Почему они молч<u>ят</u>?» (*never* я *after* ч! *Write* а *instead!*) Маша не отвечает? Ваня берёт свои книг<u>ы</u> (*never* ы *after* к! *Write* и *instead!*)   и уходит к дру́гу, Саш<u>ю</u> (*never* ю *after* ш! *Write* у *instead!*).   *Vanya finally asks Masha 'Where are the dogs? Why are they silent?' Masha does not reply. Vanya takes his books and goes off to his friend's, Sasha.*

Unit 3

1 1 ср, 2 м, 3 ж, 4 ж, 5 ж, 6 ср, 7 ср, 8 ж, 9 м, 10 м   **2**   1 компью́тер (м) 2 ра́дио (ср) 3 соба́ка (ж) 4 де́рево (ср)   5 автомоби́ль (м)   6 ла́мпа (ж)   **3** In list M the rogue is ви́за (ж), in list Ж the rogue is инжене́р (м), in list CP the rogue is эне́ргия (ж)

Unit 4

1 1 husband 2 Viktor 3 Olga 4 dog 5 student   **2** 1 соба́ка 2 теа́тр 3 конце́рт 4 кни́га 5 сын e.g. *Usually Vladimir holidays in Yalta.*   1 *The dog is playing in the garden.*   2 *The theatre is very beautiful*   3 *When does the concert start?*   4 *Where is my book?*   5 *My son is a very good footballer.*

3 1 Лéкция   2 мéсто   3 Студéнт   4 Дéдушка   5 Автомобúль   6 стадиóн

Unit 5

1 1 газéты *Most of all Viktor likes to read newspapers*   2 мáрки *Stamps are expensive*   3 компьютеры *I don't know where the computers are*   4 кинофúльмы *Yes, I often watch films*   5 телесериáлы *I don't understand why he watches television serials*   **2** 1 балерúны 2 журналúсты 3 собáки 4 самолёты 5 истóрии 6 свидáния 7 инженéры 8 мéсяцы 9 бутылки 10 пúсьма   **3** 1 жéнщины   2 мáльчики   3 дéвушки   4 мужчúны   5 кóшки   6 лóшади   7 моря   8 деклáрации   9 здáния   10 герóи   **4** 1 с, 2 а, 3 b

Unit 6

1 1 брáтья   2 именá   3 дéти   4 мáтери   5 адресá 6 глазá 7 дерéвья 8 друзья 9 люди 10 городá

2 Кроссвóрд

Unit 7

1 1 television 2 water 3 cat 4 Kremlin 5 watch   **2** 1 d 4, 2 a 1, 3 e 5, 4 b 2, 5 с 3   **3**   1 дочь   2 бáбушку   3 мать   4 дядю   5 тётю   6 стол   7 пóле   8 октрытку   9 лóшадь   10 брáта

Unit 8

1 1 Underline boats, circle, seagulls   2 underline tickets   3 underline purchases, circle customers   4 underline books, newspapers 5 circle dogs   **2** 1 телефóны   2 здáния   3 бутылки 4 поля   5 мáрки   **3** 1 инженéров   2 медсестёр   3 футболúстов   4 балерúн   5 врачéй   **4**   1 корóв   2 музыкáнтов   3 лóдки   4 магазúны   5 птиц

Unit 9

1 Что вы лю́бите бо́льше, 1 дере́вья/берега́ 2 поезда́/трактора́ 3 сту́лья/цвета́ 4 дома́/города́ **2** 1 b 4, 2 e 3, 3 a 5, 4 d 1, 5 c 2 **3** ✓ города́, дома́, люде́й и номера́ ✖ поезда́ и вечера́

Unit 10

1 1 cheese 2 ham 3 Italy 4 tourist 5 Igor, paper **2** 1 Э́то соба́ка Бори́са 2 Э́то автомоби́ль Андре́я 3 Э́то телефо́н А́нны 4 Э́то ра́дио И́горя **3** 1 вина́ 2 сы́ра 3 икры́ 4 ча́я 5 во́дки **4** 1 ветчины́ 2 пи́ва 3 хле́ба 4 говя́дины 5 шокола́да

Unit 11

1 1 ма́льчиков 2 студе́нтов 3 книг 4 пи́сем 5 помидо́ров **2** 1 часо́в 2 рек 3 музе́ев 4 танцо́ров 5 двере́й 6 море́й 7 гости́ниц 8 ня́нь 9 геро́ев 10 строи́телей **3** 1 апельси́нов 2 конфе́т 3 спи́чек 4 сигаре́т 5 бана́нов **4** 1 мно́го ста́нций 2 буке́т роз 3 нет ма́рок 4 гру́ппа враче́й 5 па́чка докуме́нтов

Unit 12

1 1 бра́тьев 2 дере́вьев 3 дете́й 4 звёзд 5 городо́в 6 англича́н 7 сынове́й 8 дочере́й 9 гра́ждан 10 ли́стьев **2** 1 сту́льев 2 апельси́нов 3 откры́ток 4 блу́зок 5 конве́ртов 6 ру́чек 7 сувени́ров 8 домо́в 9 я́блок 10 пи́сем **3** 1 лист 2 мать 3 гости́ница 4 англича́нин 5 фотогра́фия 6 у́хо 7 бу́лка 8 автомоби́ль 9 вре́мя 10 челове́к

Unit 13

1 дру́гу Ви́ктору тёте дя́де племя́ннику **2** 1 Он дал кни́гу Светла́не 2 Дочь дала́ духи́ ма́тери 3 Он дал цветы́ медсестре́ 4 А́ня дала́ мотоци́кл Андре́ю 5 Она́ дала́ письмо́ дире́ктору **3** 1 врачу́ 2 журнали́сту 3 И́горю 4 по́лю 5 у́лице 6 Ита́лии 7 Зо́е 8 ку́хне 9 писа́телю 10 свекро́ви **4** ма́тери Татья́не бра́ту Константи́ну дру́гу Анто́ну

Unit 14

1 1 Касси́рша даёт сда́чу клие́нтам 2 Ученики́ даю́т кни́ги учителя́м 3 Медсестра́ даёт лека́рство пацие́нтам 4 Гид даёт биле́ты англича́нам 5 Он даёт пода́рки друзья́м **2** 1 трамва́ям 2 дере́вьям 3 карти́нам

4 худо́жникам   5 сыновья́м 6 почтальо́нам 7
преподава́телям 8 зда́ниям 9 лошадя́м   10 официа́нткам
3   1 e 3, 2 a 1, 3 d 5, 4 c 4, 5 b 2

Unit 15

1   *In the evening I am going by _train_ with _Elena_ to Viktor's. Viktor
works in Novgorod, as an _architect_. Viktor's interested in _sport_. In
summer he plays tennis with _Sasha_ twice a week, when it's fine.*   **2**
Ве́чером я е́ду по́ездом с Е́леной к Ви́ктору. Ви́ктор
рабо́тает в Но́вгороде, архите́ктом. Ви́ктор интересу́ется
спо́ртом. Ле́том он игра́ет в те́ннис с Са́шей два ра́за в
неде́лю.   **3**   1 хле́бом 2 сала́том 3 карто́шкой 4 молоко́м
5 лимо́ном   6 пече́ньем   **4** 1 И́горем   2 профе́ссором   3
Мари́ей   4 дру́гом   5 Ка́тей

Unit 16

1   1 апте́ками   2 зда́ниями   3 предме́тами   4 писа́телями
5 откры́тиями   6 дере́вьями   7 друзья́ми   8 экску́рсиями
9 дочерьми́ 10 компью́терами   **2**   1 Ири́на интересу́ется
симфо́ниями   2 Валенти́н интересу́ется фи́льмами   3
Архите́ктор интересу́ется о́кнами   4 Гитари́ст
интересу́ется гита́рами   5 Студе́нт интересу́ется
писа́телями   **3**   1 суп с помидо́рами   2 сала́т с огурца́ми
(fleeting vowel! see Unit 5)   3 торт с оре́хами   4 моро́женое
с фру́ктами

Unit 17

1   1 Врач рабо́тает в больни́це   2 Архите́ктор рабо́тает в
зда́нии   3 Моря́к рабо́тает на мо́ре   4 Официа́нт
рабо́тает в рестора́не   5 Садо́вник рабо́тает в саду́.   **2**   1
Самолёт в аэропорту́   2 Ви́за в па́спорте   3 Шу́ба в
шкафу́   4 Компью́тер на столе́   5 Мадри́д в Испа́нии   **3**
1 ме́сте   2 бассе́йне   3 автомоби́ле   4 лаборато́рии   5
льду́   6 музе́е   7 трамва́е   8 по́чте   9 ку́хне   10 по́ле   **4**
1 c, 2 a, 3 e, 4 b, 5 d

Unit 18

1   1 дере́внях   2 города́х   3 це́нтрах   4 стра́нах   5 места́х
6 парфюме́риях   7 портфе́лях   8 поля́х 9 номера́х 10
сту́льях   **2**   1 Продавцы́ рабо́тают в магази́нах   2
Студе́нты у́чатся в университе́тах   3 Фе́рмеры рабо́тают
на фе́рмах   4 Хи́мики рабо́тают в лаборато́риях   5
Учителя́ рабо́тают в шко́лах   **3**   Тури́сты живу́т в
гости́ницах и в ке́мпингах. Они́ прово́дят некото́рое вре́мя

в музе́ях, в галере́ях, в собо́рах и к концу́ дня, в универма́гах. Они́ то́же прово́дят не́которое вре́мя в клу́бах, в са́унах и в рестора́нах.

Unit 19

1 1 d 3, 2 a 5, 3 e 4, 4 c 2, 5 b 1 **2** 1 Genitive plural 2 a врач b актёр c профе́ссор d компью́тер e учи́тель **3** 1 Бори́с зна́ет <u>бра́та</u> (animate!) Ива́на. 2 Вы хоти́те смотре́ть <u>телеви́зор</u>? 3 Она́ купи́ла <u>сту́лья</u> 4 Ви́ктор уви́дел <u>друзе́й</u> (animate!) в теа́тре 5 Мы заказа́ли <u>ку́рицу</u> с ри́сом. **4** 1 Серге́й лю́бит де́рево. 2 Мы живём в го́роде 3 О́льга дала́ Вади́му карти́ну 4 Я зна́ю студе́нтов 5 Я люблю́ е́здить по́ездом с друзья́ми 6 Он смо́трит фильм с бра́том 7 А́нна рабо́тает медсестро́й в больни́це.

Unit 20

1 1 высо́кая стро́йная же́нщина 2 ма́ленький то́лстый мужчи́на **2** 1c, 2a, 3d, 4e, 5b **3** 1 краси́вая шко́ла 2 жёлтое окно́ 3 све́жее молоко́ 4 хоро́ший журнали́ст 5 до́брое у́тро

Unit 21

1 1 <u>у́треннюю</u> 2 <u>ни́жняя</u> 3 <u>си́няя, ле́тняя</u> 4 <u>сосе́дний</u> 5 <u>за́втрашняя</u> **2** 1 плоха́я 2 после́дняя 3 нового́дние 4 молодо́е 5 ка́рие 6 большо́е **3** 1e 2a 3d 4c 5b **4** 1 молода́я актри́са 2 други́е теа́тры 3 ле́тняя програ́мма 4 плохо́е у́тро 5 после́дняя пробле́ма

Unit 22

1 1 на́ши 2 ва́ши 3 Его́ 4 твой 5 Их 6 Моя́ 7 Твой 8 её, их 9 Наш **2** 1c 2d 3b 4a 5e **3** 1 ваш 2 мой 3 ваш 4 моя́, мой **4** 1 моя́ 2 на́ши 3 ваш 4 твой 5 их

Unit 23

1 *Last year we set off on holiday in <u>our</u> car. Unfortunately Ivan lost <u>his</u> passport before we reached <u>our</u> destination. My brother, Nikolai, tried to help him find it. Nikolai is a very impatient person and soon lost <u>his</u> patience with Ivan. While they were arguing, I looked in his suitcase and found that his passport was right at the bottom. How I love <u>my</u> brothers!* **2** 1 Её 2 свой 3 Мой, свой 4 На́ши, свой 5 Их, своё **3** 1 Их дом в го́роде 2 Они́ лю́бят свой дом 3 Мы лю́бим ваш дом 4 Их мать лю́бит наш дом 5 Дом Ива́на? Я люблю́ его́ дом!

Unit 24

1 Вчера́ мы бы́ли в го́роде. В рестора́не мы ви́дели на́шего дру́га, Ива́на. Он уже́ сде́лал свои́ поку́пки. Он показа́л нам свой но́вый сви́тер, дороги́е джи́нсы и шика́рный пиджа́к **2** 1 большу́ю соба́ку 2 но́вый дива́н 3 пуши́стого кро́лика 4 дереву́нный стол 5 но́вое окно́ 6 вку́сный торт 7 шика́рную ю́бку 8 интере́сную кни́гу 9 купа́льный костю́м 10 си́нюю бро́шку **3** 1 мою́ сестру́ 2 молодо́го профе́ссора 3 дре́внего писа́теля 4 интере́сную актри́су 5 ску́чного журнали́ста

Unit 25

1 1 свои́х 2 краси́вые 3 молоды́х 4 истори́ческие 5 но́вых **2** 1 больши́х соба́к 2 краси́вых лошаде́й 3 зелёные дере́вья 4 дре́вние дома́ 5 стра́нных птиц 6 свои́х бра́тьев 7 молоды́х ко́шек 8 ма́ленькие кварти́ры 9 иностра́нные города́ 10 изве́стных писа́телей **3** 1 ма́леньких соба́к 2 хоро́шие костю́мы 3 ва́ши кни́ги 4 но́вые о́кна 5 интере́сные кассе́ты

Unit 26

1 На́ша шко́ла нахо́дится недалеко́ от краси́вого па́рка. Нале́во от на́шей шко́лы есть больша́я апте́ка, где рабо́тает мать моего́ дру́га, Ива́на. Друг мое́й сестры́ то́же рабо́тает в э́той большо́й апте́ке **2** 1 ма́ло/ру́сской во́дки 2 мно́го/францу́зского вина́ 3 ма́ло/кита́йского ри́са 4 мно́го/вку́сного сала́та 5 ма́ло/све́жей колбасы́ **3** 1 Э́то соба́ка высо́кой стро́йной же́нщины 2 Э́то ко́шка ма́ленького то́лстого мужчи́ны

Unit 27

1 1 Нале́во от у́тренних газе́т 2 Напра́во от на́ших велосипе́дов 3 Напра́во от дороги́х ю́бок 4 Нале́во от деревя́нных сту́льев 5 Нале́во от огро́мных зда́ний **2** 1 гру́ппа италья́нских тури́стов 2 гру́ппа изве́стных враче́й 3 гру́ппа но́вых студе́нтов 4 гру́ппа пожилы́х люде́й 5 гру́ппа серьёзных исто́риков **3** 1c 2a 3d 4h 5b 6g 7e 8f

Unit 28

1 1 ру́сскому студе́нту 2 больно́й стару́шке 3 пре́жнему ме́неджеру 4 на́шей ма́тери 5 молодо́му пиани́сту **2** 1 Татья́на идёт к краси́вой карти́не 2 И́горь идёт к дре́вней ва́зе 3 Вади́м идёт к большо́му

мосту́   4 А́ня идёт к сосе́днему до́му   5 Па́вел идёт к
но́вой лаборато́рии   **3** 1 Же́нщина даёт конфе́ту
большо́й соба́ке   2 Мужчи́на даёт ры́бу ма́ленькой ко́шке

Unit 29

1 1b 2d 3e 4a 5c   **2** 1 твои́м дочеря́м   2 на́шим учителя́м
3 молоды́м соба́кам   4 пре́жним директора́м   5 ру́сским
студе́нтам   **3** 1 Официа́нт подхо́дит к больши́м стола́м
2 Архите́ктор подхо́дит к ма́леньким о́кнам   3 Татья́на
подхо́дит к но́вым о́фисам   4 Ка́тя подхо́дит к свои́м
де́тям   5 Ива́н подхо́дит к ста́рым друзья́м

Unit 30

1 1 Я е́ду ра́нним по́ездом   2 Я пишу́ дешёвой ру́чкой
3 На́до мыть посу́ду горя́чей водо́й.   4 Я открыва́ю дверь
мои́м ключо́м   5 Он гла́дит руба́шку но́вым утюго́м   **2**
1 Врач хо́чет пойти́ в теа́тр с краси́вой медсестро́й   2
Ива́н хо́чет пойти́ в теа́тр с англи́йским тури́стом   3
Журнали́ст хо́чет пойти́ в теа́тр с изве́стным поли́тиком
4 Евге́ний хо́чет пойти́ в теа́тр с мое́й сестро́й   5 Муж
хо́чет пойти́ в теа́тр с молодо́й жено́й   **3** 1 све́жей
ветчино́й   2 копчёной ры́бой   3 зелёным огурцо́м (fleeting
vowel, see Unit 5)   4 дороги́м майоне́зом   **4** 1 Ко́фе с
холо́дным молоко́м   2 Чай со све́жим лимо́ном

Unit 31

1 1d 2c 3a 4b   **2** 1 но́выми друзья́ми   2 францу́зскими
гостя́ми   3 ва́жными клие́нтами   4 молоды́ми детьми́   5
ру́сскими студе́нтами   6 ста́рыми пенсионе́рами   7
на́шими бра́тьями   **3** 1 интере́сными кни́гами   2
больны́ми пацие́нтами   3 но́выми студе́нтами   4
хоро́шими газе́тами   5 ру́сскими компью́терами

Unit 32

1 1 ста́ром   2 дре́вней   3 шу́мном   4 краси́вой   5
хоро́шем   **2** 1e 2a 3d 4c 5b   **3** 1 зелёном па́рке   2
Кра́сной пло́щади   3 чёрном портфе́ле   4 жёлтой ю́бке
5 си́нем не́бе

Unit 33

1 1b 2g 3e 4d 5a 6c 7h 8f   **2** 1 краси́вых зда́ниях   2
ру́сских города́х   3 ночны́х клу́бах   4 после́дних
авто́бусах   5 высо́ких дере́вьях   **3** 1 Он рабо́тает на
шу́мных заво́дах   2 Она́ де́лает поку́пки в дороги́х

магази́нах   3 Мы чита́ем но́вости в вече́рних газе́тах   4 Вы обе́даете в ма́леньких рестора́нах   5 Они́ отдыха́ют в краси́вых па́рках

Unit 34

1 *Svetlana walks into the house and notices that all the doors and windows are <u>open</u>. The new curtains are blowing about in the wind. The door, however, is <u>shut</u>. On the table a cat lies, howling. It is clearly <u>glad</u> to see her. She is <u>furious</u> when she realizes that her son has gone out without feeding the cat. 'He is so <u>unreliable</u>!' she thinks.*   **2** 1 Э́то ме́сто свобо́дно.   2 Его́ автомоби́ль нов.   3 На́ши де́ти здоро́вы.   4 Все о́кна откры́ты.   5 Ка́ша вку́сна.   **3** 1d 2a 3e 4b 5c   **4** 1 ра́ды   2 согла́сный откры́тый закры́тый за́нятый

Unit 35

1 *My younger sister, Masha, really likes shopping. Yesterday she bought a bigger bag, a <u>newer</u> car, a more <u>expensive</u> radio, a more <u>interesting</u> book and a smaller mobile telephone*   **2** Моя́ мла́дшая сестра́, Ма́ша, о́чень лю́бит де́лать поку́пки. Вчера́ она́ купи́ла бо́льшую су́мку, бо́лее но́вый автомоби́ль, бо́лее дорого́е ра́дио,   бо́лее интере́сную кни́гу и ме́ньший со́товый телефо́н   **3** 1g 2j 3i 4a 5h 6b 7c 8f 9e 10d

Unit 36

1 You could use the short form comparative in 1, 3, 6, 7, 9, 10   **2** 1 Мой брат умне́е   2 Э́та кни́га ме́нее ску́чная   3 Его́ маши́на деше́вле   4 Мы купи́ли бо́лее но́вый дом   5 Вы не зна́ете, где бо́лее удо́бный стул?   6 Э́то про́ще   7 До Москвы́ да́льше   8 Мы получи́ли бо́лее ва́жное письмо́   9 Э́то письмо́ коро́че   10 Э́то ра́дио доро́же   **3** 1 Вади́м 2 Ива́н

Unit 37

1 1b 2d 3a 4e 5c   **2** 1 О́льга намно́го добре́е Ири́ны   2 Андре́й намно́го серьёзнее Константи́на   3 Он намно́го энерги́чнее меня́   4 Мой брат намно́го лени́вее мое́й сестры́   5 Ба́бушка намно́го моло́же де́душки   **3** 1 Э́то бо́лее серьёзная пробле́ма, чем его́   2 Го́род Москва́ бо́льше, чем Но́вгород. (Го́род Москва́ бо́льше Но́вгорода)   3 Он ста́рше меня́   4 Ваш телеви́зор лу́чше моего́   5 Я люблю́ бо́лее энерги́чную соба́ку

Unit 38

1 1 Э́то са́мый краси́вый парк   2 Ива́н (са́мый) лу́чший

футболи́ст 3 Вот са́мая энерги́чная медсестра́ 4 Я
чита́ю са́мую интере́сную кни́гу 5 Он живёт в са́мой
ма́ленькой кварти́ре **2** 1 Он оди́н из (са́мых) лу́чших
гитари́стов 2 Это са́мый краси́вый пляж 3 Чисте́йший
вздор! 4 Где ближа́йшая остано́вка авто́буса? 5 Это
са́мая серьёзная пробле́ма **3** 1 Зима́ са́мое холо́дное
вре́мя го́да. 2 Са́мый жа́ркий кли́мат. 3 Во́дка са́мый
кре́пкий напи́ток 4 Это са́мая краси́вая кварти́ра

Unit 39

1 1 глу́по 2 прия́тно 3 хорошо́ 4 тепло́ 5 логи́чески
6 го́рдо 7 впечатля́юще 8 саркасти́чно 9 эгоисти́чески
10 ще́дро 11 ти́хо 12 шу́мно **2** 1 Нет, сего́дня тепло́
2 Нет, пиани́ст блестя́ше игра́ет 3 Нет, студе́нт
ме́дленно рабо́тает 4 Нет, де́ти ти́хо игра́ют 5 Нет,
брат энерги́чно игра́ет **3** 1 Испа́нец говори́т по-
испа́нски 2 Ру́сский говори́т по-ру́сски 3 Англича́нин
говори́т по-англи́йски 4 Япо́нец говори́т по-япо́нски

Unit 40

1 1b 2e 3d 4a 5c **2** 1 Пиани́ст хорошо́ игра́ет, но
гитари́ст игра́ет ещё лу́чше 2 Мой брат лени́во игра́ет,
но твой брат игра́ет ещё лени́вее 3 Тенниси́ст энерги́чно
игра́ет, но футболи́ст игра́ет ещё энерги́чнее 4
Баскетболи́ст глу́по игра́ет, но хоккеи́ст игра́ет ещё глу́пее
5 Игро́к в гольф ме́дленно игра́ет, но игро́к в кри́кет
игра́ет ещё ме́дленнее **3** 1 Ка́тя ти́ше говори́т, чем её
сестра́. 2 И́горь гора́здо усе́рднее рабо́тает, чем
Валенти́н 3 Татья́на поёт ещё ху́же, чем Зо́я 4 Чем
ра́ньше, тем лу́чше 5 Как мо́жно скоре́е **4** 1 лу́чше
всех 2 лу́чше всего́ 3 лу́чше всех

Unit 41

1 1 сто ми́нус два́дцать бу́дет во́семьдесят 2 два плюс
шестна́дцать бу́дет восемна́дцать 3 три́дцать три плюс
сто два бу́дет сто три́дцать пять 4 два́дцать де́вять
ми́нус пятна́дцать бу́дет четы́рнадцать 5 во́семьдесят
пять ми́нус пятьдеся́т четы́ре бу́дет три́дцать оди́н **2** 1b
2c 3e 4a 5d **3** 1 42-93-12 со́рок два девяно́сто три
двена́дцать 2 84-53-55 во́семьдесят четы́ре пятьдеся́т три
пятьдеся́т пять 3 20-30-40 два́дцать три́дцать со́рок 4
36-62-73 три́дцать шесть шестьдеся́т два се́мьдесят три 5
18-11-26 восемна́дцать оди́ннадцать два́дцать шесть **4**
100 is the numeral involved. The advice is that it's more important

to have 100 friends than 100 roubles (i.e. friendship is more important than money).

Unit 42

1 *Boris recently went to two book shops and bought three books. Yesterday he was reading his new book on chemistry. He read about 60 different experiments in 32 countries. Ninety-six chemists had got results, but in 44 laboratories there had been accidents* **2** 1 четырёх 2 шести́десяти 3 двацати́ трёх 4 девяно́ста двух 5 ста десяти́ **3** 1 сорока́ 2 восемна́дцати 3 семи́десяти трём 4 трёмста́м 5 шестиста́м **4** 1 тремя́ 2 десятью 3 двумяста́ми 4 двадцатью́ 5 пятью́ **5** 1 двена́дцати 2 восьми́десяти шести́ 3 сорока́ пяти́ 4 оди́ннадцати 5 ста

Unit 43

1 1 Два журна́ла 2 Шесть неде́ль 3 Со́рок челове́к 4 Два́дцать три ко́шки 5 Оди́ннадцать часо́в 6 Сто рубле́й 7 Девятна́дцать киломе́тров 8 Ты́сяча книг 9 Сто четы́ре ма́льчика 10 Сто пять де́вушек **2** 1 Две больши́е соба́ки 2 Три ма́леньких теа́тра 3 Сто де́сять но́вых студе́нтов 4 Пять ста́рых домо́в 5 Три́дцать два энерги́чных ма́льчика **3** 1 пяти́ ста́рым профессора́м 2 двадцати́ серди́тым клие́нтам 3 оди́ннадцати шу́мным хулига́нам **4** 1 The phrase с пятью́ но́выми студе́нтами is *all* in the instrumental, because of the preposition с, which takes the instrumental 2 32 students are an animate object, but there is no animate accusative for compounds of 2, 3, 4 3 There is an animate accusative for 2, 3, 4 on their own 4 The preposition о is followed by the prepositional, so the whole phrase is in the prepositional 5 Books are inanimate – so the numeral and its adjective and noun behave as they would do if the numeral and its phrase were the subject (numeral + nom. pl. adj. + gen. sing. noun).

Unit 44

1 1 Апре́ль четвёртый ме́сяц го́да 2 Ноя́брь оди́ннадцатый ме́сяц го́да 3 А́вгуст восьмо́й ме́сяц го́да 4 Май пя́тый ме́сяц го́да 5 Ию́ль седьмо́й ме́сяц го́да **2** 1 Вади́м купи́л ту́фли три́дцать восьмо́го разме́ра 2 Татья́на купи́ла ту́фли тридца́того разме́ра 3 А́нна купи́ла ту́фли три́дцать второ́го разме́ра 4 Андре́й купи́л ту́фли со́рок тре́тьего разме́ра 5 Еле́на купи́ла ту́фли три́дцать шесто́го разме́ра **3** 1 Бага́ж на второ́м этаже́ 2 Фотоаппара́ты на тре́тьем этаже́ 3 Ту́фли на четвёртом

этажé   4 Кни́ги на пя́том этажé   5 Сувени́ры на шесто́м
этажé   **4**   1 Фотогра́фия шко́лы на страни́це пятьдеся́т
второ́й   2 Фотогра́фия теа́тра на страни́це две́сти
два́дцать девя́той   3 Фотогра́фия у́лицы на страни́це
во́семьдесят седьмо́й   4 Фотогра́фия актёра на страни́це
шестьдеся́т пе́рвой   5 Фотогра́фия актри́сы на страни́це
деся́той

Unit 45

1   1 без че́тверти пять   2 де́вять часо́в   3 два́дцать
мину́т шесто́го   4 без десяти́ семь   5 полови́на
двена́дцатого   **2**   1 По́езд в Новосиби́рск отхо́дит в семь
пятна́дцать   2 По́езд в Тверь отхо́дит в четы́рнадцать
пятьдеся́т пять   3 По́езд в Я́лту отхо́дит в два́дцать оди́н
три́дцать пять   4 По́езд в Воро́неж отхо́дит в
девятна́дцать три́дцать   5 По́езд в Ки́ров отхо́дит в
семна́дцать де́сять   **3**   1 Он встаёт в семь часо́в   2 Он
за́втракает в че́тверть восьмо́го   3 Его́ рабо́чий день
начина́ется без че́тверти де́вять   4 Он обе́дает без
тридцати́ пяти́ два   5 Его́ рабо́чий день конча́ется в
полови́не шесто́го

Unit 46

1   1 Сего́дня шесто́е ноября́   2 Сего́дня два́дцать пя́тое
а́вгуста   3 Сего́дня седьмо́е января́   4 Сего́дня тре́тье
октября́   5 Сего́дня два́дцать девя́тое февраля́   6 Сего́дня
шестна́дцатое апре́ля   7 Сего́дня два́дцать пя́тое ию́ня   8
Сего́дня пе́рвое сентября́   9 Сего́дня три́дцать пе́рвое
декабря́   **2**   1 Деся́того а́вгуста я бу́ду в Вене́ции   2
Шестна́дцатого а́гвуста я бу́ду в Берли́не   3 Двадца́того
а́вгуста я бу́ду в Москве́   4 Два́дцать пя́того а́вгуста я
бу́ду в Ки́рове   5 Тридца́того а́вгуста я бу́ду в Но́вгороде
3   1 Я пое́ду во Фра́нцию восемна́дцатого а́вгуста   2 Мы
получи́ли письмо́ тре́тьего апре́ля   3 Он позвони́л мне
тридца́того января́   4 Её день рожде́ния седьмо́го ма́рта.
5 Они́ уе́хали из Герма́нии два́дцать второ́го ноября́   **4**
1 Пу́шкин роди́лся в ты́сяча семьсо́т девяно́сто девя́том
году́   2 Ле́рмонтов роди́лся в ты́сяча во́семьсот
четы́рнадцатом году́   3 Блок роди́лся в ты́сяча во́семьсот
восемьдеся́том году́   4 Ахма́това родила́сь в ты́сяча
во́семьсот во́семьдесят девя́том году́   5 Пастерна́к
роди́лся в ты́сяча во́семьсот девяно́стом году́   6 Цвета́ева
родила́сь в ты́сяча во́семьсот девяно́сто второ́м году́

Unit 47

1 1 Ско́лько сто́ит деревя́нный стол? Ты́сяча две́сти пятьдеся́т рубле́й   2 Ско́лько сто́ит япо́нский телеви́зор? Три ты́сячи рубле́й   3 Ско́лько сто́ит конве́рт? Три рубля́ два́дцать копе́ек   4 Ско́лько сто́ит кра́сная ру́чка? Пятна́дцать рубле́й пятьдеся́т копе́ек   5 Ско́лько сто́ит буты́лка кра́сного вина́? Со́рок рубле́й   **2** 1 Ба́бушке во́семьдесят оди́н год   2 Ма́тери пятьдеся́т пять лет   3 Отцу́ (fleeting vowel!) пятьдеся́т четы́ре го́да   4 Сы́ну три́дцать два го́да   5 До́чери три́дцать лет   6 Вну́ку шестна́дцать лет   **3** 1 четы́ре килогра́мма хле́ба   2 полкило́ мя́са   3 пять килогра́ммов са́хара   4 три килогра́мма помидо́ров   5 шесть килогра́ммов апельси́нов

Unit 48

1 1 Он   2 Они́   3 Вы   4 Мы   5 Они́   **2** 1 Он   2 Оно́   3 Она́   4 Они́   5 Они́   **3** 1 ты   2 ты   3 ты   4 вы (unless you know your boss very well!)   5 вы   **4** 1e 2d 3b 4a 5c

Unit 49

1 1b 2c 3e 4a 5d   **2** 1 Сего́дня я звоню́ тебе́   2 Сего́дня О́льга звони́т нам   3 Сего́дня он звони́т вам   4 Сего́дня Са́ша звони́т ей   5 Сего́дня ты звони́шь ему́   **3** 1 У тебя́ боли́т голова́   2 У неё боли́т голова́   3 У вас боли́т голова́   **4** 1 Я приглаша́ю его́ на вечери́нку   2 Я приглаша́ю их на вечери́нку   3 Я приглаша́ю вас на вечери́нку

Unit 50

1 1 Это его́ дом? Да, его́   2 Это их соба́ка? Да, их   3 Это ваш па́спорт? Да, мой (наш)   4 Это моё письмо́? Да, твоё (ва́ше)   5 Это на́ша фотогра́фия? Да, ва́ша   **2** 1 Ка́тя, вот твоё письмо́. Нет, это не моё   2 Ви́ктор вот твой сви́тер. Нет, это не мой   3 Са́ша и Аня, вот ва́ши кни́ги. Нет, это не на́ши   4 Светла́на и Та́ня, вот ва́ши фотогра́фии. Нет, это не на́ши   5 Андре́й, вот твоя́ руба́шка. Нет, это не моя́   **3** 1d 2c 3e 4a 5b

Unit 51

1 1c 2e 3a 4d 5b   **2** 1 Каку́ю кварти́ру вы покупа́ете?   2 Како́й автомоби́ль вы покупа́ете?   3 Како́е окно́ вы покупа́ете?   4 Како́й велосипе́д вы покупа́ете?   5 Каки́е кни́ги вы покупа́ете?   **3** 1 Чей это га́лстук?   2 Чей это чемода́н?   3 Чья это ю́бка?   4 Чьё это пла́тье?   5 Чьи э то носки? **4** 1 Какую газету вы читаете? 2 О чём вы думаете (ты думаешь)? 3 С кем вы идёте (ты идёшь) в магазин? 4 Что это? Книга или журнал? 5 Чьи это дети?

Unit 52

1 1 Вы предпочитаете это пальто или то пальто, вон там? 2 Вы предпочитаете эту шапку или ту шапку, вон там? 3 Вы предпочитаете этот шарф или тот шарф, вон там? 4 Вы предпочитаете эту рубашку или ту рубашку, вон там? 5 Вы предпочитаете эти туфли или те туфли, вон там? **2** 1 Кто это? Это наш врач 2 Они живут в этом доме 3 Вчера мы были в театре с Борисом и Сергеем. Тот работает врачом 4 Вы уже знаете об этой проблеме? 5 Вот та же книга! 6 Он получил тот же самый галстук 7 Мы читаем ту же газету 8 Они работают на этих заводах 9 Я иду в театр с такими интересными друзьями. 10 Лучшие магазины на этой улице **3** 1 В каком городе ты живёшь? 2 Кто это? 3 Это такая красивая фотография! 4 Какую шапку ты предпочитаешь?

Unit 53

1 1b 2c 3e 4a 5d **2** 1 Можно купить марки в любом магазине 2 Сам композитор идёт на концерт 3 Есть такие города по всей Англии 4 У меня подарки для каждого ребёнка 5 Он идёт к самому директору **3** 1 Мы работаем каждый день 2 Актриса сама идёт в театр 3 Я подожду у самой библиотеки 4 Все наши друзья идут на концерт 5 Какие билеты вы хотите? Любые. **4** 1 в любом магазине 2 в каждом магазине 3 во всех магазинах 4 в самом центре

Unit 54

1 *The tourist came into his room and shut the door behind him*. He saw in front of him* a large room with a bed, a chair and a washbasin, but no towels. He was glad he had brought some with him*. As he was feeling* rather tired, he decided to have a wash and a sleep, although he imagined* that the bed would not be very comfortable.* **2** 1d 2a 3b 4e 5c **3** 1 Он хорошо ведёт себя 2 Я представляю себе, что это трудно 3 Закрой за собой дверь! 4 Я плохо чувствую себя 5 Мы купили шампанское для себя **4** 1 Что вы купили для себя? 2 Он думает только о себе 3 Я беру с собой вино 4 Мы берём с собой собаку

Unit 55

1 1 Óльга, котóрая живёт в Ки́рове, продавщи́ца 2 Наши друзья, котóрые живу́т в Можа́йске, учителя́ 3 Виктор, котóрый живёт в Москве́, перевóдчик 4 Cáша, котóрый живёт в Вор́онеже, юри́ст 5 Аня, котóрая живёт в Я́лте, медсестра́ 6 Вади́м, котóрый живёт в Обни́нске, гид **2** 1 Велосипéд, котóрый Óльга купи́ла, большóй 2 Джи́нсы, котóрые Óльга купи́ла, мóдные 3 Цветы́, котóрые Óльга купи́ла, краси́вые 4 Юбка, котóрую Óльга купи́ла, кор́откая **3** 1 Друг, к котóрому мы идём, музыка́нт 2 Здания, в котóрых они рабóтают, óчень больши́е 3 Врач, с котóрым она говори́ла, óчень дóбрый 4 Фильм, о котóром вы говори́те, не óчень хорóший. 5 Студéнты, от котóрых мы получи́ли письмó, рабóтают в А́фрике. **4** 1 Собáка, котóрую ты сфотографи́ровал, óчень ста́рая 2 Шкóла, о котóрой ты говори́шь, óчень хорóшая

Unit 56

1 1d 2e 3b 4a 5c **2** 1 кто 2 кто 3 что 4 что 5 что 6 что

Unit 57

1 *Someone called to see you this morning. He said something about a meeting tomorrow. For some reason he didn't want to talk to me. He just said that if you can't be on time you should ring anyone in the office* **2** Ктó-то позвони́л тебé сегóдня у́тром. Он сказáл чтó-то о совеща́нии за́втра. Он почему́-то не хотéл говори́ть со мной. Он сказáл тóлько, что éсли вы не смóжете приéхать вó-время, на́до позвони́ть комý-нибудь в óфисе. **3** 1 чтó-то 2 когда́-нибудь 3 чтó-нибудь 4 гдé-нибудь 5 когó-то 6 какóм-то óфисе

Unit 58

1 1 вы зна́ете 2 ты понима́ешь 3 я ка́шляю 4 она́ рабóтает 5 они́ отвеча́ют 6 мы спра́шиваем 7 он покупáет 8 мы гуля́ем 9 вы слу́шаете 10 ты умéешь **2** 1 Вы слу́шаете ра́дио 2 Мы игра́ем в тéннис 3 Ты покупáешь чай. 4 Она́ понима́ет вопрóс? 5 Я зна́ю дирéктора **3** 1 покупáю 2 отвечáет 3 понима́ем 4 игра́ешь 5 гуля́ют

Unit 59

1 1 я смотрю́ 2 ты стрóишь 3 онó стóит 4 вы ку́рите 5 они́ ва́рят 6 мы готóвим 7 я лежу́ 8 она́

стои́т   9 вы слы́шите   10 ты говори́шь **2** 1 Вы
слы́шите ра́дио   2 Мы стои́м у окна́   3 Они́ стро́ят дом
4 Она́ смо́трит фильм?   5 Ты звони́шь дире́ктору   **3** 1
звоню́   2 слы́шите   3 стои́т   4 смо́тришь   5 стоя́т

Unit 60

1 1 я люблю́   2 я сплю   3 я говорю́   4 я сижу́   5 я
лажу́   6 я стою́   7 я прошу́   8 я смотрю́   9 я кормлю́
10 я звоню́ **2**   1 сиди́т   2 гото́влю   3 во́зит   4 ношу́
5 лети́те **3** 1b 2e 3a 4c 5d

Unit 61

1 1 мы берём   2 я живу́   3 вы пьёте   4 они́ кладу́т
5 он идёт   6 ты поёшь   7 я лью   8 они́ ждут   9 я пью
10 мы живём **2** 1 я 2 они́ 3 мы 4 ты 5 они́ 6 вы 7 он
(она́, оно́) **3** Ива́н поёт. Вади́м пьёт **4** 1 Ива́н пьёт
во́дку   2 О́льга живёт в кварти́ре   3 Он ждёт в теа́тре
4 Мы берём биле́ты   5 Они́ пою́т сего́дня ве́чером

Unit 62

1 1 Я ча́сто пишу́ моему́ дру́гу   2 Сего́дня мы е́дем в
центр го́рода   3 Он не мо́жет прийти́ в теа́тр   4 Вы не
о́чень ча́сто мо́ете посу́ду   5 Почему́ ты пла́чешь?   6 Они́
и́щут свои́ паспорта́   7 Тури́ст не хо́чет смотре́ть фильм
8 Кому́ вы пи́шете?   9 Вы е́дете в музе́й и́ли в цирк?   10
Нет, спаси́бо, я не хочу́ ко́фе **2**   1 они́   2 он   3 они́   4 я
5 ты   6 он   7 они́   8 вы   9 мы   10 ты

Unit 63

1 1 я танцу́ю   2 ты даёшь   3 он рекоменду́ет   4 мы
встаём   5 вы сове́туете   6 они́ риску́ют   7 она́ узнаёт   8
я испо́льзую   9 мы тре́буем   10 они́ путеше́ствуют **2**   1
Мой брат – инжене́р   2 Сего́дня хо́лодно   3 На столе́
есть ключ   4 В дере́вне нет магази́нов **3** 1 У Вади́ма
есть дом.   2 У Бори́са нет автомоби́ля.   3 У Та́ни есть
телеви́зор.   4 У Зо́и есть кварти́ра   5 У И́горя нет ко́шки.
6 У Серге́я нет компью́тера. **4**   1e 2d 3a 4c 5b

Unit 64

1 1 я умыва́юсь 2 он причёсывается **2** 1c 2a 3f 4j 5d 6b 7h
8e 9i 10g **3** 1 Я одева́юсь в во́семь часо́в   2 Он
умыва́ется в семь часо́в   3 Они́ раздева́ются в де́сять
часо́в   4 Конце́рт конча́ется в де́сять часо́в   5 Вы
ложи́тесь спать в оди́ннадцать часо́в

Unit 65

1 Imperfective: 1 speaking, 3 to read, 4 playing; perfective: 2 to write, 5 to return **2** 1 говори́ть 2 написа́ть 3 чита́ть 4 игра́ть 5 верну́ться **3** 1 Он предпочита́ет чита́ть газе́ты 2 Я хочу́ посла́ть э́то письмо́ сего́дня 3 Актёр начина́ет говори́ть в семь часо́в 4 Мы продолжа́ем смотре́ть телеви́зор 5 Они́ лю́бят отдыха́ть на пля́зе 6 Я хочу́ взять кни́гу сейча́с 7 Мы хоти́м купи́ть э́ту соба́ку 8 Вы предпочита́ете слу́шать ра́дио? 9 Вы хоти́те верну́ться сего́дня?

Unit 66

1 *On Saturday I fly to Saint Petersburg at 10am. While I am there I will have meetings with Russian representatives of the company, but I hope that I will also visit some museums and theatres. I promise that I will ring you as regularly as I can during my stay, or else I will use e-mail at the hotel* **2** 1 Он ча́сто бу́дет звони́ть дру́гу 2 Ба́бушка бу́дет отдыха́ть до́ма 3 Мы бу́дем игра́ть в гольф ка́ждый день 4 За́втра я бу́ду занима́ться уро́ками 5 В университе́те он бу́дет изуча́ть исто́рию **3** 1b 2e 3c 4a 5d

Unit 67

1 *I will ring you tomorrow at 10am, then I will write a letter to the director. As far as I know, he will be visiting lots of offices in England, but he has promised that he will visit our office on Tuesday. He will be considering all our proposals before his departure. Hopefully he will sign the contract on Tuesday* **2** 1 позвоню́ 2 накормлю́ 3 пообе́даю 4 куплю́ 5 вы́учу **3** 1 Во вто́рник я куплю́ пода́рки 2 В сре́ду я позвоню́ ма́ме 3 В четве́рг я напишу́ письмо́ бра́ту 4 В пя́тницу я вы́учу грамма́тику 5 В суббо́ту я отремонти́рую маши́ну 6 В воскресе́нье я закажу́ биле́ты

Unit 68

1 1 О́льга за́втракала 2 Меня́ зову́т Еле́на, я мы́ла посу́ду 3 Он игра́л в ка́рты 4 Мы смотре́ли телеви́зор 5 Вы возвраща́лись в о́фис 6 Они́ писа́ли пи́сьма 7 Бори́с и Светла́на гото́вили обе́д **2** *When we used to live in a flat it was impossible to have a dog, but when we moved into a house with a garden, we bought one. He was a large black mongrel and he loved to play in the garden. One day he was barking by the gate when the postman arrived. He thought the dog was aggressive* *and refused to come in*   **3**   1 process, not necessarily complete; it went on for 2 hours   2 action of playing is interrupted   3 description of where you were; быть exists only in imperfective   4 action of walking is interrupted   5 habit in the past

Unit 69

1   1 Хорошо́! Вади́м уже́ вы́мыл посу́ду   2 Хорошо́! вы уже́ пригото́вили обе́д   3 Хорошо́! они́ уже́ сде́лали поку́пки   4 Хорошо́! На́дя уже́ накорми́ла соба́ку   5 Хорошо́! И́горь уже́ вы́стирал бельё   **2**   *She had already finished the book when the 'phone rang. It was Boris, inviting her to the theatre. She refused politely, because she had already agreed to go to the cinema with Sergei. While she was speaking to Boris, her brother rang the doorbell. She hung up quickly and rushed to the door. Her brother was looking tired. 'I have brought the plants you asked for,' he said.*   1 И́горь и Зо́я ремонти́ровали автомоби́ль, когда́ Бори́с позвони́л   **3**   2 И́горь и Зо́я стира́ли бельё, когда́ стира́льная маши́на слома́лась   3 И́горь и Зо́я сажа́ли дере́вья в саду́, когда́ сын верну́лся   4 И́горь и Зо́я де́лали поку́пки, когда́ Зо́я потеря́ла де́ньги

Unit 70

1   1 е́здил   2 бе́гает   3 пла́вал   4 лета́ем   5 вози́ла   **2**   1 е́дет   2 бе3и́т   3 плывёт   4 лете́ли   5 везла́   **3**   1 пое́дет   2 побегу́   3 поплывёт   4 полете́ли   5 повезла́   **4**   1 несёт   2 понёс   3 нёс

Unit 71

1 1 выхожу́   2 подхожу́   3 приезжа́ет   4 вхожу́   5 приезжа́ю   6 выхожу́   7 прохожу́   8 вхожу́   **2**   1 в 2 к 3 до 4 из 5 на 6 из 7 ми́мо 8 с 9 от 10 че́рез   **3**   1 Я вхожу́ в теа́тр   2 Он вно́сит кни́ги в ко́мнату   3 Мы вы́бегаем из па́рка   4 Они́ перево́дят соба́ку че́рез у́лицу

Unit 72

1   1 напи́шет   2 пропылесо́сит   3 вы́стирает   4 вста́нет   5 почи́стит   **2**   1 прие́дет во́время   2 не забу́дет свои́ де́ньги   3 позвони́т профе́ссору   4 напи́шет письмо́ (своему́) бра́ту   5 прода́ст (свой) мотоци́кл   6 даст мне пода́рок   7 зака́жет биле́ты   8 ку́пит соба́ку   9 сде́лает поку́пки   10 вернётся ра́но   **3**   1 We are always glad if they send us a card ✓   2 They will not be pleased if you don't send them a card ✗   3 You are never satisfied if the food is cold ✓ 4 If you don't ring me tonight I will be furious ✗

Unit 73

1 1b 2e 3a 4c 5d **2** 1 Éсли бы у них бы́ли де́ньги, они́ постро́или бы да́чу 2 Éсли бы у нас бы́ли де́ньги, мы купи́ли бы пода́рки для друзе́й 3 Éсли бы у него́ бы́ли де́ньги, Па́вел сиде́л бы до́ма 4 Éсли бы у неё бы́ли де́ньги, Ка́тя купи́ла бы но́вую оде́жду 5 Éсли бы у вас бы́ли де́ньги, вы доста́ли бы биле́ты в Большо́й **3** 1 Éсли бы то́лько мы не забы́ли, Áня не рассерди́лась бы на нас. 2 Éсли бы то́лько она́ зна́ла об э́том, она́ позвони́ла бы ему́. 3 Éсли бы то́лько мы пришли́ во́время, мы уви́дели бы их. **4** 1 Бы́ло бы лу́чше, е́сли бы она́ согласи́лась на э́то 2 Бы́ло бы лу́чше, е́сли бы у него́ был телефа́кс 3 Бы́ло бы лу́чше, е́сли бы я знал/зна́ла его́ а́дрес

Unit 74

1 1h 2c 3j 4a 5f 6b 7i 8g 9d 10e **2** 1 спи 2 напиши́ 3 бери́ 4 купи́ 5 поблагодари́ **3** 1 забу́дьте 2 отдыха́йте 3 слу́шайте 4 рабо́тайте 5 улыба́йтесь **4** 1 Не забу́дьте биле́ты1 2 Не кури́ть1 3 Переда́йте ключ, пожа́луйста 4 Дава́й/Дава́йте позвони́м Та́не

Unit 75

1 1 Ви́ктор никогда́ не поёт пе́сни 2 Ви́ктор нигде́ не слу́шает поп-му́зыку 3 Ви́ктор ни с кем не слу́шает поп-му́зыку 4 Ви́ктор ничего́ не зна́ет о му́зыке **2** 1 Я не люблю́ смотре́ть фи́льмы 2 Здесь нет кинотеа́тра 3 Я ниче́м не занима́юсь в свобо́дное вре́мя 4 Я нигде́ не люблю́ отдыха́ть **3** 1b 2c 3d 4e 5a

Unit 76

1 1e 2a 3h 4b 5g 6j 7i 8f 9c 10d **2** 1 Ива́ну и Мари́и не́когда смотре́ть телеви́зор 2 Ива́ну и Мари́и не́чем писа́ть пи́сьма 3 Ива́ну и Мари́и не́кого приглаша́ть на обе́д 4 Ива́ну и Мари́и не́чего пить 5 Ива́ну и Мари́и не́кому звони́ть **3** 1 Вам не́чего бу́дет де́лать 2 Бори́су не́ с кем бы́ло говори́ть 3 Не́чего есть 4 Врачу́ не́когда бы́ло отдыха́ть 5 Нам не́чего бы́ло чита́ть

Unit 77

1 1 пора́ 2 нельзя́ 3 мо́жно 4 на́до 5 нельзя́ **2** 1c 2a 3b **3** 1 Ему́ на́до отдыха́ть в больни́це 2 Нам пора́ бы́ло идти́ 3 Мо́жно (возмо́жно) бу́дет пла́вать 4 Нет, вам (тебе́) нельзя́ смотре́ть телеви́зор 5 Да, вам (тебе́) на́до рабо́тать

Unit 78

1 1c 2a 3e 4b 5d **2** 1 Я спроси́л(а), прие́дет ли Бори́с за́втра. 2 Я спроси́л(а), заплати́ла ли О́льга за кни́ги 3 Я спроси́л(а), пожа́ловались ли клие́нты на това́ры 4 Я спроси́л(а), позвони́л ли Бори́с дире́ктору 5 Я спроси́л(а), вернётся ли О́льга **3** 1 Мы спроси́ли, мо́жно ли поза́втракать в 8 часо́в 2 Он спроси́л, пошёл ли друг на дискоте́ку 3 Он нам сказа́л /Он сказа́л нам, когда́ вернётся 4 Ты не зна́ешь, получи́ла ли она́ письмо́? 5 Я хочу́ знать, подпи́шет ли дире́ктор контра́кт

Unit 79

1 1 Врач тре́бует, что́бы спортсме́н не кури́л 2 Гид рекоменду́ет, что́бы тури́сты обе́дали в рестора́нах 3 Профе́ссор тре́бует, что́бы студе́нты прочита́ли всю кни́гу 4 Я хочу́, что́бы мой сын стал врачо́м 5 Де́ти, хотя́т, что́бы роди́тели купи́ли дороги́е игру́шки **2** 1c 2e 3d 4b 5a **3** 1 Я хочу́, что́бы вы позвони́ли (ты позвони́л/а) мне за́втра. 2 Врач хо́чет, что́бы пацие́нт лежа́л в посте́ли. 3 Профе́ссор тре́бует, что́бы студе́нты рабо́тали в библиоте́ке 4 Милиционе́р предлага́ет, что́бы вы пошли́ (ты пошёл/ты пошла́) домо́й 5 Я приказа́л(а), что́бы они́ се́ли

Unit 80

1 1 Мы хоти́м купи́ть телеви́зор, что́бы смотре́ть ма́тчи 2 Вы хоти́те позвони́ть дру́гу, что́бы пригласи́ть его́ на конце́рт 3 Ты хо́чешь написа́ть письмо́, что́бы переда́ть но́вости 4 Они́ хотя́т посеща́ть Москву́, что́бы ви́деть интере́сные места́ 5 Тури́сты хотя́т посеща́ть пля́жи, что́бы отдыха́ть **2** 1 Бори́с позвони́л, что́бы она́ отве́тила на вопро́с 2 Бори́с позвони́л, что́бы он извини́лся 3 Бори́с позвони́л, что́бы мы обсуди́ли ситуа́цию 4 Бори́с позвони́л, что́бы вы пригласи́ли его́ на обе́д 5 Бори́с позвони́л, что́бы они́ заказа́ли биле́ты **3** 1 позвони́ть 2 что́бы позвони́ть 3 что́бы друг позвони́л

Unit 81

1 1 Им ску́чно 2 Мне хо́лодно 3 Ей жаль соба́ку 4 Ему́ нра́вится пла́вать. 5 Тебе́ хо́чется пить 6 Вам удало́сь найти́ ключ. **2** 1b 2e 3c 4a 5d **3** 1 Ему́ нра́вится актри́са 2 Врачу́ нра́вится больни́ца 3 Профе́ссору нра́вятся студе́нты 4 Вам понра́вилась экску́рсия 5 Она́ нравится мне   **4** 1 Мне надоéло   2 Мне жáрко   3 Мне хýже

Unit 82

1 1 Я пью и винó и вóдку   2 Я не игрáю ни в крúкет, ни в футбóл   3 Я люблю óперу, а он любит балéт   4 Я не идý на концéрт, потомý что прогрáмма неинтерéсная   5 Я не знáю, где он рабóтает   **2** 1 Онá обещáла написáть письмó, но онá забыла   2 Он изучáет математику и физику   3 Сергéй печáлен, и никтó не обращáет внимáния на негó   4 Турúсты сердúты, потомý что в гостинице хóлодно.   5 Дирéктор дýмает, что клиéнт довóлен   **3** 1 а 2 когдá 3 úли 4 из-за тогó, что 5 где 6 но 7 ни... ни   **4** 1 Я рад (рáда), потомý что (так как/из-за тогó, что) он купúл билéт   2 Я хочý пойтú на концéрт, но билéтов нет   3 Вы хотúте два билéта úли три?

Unit 83

1 1 Дом в гóроде   2 Цéрковь в дерéвне   3 Кнúга в шкафý   4 Автомобúль на ýлице   5 Компьютер в óфисе   6 Брúстоль на зáпаде Áнглии   7 Пóезд на стáнции   8 Тигр в зоопáрке   9 Почтальóн на пóчте   10 Пианúст на концéрте   **2** 1 Секретáрь идёт на рабóту   2 Вúктор идёт на стадиóн   3 Учúтель идёт в шкóлу   4 Студéнт идёт на лéкцию   5 Собáка идёт в сад   **3** 1 шкóле 2 сéвере 3 рабóту 4 Крáсной Плóщади 5 Фрáнцию   6 вокзáл 7 Крымý 8 бассéйне 9 Москвý 10 садý

Unit 84

1 1 мéжду 2 у 3 под 4 пéред 5 над 6 за   **2** 1 Óльга дýмает, что рýчка под кнúгами, но онá у телефóна   2 Óльга дýмает, что билéты за зéркалом, но онú под пáспортом   3 Óльга дýмает, что автомобúль пéред дóмом, но он за дóмом   4 Óльга дýмает, что портрéт над камúном, но он над столóм   5 Óльга дýмает, что холодúльник мéжду шкафáми, но он за двéрью

Unit 85

1 1 от 2 к 3 по 4 мúмо 5 из 6 чéрез   **2** 1 ýлицу 2 кáссе 3 когó 4 Итáлии 5 кáссы   **3** 1 Онá не любит ходúть по магазúнам   2 Профéссор спешúт к студéнтам   3 Собáка перехóдит чéрез ýлицу

Unit 86

1 1 понедéльник, e   2 втóрникам, g   3 э́тот момéнт, j   4 пя́тницу, b   5 срéдам, a   6 воскресéньям, c   7 четвергáм, i

8 четвергáм, d   9 пя́тницу, f   10 суббóту, h   **2** 1 в
понедéльник, в пя́тницу и в суббóту 2 во втóрник 3 в
воскресéнье

Unit 87

1 1 в э́том годý   2 на э́той недéле   3 в мáрте   4 в ию́не
5 в бýдущем годý   6 в февралé   7 в э́том мéсяце   8 в
áвгусте   9 на бýдущей недéле   10 в двáдцать пéрвом вéке
2 1 День рождéния Сергéя в мáрте   2 День рождéния
А́ни в апрéле   3 День рождéния Татья́ны в сентябрé   4
День рождéния сестры́ в декабрé   5 День рождéния брата
в январé   6 День рождéния мужа в октябрé   7 День
рождéния Кáти в áвгусте   8 День рождéния Вади́ма в мáе
9 День рождéния Зóи в ию́не   10 День рождéния И́горя в
ноябрé   **3** 1 В декабрé мы лю́бим катáться на лы́жах   2
В áвгусте мы лю́бим лежáть на пля́же   3 В февралé мы
лю́бим сидéть дóма   4 В ию́ле мы лю́бим гуля́ть в
дерéвне

Unit 88

1 1 во врéмя 2 за 3 чéрез 4 назáд 5 пóсле 6 с ... до 7 за
2 1 пóсле того, как, g   2 во врéмя, d   3 за, а   4 чéрез,
f   5 назáд, b   6 до, i   7 с, j   8 за, h   9 во врéмя, с   10 до
того, как, е

Unit 89

1 1 крóме   2 для   3 без   4 прóтив   5 в   6 по   7 о   8
при   9 за   10 на   **2** 1d Мы поблагодари́ли её за
подáрок,   2а Они́ живýт в дóме напрóтив больни́цы,   3b
Вы за и́ли прóтив э́той идéй?,   4е Крóме Бори́са все
довóльны,   5с Они́ ходи́ли на дискотéку без меня́!
3 1 Я купи́л(а) духи́ для неё.   2 Спаси́бо за предложéние.
3 О чём вы говори́ли?

Unit 90

1 1 в с,   2 у f,   3 на е,   4 за h,   5 с g,   6 к b,   7 в а,   8
на d   **2** 1 Бори́с игрáет в футбóл 2 Татья́на игрáет на
флéйте   **3** 1 Мы серди́мся на тебя́/вас   2 Мы надéемся
на лýчшее   3 Он отвечáет на мой вопрóс   4 Не нáдо
жáловаться на письмó   5 Плати́те за кни́ги в кáссу   6
Они́ продаю́т стул за двéсти рублéй   7 Мы покупáем стул
у А́ни   8 вы игрáете на гитáре?   9 Посмотри́те на собáку!
10 Обы́чно мы начинáем с пéрвой страни́цы

adjective A word which describes a noun: a *boring* film.

adverb A word which gives us information about the way in which an action is carried out: he sings *well*; she sings *very badly*.

animate noun A person or an animal.

article Words meaning *a, an, the, some*. There are no articles in Russian.

aspects Most Russian verbs exist in two forms, imperfective and perfective. The imperfective is concerned with process or description and the perfective is concerned with result and successful completion.

case There are six cases in Russian – nominative, accusative, genitive, dative, instrumental, prepositional. A case indicates what role nouns, adjectives and pronouns are playing in the sentence and the endings of these words change according to their case.

clause A group of words that contains a verb. A main clause can be followed by a subordinate clause: *Champagne is a drink* (main clause), *which I love* (subordinate clause).

comparative Adjectives and adverbs in the comparative indicate *more/less*: This is a *more* boring film; he sings *less* well than his sister.

conjugation The way verb endings change when in a tense.

conjunction Words which link sentences or phrases (e.g. *and, but, because*).

declension The way noun endings change when not in the nominative case.

gender A category of noun. In Russian there are three categories: masculine, feminine and neuter.

infinitive The form of the word meaning *to* (e.g. *to do, to read, to write*). In Russian most verbs have two infinitives, the imperfective and the perfective.

negative A word or phrase denying or contradicting something: I *never* watch television; he *can't* sing.

noun Word used to name a person, an animal, an object or an abstract quality: *Viktor, Moscow, postman, happiness.*

object Person or thing that has an action done to it.

preposition Word used before a noun or pronoun to show position, time, method: *in, at, from, with.*

pronoun A word used in place of a noun or phrase: *him, she, this, which, who*

relative clause Part of a sentence introduced by a relative pronoun: These are my friends *who live in Russia.*

subject Person or thing doing an action.

superlative Adjectives and adverbs in the superlative indicate *most*: *This is the most boring film; he sings best of all.*

tense Tells us when the action of the verb takes/took/will take place:

He reads	present tense
He will read	future tense
He was reading	past tense
He read	past tense
He had read	past tense

verb Words which describe actions, feelings and states.

russian
daphne west

- Do you want to cover the basics then progress fast?
- Have you got rusty Russian which needs brushing up?
- Do you want to reach a high standard?

Russian starts with the basics but moves at a lively pace to give you a good level of understanding, speaking and writing. You will have lots of opportunity to practise the kind of language you will need to be able to communicate with confidence and understand the culture of Russian speakers.

teach
yourself

beginner's russian
rachel farmer

- Are you new to language learning?
- Do you want lots of practice and examples?
- Do you want to improve your confidence to speak?

Beginner's Russian is written for the complete beginner who wants to move at a steady pace and have lots of opportunity to practise. The grammar is explained clearly and does not assume that you have studied a language before. You will learn everything you need to get the most out of a holiday or to go on to further study.

teach yourself

beginner's russian script
daphne west

- Do you want help with writing Russian?
- Are you planning a business trip or holiday?
- Are you learning Russian?

Beginner's Russian Script will help you get to grips with reading and writing Russian, whether you are studying the language or planning a trip for business or pleasure. The step-by-step approach will build your confidence to read and write in a variety of real contexts.

teach yourself

russian language, life & culture
stephen webber & tatyana webber

- Are you interested in the story of Russia and the Russians?
- Do you want to understand how the country works today?
- Are you planning a visit to Russia or learning Russian?

Russian Language, Life & Culture will give you a basic overview of Russia – the country, its language, its people and its culture – and will enrich any visit or course of study. Vocabulary lists and 'Taking it Further' sections at the end of every chapter will equip you to talk and write confidently about all aspects of Russian life.